£ 1-00

THE THEATRE ADDICT'S ARCHIVE

EDITED BY
SHERIDAN MORLEY

ELM TREE BOOKS · LONDON

For Kate and Edward and Jonathan, my three godchildren, in the hope that one day they may feel inclined to join the rest of us addicts

*First published in Great Britain 1977
by Elm Tree Books/Hamish Hamilton Ltd
90 Great Russell Street, London WC1B 3PT*

Copyright © 1977 by Sheridan Morley

ISBN 0 241 89806 4

*Printed in Great Britain
by Ebenezer Baylis and Son Ltd
The Trinity Press, Worcester, and London*

CONTENTS

ACKNOWLEDGEMENTS

'The Boy Actor' by Noël Coward is reprinted by permission of Curtis Brown Ltd; 'So You Want to be an Audience?' by Alan Brien by permission of Alan Brien Esq. and *Punch*; 'It all Began with Growcott' by Ralph Richardson from *Encore, The Sunday Times Book* (Michael Joseph) by permission of Sir Ralph Richardson; 'The Hell of the Greasepaint, the Bore of the Crowd' by Basil Boothroyd by permission of Basil Boothroyd Esq. and *Punch*; from *I know the face, but . . .* by Peter Bull (Peter Davis Ltd) by permission of Peter Bull Esq.; from *James Agate: An Anthology* edited by Herbert van Thal by permission of Rupert Hart-Davis Ltd/Granada Publishing Ltd; from *Distinguished Company* by John Gielgud by permission of Heinemann Educational Books Ltd; 'The Gielgud Hat' by Alec Guinness from *Encore, The Sunday Times Book* (second year) (Michael Joseph) by permission of *The Sunday Times*; from *A Musing Morley* by Robert Morley by permission of Robson Books Ltd; from *A Thurber Carnival* by James Thurber (Hamish Hamilton) copyright © 1945 James Thurber; from *Henry Irving* by Laurence Irving (Faber and Faber Ltd) by permission of Richard Scott Simon Ltd; from *Isadora* by Sewell Stokes by permission of Granada Publishing Ltd; from *The Entertainer* by John Osborne (Faber and Faber Ltd) by permission of David Higham Associates Ltd; from *The truth about 'Pygmalion'* by Richard Huggett by permission of William Heinemann Ltd; from *Sybil Thorndike* by Russell Thorndike by permission of Curtis Brown Ltd; from *Gerald: A Portrait* by Daphne du Maurier (Victor Gollancz Ltd) by permission of Curtis Brown Ltd; from *Tyrone Guthrie on Acting* by permission of Cassell & Collier Macmillan; from *Around Theatres* by Max Beerbohm by permission of Rupert Hart-Davis Ltd/ Granada Publishing Ltd; 'The Art of Rehearsal' by George Bernard Shaw by permission of The Society of Authors on behalf of The Bernard Shaw Estate; from 'Friends and Neighbours' in *Long, Long Ago* by Alexander Woollcott copyright 1943 by The Viking Press, Inc., © renewed 1971 by The Viking Press, Inc. reprinted by permission of The Viking Press; 'Why I am Not an Actor' by Michael Parkinson by permission of Michael Parkinson Esq. and *Punch*; from *Lost Empires* by J. B. Priestley by permission of William Heinemann Ltd; 'You Out

There' by Ned Sherrin by permission of the *Telegraph Sunday Magazine*; 'To The Lady Behind Me at the Theatre' by A. P. Herbert by permission of Lady Gwendolen Herbert and *Punch*; *Lyrics on Several Occasions* is published by Elm Tree Books.

INTRODUCTION

A SEDUCTIVE invitation but a mixed blessing: to be asked to edit an anthology such as this is to be given the chance to impose your personal choice on other people, and there's nothing better than that, always provided of course that they happen to like it. On the other hand, like participation in *Desert Island Discs*, it's also an incitement to horrific self-exposure. By their inclusions and their exclusions shall ye know them: how many people—lawyers, actors, painters, writers, statesmen— do I now enjoy and/or admire the less since they've told me what their eight favourite records are?

Equally, if I told you that these were my favourite examples of theatrical prose and verse, what would you make of me? In fact, of course, they are not necessarily my top thirty nor yet a cross-section of family favourites; simply an arrangement of the theatrical writing which I thought would best fit into an archive of this kind.

The qualification is important, because it may explain some of the omissions: among the best theatre books I know, for instance (or rather among the best theatre books I thought I knew) are Emlyn Williams' *George*, Moss Hart's *Act One* and Noël Coward's *Present Indicative*. Reading them all again with an eye to filing them in the archive I discovered a) that they don't lend themselves to extraction and, more surprisingly, b) that they aren't books about the theatre at all. They're books about the childhood of people who sooner or later went into the theatre, and therefore belong in an altogether different archive.

Similarly, there are a number of excellent theatre novels (Margaret Drabble's *The Garrick Year*, Michael Blakemore's *Next Season* and Garson Kanin's *One Hell of an Actor* to name but three) which don't fit in here because carefully plotted novels in extract have a habit of becoming incomprehensible to the first-time reader. Then again, there are a huge number of excellent theatre essays which have, however, already turned up in hardcover theatre anthologies over the past few decades (James Fox's *Life and Death of Joe Orton*, for example, or the Tynan profiles) and that, when I discovered that my first selection for the archive ran to more than twice the maximum possible length of the book, became an iron rule for deciding what to drop.

Other rules for cut-outs had to do with immediacy: an overnight review of a show which closed in 1943, however brilliantly written, is not likely to be of much use tomorrow and so critics tend to be poorly represented here unless (like Shaw, Beerbohm and Agate) they were conscious enough of posterity to wear historian's hats as well. Equally, playwrights come off badly since they tend to write only plays, and plays in extract again have a habit of becoming pretty hard to follow. I'd otherwise like to have included something from Ben Travers, something from Rattigan, John Mortimer, Tom Stoppard, Michael Frayn, Peter Nichols and others who have added much to the gaiety not only of nations but also of me, but there again the material simply came in the wrong shape for an archive of extracts.

I'm also only too aware that this is inclined to be a book about the theatre's immediate past rather than its immediate present, partly because the nature of an archive presupposes the preservation of that past, and partly because the theatrical present is anyway largely uncontainable.

So much for what you won't find here: what you will find here is a selection of theatre writing from the past hundred or so years, heavily biased towards personal memoirs because in the end the theatre of any country can only be as good as the people who act and direct and design and write for it.

A note about the editor: I am the son and grandson and godson of actors, and I was brought up to regard the theatre not as a mystic temple of the arts but as a place relatives went every night to earn our living. Though neither born in a trunk nor carried on as a babe in my father's arms (I was always a heavy child), I did make three matinée appearances as a boy actor in New Zealand in 1950, a public début which local theatregoers have subsequently led me to believe was peculiarly disastrous but which a quarter of a century later I can still remember much enjoying. It was however soon clear to me (and to a large number of New Zealanders) that I was never going to be an actor, though I did in fact inflict myself in a number of minor roles on paying customers at university theatres in Oxford and Honolulu during the early 1960s.

Brave is the actor's child who becomes a professional actor: if he/she does well there is an unspoken suspicion of nepotism, if badly a kind of amazement that the career hasn't worked out better, considering the family background against which it started. It seemed to me an uneven contest, and I was never taught how to be a good loser; on the other hand, the theatre was all I ever really knew or cared about or understood. At Oxford I started reviewing it (as a student critic it was I who advised Michael York that he would never be able to make a living as an actor, and I who begged a large number of others to take up the profession, many of whom can still be seen at the very back of crowd shots in occasional BBC2 classic serials) and the joy of making my living in the theatre without having to be an actor is one I have cherished almost ever since.

Because Fleet Street does not exactly hold out its arms towards 21-year-old theatre critics of limited journalistic experience, I started my working life away from the theatre, writing and subsequently reading television news bulletins for ITN; in some curious way, though, the experience of condensing and retelling the details of air crashes and ambassadorial visits and town-planning decisions to an audience who might or might not much care was a wonderful training. As Tynan kept pointing out, a theatre critic ought in the end to be no more and no less than a good reporter, there to tell his readers what was going on in a certain theatre on a certain night. It is not my job to analyse for you the significance of Pinter's cricketing symbolism: it is my job to tell you what Gielgud and Richardson looked like and sounded like and were like in *No Man's Land*, and that difference is what separates the professional critic from the professor of drama.

This book is therefore going to be about the actuality of theatre, not the theory of it; it reflects a little of the ten years for which I've been making most of my living as a regular magazine critic, and a lot of the eighty or ninety years which conditioned what I saw in that time. You want the best memories, to misquote an old Keith Prowse ad., we have them here. Now read on.

SHERIDAN MORLEY

Those ingenious and formidable brothers the Shuberts, who own hundreds of theatres—and somehow make them pay—not long since asked 30,000 of their patrons what had induced them to go to certain plays. Nearly 12,000 replied that they went on the recommendation of their friends; 6,918 were persuaded thither by newspaper advertisements and 6,884 by theatrical criticism. Only 1,200 were drawn by the magic of starry names. The other aids to theatre going were negligible by comparison.

Arnold Bennett: *The Evening Standard,* 28 March 1929.

Since this is going to be an unashamedly personal collection of favourites, we may as well start the way we mean to continue: Noël Coward (1899–1973) was the subject of the first biography I wrote and later he became a god-father to my son. By the time I first met Coward he was already into his sixties and about to make that extraordinary final leap from Jamaican tax exile via the Hay Fever *revival at the National to grand old man of the British theatre. Fifty years, sixty plays and more than two hundred songs earlier, he'd started out from Teddington into the London of 1911 and this poem (first published in 1967) is about his memories of that time. His first 'Christmas play' was* The Goldfish, *in which he played Prince Mussel for one and a half guineas a week, half a guinea less than an actor called Alfred Willmore was getting in the same cast: Willmore later became better known as Micheàl MacLiammòir. Coward got the job from a Miss Lila Field, for whom at the audition in Baker Street he'd sung* Liza Ann *unaccompanied, an achievement he followed up with a brisk tap dance while his mother, in the absence of a pianist, sang. Miss Field, duly impressed, told Mrs Coward that she'd engage her boy as Prince Mussel for the aforementioned fee, following which there was a terrible pause until Mrs Coward plucked up the courage to say that alas she would not be able to afford it. Miss Field laughed, explain that it was she who would be paying, and Noël Coward had his first job. To celebrate, he took his mother to tea at Selfridge's: 'I was a precocious child' he recalled later 'and, when washed and smarmed down a bit, passably attractive'.*

The Boy Actor

I can remember. I can remember.
The months of November and December
    Were filled for me with peculiar joys
So different from those of other boys
    For other boys would be counting the days
Until end of term and holiday times
    But I was acting in Christmas plays
While they were taken to pantomimes.
    I didn't envy their Eton suits,
Their children's dances and Christmas trees.

I

My life had wonderful substitutes
For such conventional treats as these.
    I didn't envy their country larks,
Their organized games in panelled halls:
    While they made snow-men in stately parks
I was counting the curtain calls.

    I remember the auditions, the nerve-racking auditions:
    Darkened auditorium and empty, dusty stage,
    Little girls in ballet dresses practising 'positions',
    Gentlemen with pince-nez asking you your age.
    Hopefulness and nervousness struggling within you,
    Dreading that familiar phrase, 'Thank you, dear, no more.'
    Straining every muscle, every tendon, every sinew
    To do your dance much better than you'd ever done before.
    Think of your performance. Never mind the others,
    Never mind the pianist, talent must prevail.
    Never mind the baleful eyes of other children's mothers
    Glaring from the corners and willing you to fail.

I can remember. I can remember.
The months of November and December
    Were more significant to me
Than other months could ever be
    For they were the months of high romance
When destiny waited on tip-toe,
    When every boy actor stood a chance
Of getting into a Christmas show,
    Not for me the dubious heaven
Of being some prefect's protégé!
    Not for me the Second Eleven.
For me, two performances a day.

    Ah those first rehearsals! Only a very few lines:
    Rushing home to mother, learning them by heart,
    'Enter Left through window'—Dots to mark the cue lines:
    'Exit with the others'—still it *was* a part.
    Opening performance; legs a bit unsteady,
    Dedicated tension, shivers down my spine,
    Powder, grease and eye-black, sticks of make-up ready
    Leichner number three and number five and number nine.
    World of strange enchantment, magic for a small boy
    Dreaming of the future, reaching for the crown,
    Rigid in the dressing-room, listening for the call-boy
    'Overture Beginners—Everybody Down!'

2

I can remember. I can remember.
The months of November and December,
    Although climatically cold and damp,
Meant more to me than Aladdin's lamp.
I see myself, having got a job,
Walking on wings along the Strand,
Uncertain whether to laugh or sob
And clutching tightly my mother's hand,
    I never cared who scored the goal
Or which side won the silver cup,
    I never learned to bat or bowl
But I heard the curtain going up.

From *Not Yet the Dodo and Other Verses*, 1967.

Actors, even child actors, are perhaps reviewed too often; audiences on the other hand are never reviewed often enough. Usually more dramatic, varied, amazing, unpredictable, funny and enthralling than what they are in fact assembled to watch, audiences are a constant source of interest and education and delight and sometimes horror which is why I've included two reports on them. This, the first, is by Alan Brien (b. 1925) who spent the ten years 1958–68 as a theatre critic first on The Spectator *and then on the* Sunday Telegraph *before taking up a film column elsewhere. I have him to thank not only for some of the most enjoyable and accurate theatre writing of the '60s, but also for teaching me that in moments of real depression there is a macabre pleasure to be derived from wandering around London's theatres looking to see how often and how accurately you've been quoted on the posters outside. I write as the proud author of 'hilarious' and 'one of the best revivals of* The Wild Duck *since the war', though not alas as the author of 'it will run and run', widely attributed to Mr Fergus Cashin.*

So You Want to be an Audience?

WHAT THE British theatre needs more than anything else is an audience. An audience is much more difficult to corral than a playwright, a critic or an actor. After all, it consists of people who hand over real money to appear in theatres. And why should they? Why should they have to strain over the fine print in the newspapers where the plays are indexed under the alphabetical order of theatres which is just about as sensible as listing books in a library under the names of the publishers? When they find the name of the play, they then have to try to remember what they have heard about it. 'Isn't that the comedy about the young man who tries to gas himself?' 'No, I think it's the one where they keep eating all that food on the stage and ringing each other up on the telephone.' 'Are you sure it isn't the musical based on Shakespeare with an all-Negro cast?' 'But if Princess Margaret hasn't been then it must be too intellectual for your mother, dear.' This is only the beginning.

When you have found a play dull enough to suit everybody in the party, you have to find a night far enough off to suit everybody in the party. You book the seats, preferably through an agent. If you go to the box-office there are always six people in the queue. Two of them are arranging free seats and whisper through the glass arch as if they were ordering contraceptives by the gross. One speaks only broken English and is constantly having unimportant points of grammar corrected by friends on the sideline. The fourth refuses to believe that Drury Lane and Covent Garden are not the same theatre and suspects that some metropolitan confidence trick is being played upon him because he has a Northern accent. The fifth has not been to the theatre since Gladys Cooper was carried on in a shawl and is shocked to find that he cannot get a front stall for 5s. 6d. The sixth one is you. When you reach the kiosk you can see only the top, grey, sausage curls of the box-office attendant. She is explaining the plot to a customer on a subterranean telephone. (When *you* telephone, she is always too busy talking to real customers to answer your silly questions.) There is a man there in a dinner jacket, smoking a Wills Whiff and smiling a glazed smile. On no account is he permitted to speak to a customer.

Having handed over the money for the tickets, shuffled your party because of last-minute confusions so that it now entirely consists of people you dislike, including two whose names you can never remember, managed to sneak away from work early in order to go home and change into your most expensive and most out-of-date clothes, bolted a *wiener schnitzel* rolled in sawdust and topped by ice-cream with five colours and no flavour, you are actually in the foyer among the gold basket work, the dandruffed greenery, and a crowd of bad-tempered people who have turned up five minutes late only to have to wait a quarter of an hour for their partners.

The staff of the theatre are cunningly arranged by the man with the Wills Whiff so that they become scarcer and ruder as you tread the red felt into the bowels of the theatre. Invariably when you arrive inside you find that the stage has been moved since last you were there so that it is now sited at some architecturally impossible end of the auditorium. You too are placed so that you will have the longest and most complicated trek to your seat. The attendants, dressed in the chocolate and puce satin costumes of a 1930s accordion band, make no move until they see which way you are going to play your hand. If you attempt to pose as a regular and guide your friends to the right row, the attendants immediately seize the tickets suspiciously and begin to throw doubts on the date and the number. Only the muffled oaths of the party behind you save you from being searched for contraband copies of the reviews. They refuse to sell you a programme and urge you on into what appears to be a plush cattle market. If you behave like a newcomer to the bright lights and ask for guidance, the attendant pushes aside your ticket stub as if it were contaminated and urges you on just the same. Only ten minutes after the advertised curtain time, you have walked twice round the auditorium, passed once along an entire row without stepping on anything but other people's toes, been impaled on two hat-pins, had two cigarettes stubbed out on your behind, ripped open your fly-buttons on corners, and been directed back to a block of seats only fifteen inches away from your original entrance point. It is no use complaining to the attendant there—she is indistinguishable from the original attendant but she is not the same.

The theatre, you soon discover, has been designed for some vanished race of dwarfs with bat ears and hawk eyes. The original audience could see round pillars, catch a mumbled aside bounced off the prompter, and divine which of three blurred pink young men in identical sports jackets is actually moving his lips at any moment. You arrange your enormous legs at right-angles to your torso, vainly attempt to claim one of the seat-arms for one elbow (one of them must be yours whichever end of the row you count from) and try to breathe in without producing a wheeze which groans along the woodwork, ricochets back through the iron supports and ends by twanging the broken springs in your upholstery. Soon you actually begin to hear words, even scraps of sentences and snatches of sound effects. None of them, however, seems to have anything to do with the play. 'If Ethel thinks I am going to carry her trays she can just go and . . .' 'I've taken the order from the bald head with the dyed hair in Row C, thank you very much.' 'How many tonics do you want with these whiskies, Ada?' Occasionally even this contemporary dialogue is drowned by the sound of some sporty employee tobogganing down the stone steps from the gallery on a tin tray while her supporters rattle their spoons in chipped mugs as encouragement. Really luxurious theatres even have synchronised lavatories which all flush juicily and refill at the same moment—usually when the hero is saying 'My God, Bettina—we might be in the middle of the desert'.

While this demonstration of the alienation-effect is being staged in the corridors, the audience has been wedged in silent gloom. But then the late-comers begin to arrive. They all have seats in the middle of the row (the Lord Chamberlain's regulations forbid centre aisles in most theatres). They stumble on in a brandy haze under the impression that the theatre is empty. There is invariably a fat man in charge who insists on finishing his anecdote—'and then I said to old Jaggers, I said "One man's mate is another man's poison," just like that'. His entrance is sometimes the only really dramatic lighting effect of the evening. He stands there, silhouetted like a frog-footman against the bare bulbs of the corridor, arranging his party with Freddy next to Barbara and Cyril on the end with George. With his appearance begins the coughing —brilliantly syncopated and timed so that as each burst appears to have

6

died away some virtuoso of the trachea will introduce the theme again on a different note from a different part of the house. On a really wet evening, the team is augmented by a distinguished foreign hiccuper.

All theatres have bars or what appear to be bars. But they have not been arranged for your entertainment. The purpose of the pseudo or theatre bar is to discourage you from leaving your seat. No matter how long the counter, there are never more than two women behind it. They have been chosen for the honour because in the whole of their long lives they have never been in a real or public bar. They have heard of only two drinks—a 'short' and a 'light ale'! Both, they know, must be kept warm. There is a little ice—for medicinal purposes—kept in a black plastic egg-cup, but this has usually melted during the first act. Only the first six customers are ever served. They cluster in threes around each woman. The rest of the counter is a no-drink zone. Many of the audience do stand there for the enitre interval, but only because they are unable to get out.

The second half of the play is much the same as the first. A few coughers now introduce a fruitier, more trombone-like quality into their solos. The late-comers are also late-getters-back. The lavatories gurgle and fizz without the touch of human hand. A professional laugher, whom the management share with the theatre next door, has been installed in the circle. He laughs as if he wanted to make sure that he was correctly quoted next day—'Ha. Ha. Ha. Haah'. In surburban theatres he is sometimes given a round of applause. (In West End theatres, applause is reserved for sets so preposterously impractical and garish that even the front row notices them; for any piece of business lasting more than ten seconds and unaccompanied by dialogue; for any Philistine witticism or topical reference; and for actresses who have written autobiographies.)

The end of the play is never known to take the audience by surprise. Even if the characters are still in the middle of the exposition, and the three stars have not yet appeared, there is one unmistakable sign. The sound of the male attendants—that is, those with epaulettes—grinding open the outside exit doors, the sudden rush of cold wind rustling the chocolate boxes on the floor, and the distant hooting of the taxis as they rush off home to the suburbs before they can be hired by theatregoers.

I think the British theatre is livelier than it has been for many years. It must be. Because the audiences still brave all its terrors.

From *Punch*, 1969.

Of all our leading actors, Ralph Richardson (b. 1902) alone has neither published an autobiography nor ever been the subject of a full-length biography. What we therefore know about his early life stems almost entirely from the following memoir which he wrote for the Sunday Times *in 1960. It is included here partly for that rarity value, partly in the hope that he might one day be encouraged to write the rest of it, and mainly because it establishes the origins of a career which has spanned half a century of the English theatre and contained throughout that element of on-stage danger and unpredictability which is the hallmark of the truly great actor.*

It all Began with Growcott

IT WAS in Cheltenham, in 1902, that I was born. I had two elder brothers but I do not remember much of them or my father, or Cheltenham, as I left it when I was four because my father and mother decided to separate. I have never known what the quarrel was about. I believe it was something quite trifling, but they never saw each other again and my mother took me away with her. I was a mother's boy until I was eighteen.

Snapshots remain of family life before the age of four. Once out of kindness my brothers took me on their bicycle to the Cheltenham goods yards to see the engines shunting. Christopher, the eldest, the captain of the ship, Ambrose, the next on the step behind, and myself on the handlebars in front. As if yesterday, I can feel the rush of fast wind for the first time on my face.

Afterwards my brothers were punished for this offence. Mother's darling's life had been risked, and in my father's studio I saw my father beating Ambrose, the first glimpse of jungle life. But my brothers never visited their discomfort on me—indeed, I remember when they wanted to go out for the afternoon together, and I was disconsolate at being left, they turned the nursery table up on its side and with crayons drew gauges and a furnace door on the underneath of the table and put me inside the legs, which they told me were levers, and said now I was the engine driver and that I had a long run before me, all the way to

London. It might take all afternoon. Off they went, leaving me happy with my first matinée performance.

My father was art master at the Ladies' College at Cheltenham. Perhaps he was rather tough on my brothers, but he was very gentle to me. I remember being given a stuffed monkey which frightened me out of my wits. My father was very understanding, and said he would keep it for me in the cupboard in his studio until I felt equal to possessing it, and I can see him very sharply, I don't know how long after, reaching up to the cupboard at my request, to give it back.

My father was a shortish man with a beard and cold blue eyes. I would see him off in the front garden on his way to work at the College; I remember him looking down at me and producing from a multi-coloured waistcoat a penny and very politely handing it to me, and then bowling off in a cab with yellow wheels. In the years that followed I was told that he was not a very good man, but I remembered the penny and the yellow wheels and had my doubts of his wickedness. Fourteen years later, when I met him again, I at once recognised the coloured waistcoat.

And then one day, in a cab with a deal of luggage on it, my mother ran away, taking me with her. We went to live in a bungalow at Shoreham-by-Sea, in Sussex. I remember the end of the journey very well, which was after dark, and hearing an extraordinary noise in the air—the bungalow was right on the beach. I was told the sound was the sea, and that in the morning it would be shown to me.

Shoreham-by-Sea in those days was a fine place for a little boy. The bungalow itself consisted of two complete railway carriages with all the original doors and windows. The carriages were joined by a tin roof. Those who have lived under tin roofs are alone in experience of storms. The noise made when the rain rattles, or the hail and thunder echoes, is awesome. The carriages made between them a large room. There was a front porch and veranda and a kitchen at the back. So we had a front door and a back door as well as about twenty side doors, these with brass handles and leather-strapped windows. It was a very good and inexpensive contrivance; the railway stock was beautifully made. We had lamps and candles for illumination and we caught the rain water off the tin roof into a butt, and we boiled it for drinking.

We had an old nanny of my mother's to look after us. Even as a child I realised her cooking was simple; my mother could not cook. Joey had been in the service of the Bird family who made custard powder. Loyalty to her late employers was enduring; as I remember, we ate nothing but Bird's custard and stewed rhubarb.

There were few bungalows in 1906. That meant few neighbours, and I was much on my own. I had one friend for a time, until I was accused

9

of murder. My friend was the daughter of Mrs Pankhurst. Mrs Pankhurst must have lived close to us, because I remember the grocer's boy throwing eggs from his basket at a Suffragette meeting she held in the garden—not a garden really—on her piece of beach.

One day when the little girl and I were playing together I took an iron hoop that had come off a barrel and I twirled it round and round on a stick. The hoop flew off the stick and struck little Miss Pankhurst on the head. It was terrible. Blood streamed down her face—she screamed—Mrs Pankhurst emerged from her bungalow. She could be very dramatic. She was then. 'You brute!' she stormed. 'You have killed my daughter!' It turned out to be a graze on the scalp. Many notes of apology were sent, but we were never allowed to play together again.

This must have been about 1910, because I remember being woken up to be shown Halley's Comet, which appeared in May of that year.

Although I was much on my own there was a lot to amuse a boy at Shoreham; apart from the sea itself there were wooden breakwaters to climb, no trees or grass or shrubs, always stones and shingle, always shingle. I did a great deal of play-acting for my own amusement, always dressed up as something or other, and put in a lot of falling dead and rolling over on the soft shingle. It was useful practice for me, as it turned out, for still today I can manage quite a neat fall.

My mother's sister-in-law lived at Lancing, and there were wonderful visits that my mother and I paid her. She was gay and warmhearted. Georg Hackenschmidt, the world's champion wrestler, was a neighbour. He was extremely gentle to me, and used to take me on his great shoulders to wade in water too rough for me, with a huge shrimping net. We would catch all kinds of things and take them up to the bungalow and fry them mixed with eggs into a wonderful omelette. I have never tasted anything to equal it since. He was a Russian. Perhaps it was a Russian dish?

I am sorry that many of my early memories are of nothing more romantic than things to eat, but smells and savours have a trick of remaining with us. If I ever catch it, I can instantly recognise the kind of soap they used to wash the floor with at my first school, which was a convent school at Shoreham. The nuns told me to learn chapters from the Old Testament by heart, without ever attempting to give any explanation of their meaning. I do not remember the Old Testament very well, but I do remember the French chocolate they gave me with bread and butter for lunch.

The next eight years were without thread. I did not enjoy my school days and I brought little joy to my masters or schoolmates. During the whole of this period I had only three friends: George Pensotti, Cyril Shaw and George Loftus. I am grateful to them for their friendship.

I was always the bottom of the class but as I shot up fairly tall they had to move me to the bigger boys' class for very shame.

Every subject at school bored me. That was all. I never got into very serious trouble; I was not passionate enough and had not the character to be rebellious. I think I was just a big oaf. The schools I went to— there were several—were Roman Catholic institutions. The masters were 'brothers'. The religious side interested me, and I was sent to one school that was a seminary. I think my mother rather hoped I might become a priest. From this school I ran away. I could recite *The Lays of Ancient Rome* a little better than the rest of the class, but this accomplishment was not considered by masters or schoolmates to be a worthy one, and I think I had the tact not to press it. A few times I was a boarder, but mostly a day boy. The latter years of my school life were during the first world war. The last two of them were spent with a private tutor who specialised in backward boys, Ernest de la Grave. This tutor was the only educationalist with whom I struck up a friendship. As a matter of fact, I ended up by selling him lessons, and I'll explain about that later.

About 1910 my mother left Shoreham-by-Sea and we took a little house in South London, at Norwood. We did not miss our Halley's Comet there, for we were very close to the Crystal Palace and every Thursday night there was a Brock's benefit, when they shot up rains of rockets. We got quite bored with them in time, and did not even go to the window.

We moved about a good deal, from one part of Norwood to another, then to Brighton, where we kept changing from flats to small hotels and boarding houses. I was always catching things—mumps, scarlet fever or diphtheria. The last was supposed to have left me with a weak heart, so that I was forbidden games at school. This, and my rather rare appearances at my desk in term-time—either I was laid up and my mother nursing me, or she was ill and I'd stay to look after the house— did not contribute to the success of my school life. My mother had rather a lonely life, without many friends or resources to interest her, and I think she made a bit of a hobby of her health, which was not really so bad—she lived to a very good age.

My mother spoiled me. She lavished a great deal of love and affection on me. She had not been brought up with many practical ideas about house management. She had studied art and had met my father when they were both art students in Paris. Cookery was a closed book to her, but the results of that science interested me, so I did the cooking.

My mother was a devout Roman Catholic, though my father was a Quaker. So I was brought up as a Catholic, and at Brighton was an altar boy, which I enjoyed; but I was a poor Latin scholar and I 'winged' much of the more difficult Latin responses, being sure only of the beginning and the end. People sometimes say to me in the theatre, 'You never dry up, you always say something'; perhaps it was at the altar that I acquired this knack.

My mother's means were slender. One could not employ a chauffeur now for what we lived on at those times, but we had no feeling of want; indeed, we felt rather grand. My mother wrote on crested notepaper from addresses that were modest—a childish vanity, but a little vanity can be a solace in some circumstances. My mother's carelessness about money preserved her from feeling unhappy at finding herself with less than she had had. For my part, I remembered no other circumstances, missed nothing, but must have been very careful about money, for it seems, from the diaries I kept, that I lent it freely to my friends, and I do not seem to have been the loser. There are frequent entries like: 'Cyril Shaw paid me the 3*d.* he owed me.'

The diaries I kept were dirty, scruffy, blotty things with shocking handwriting compared with my parents' notebooks. My mother wrote beautifully at twelve, and I have a sketchbook of my father's at fourteen which is very neat—of course he was to become a professional artist; but I have some notebooks of my grandfather, David, who was a leather manufacturer, which are quite fine. He spoke several languages when young, and was a keen naturalist. I believe he was disappointed with my father when he told him he wished to become a painter instead of going into the family leather works: he looked on painting as a delightful hobby.

His own drawings were excellent, better, I think, than those of my professional father. My grandfather believed in business first and art for fun; he was a very keen Quaker. I don't know what he'd have thought of the stage as a career.

I remember him when I was about twelve or fourteen. He lived in Newcastle upon Tyne and ran the Elswick Leather Works which he made successful. He came to take me out in London one day when he was about eighty. Wonderful white beard and very ironic, like a pirate in a good mood. It was my day, he said, and we'd do exactly what I liked. I took him to the Crystal Palace and we spent hours on the switchbacks; he never turned a whisker. I was told afterwards I might have killed him. To me, he behaved as if he were the same age as myself. When he did die he was eighty-five and he did it to perfection. He was never ill, but one evening he told my grandmother that he felt a little tired, and giving her a kiss said he would go up to bed. Half an hour later she went up and

found him in bed with his spectacles on his nose and a book in his hand
—dead.

In 1919 my friend Cyril Shaw left school and got a job in an insurance
office in Brighton. He was a bright and industrious chap and got on well
there. After a time he told me there was a vacancy at the office which,
if I liked, he thought he could get me. My mother thought I was young
to stop schooling, but I pointed out to her that I never learnt anything
much, and wheedled her into applying for the job; with Cyril Shaw
backing me up, I landed it. The salary was 10s. a week.

As it turned out, it was more than I was worth; to me, it was a
fortune. The offices, in the centre of Brighton, were handsome, with tall
red pillars. I regarded the place as my own; I was a tycoon. My health
immediately improved and I never missed a day's work.

The work was of a beginner's class in the office; it was, in fact, that of
the 'office boy'. I filled the inkwells and changed the blotting paper.
This I did very well indeed. I like things neat and tidy. I had a knack
with an inkwell. I changed the pen nibs every day, and the boss's at
lunchtime as well. This service was appreciated.

I also kept the post and the post book. This I did not do so well; someone always had to add it up for me, I was hopeless with figures, and
scatterbrained with the letters themselves. I brought the boss's letters
in to him to be signed with something of an air. He was a Mr Barry, a
kindly, good-looking, elegant little man, carefree and gay. I invented
for him a character of an office boy of immense solemnity and a marvel
of neatness and efficiency that seemed to rebuke his easiness. It came off
effectively with him. I suspect that I have a talent as a butler. If I half-
unconsciously pulled his leg in my pantomine, I sincerely admired him.

My schooling had not even given me the power of concentration, and
my post suffered in consequence. I put letters in the wrong envelopes.
The insurance company paid out a number of claims, some of them of
quite large sums of money. There were several instances under my
management of the post when persons must have been very surprised on
opening an envelope addressed to them to find themselves unaccountably
the recipient of a plum. The staff of the insurance company were remarkably charitable, kind and indulgent to me over these mistakes. As far as
possible they hushed them up; when the Boss had to know, he forgave.

The experience of my schooldays had given me the impression that
the world was populated with unfriendly persons who only waited for
evidence of my undoubted guilt to pounce upon me with punishment.
In the little world of business in which I next found myself I discovered
the complete opposite: friendship extended toleration in practice.

The staff at the office was not large. Immediately senior to me was my friend, Shaw, and then there came the book-keeper, Mr Lewis. My own book-keeping being bad, I did not win favour in the eyes of Mr Lewis. There were the two shorthand-typewriting girls, Vera Bell, with her jolly, banging, bell-ringing Remington, and her senior, whose name I have forgotten, discreet and a little mysterious, with a typewriter that exactly suited her—a smart dark green Oliver, quieter in action, discreet, with a mellow striking bell.

Last before the boss was Mr Lines the manager, the commander of the office, with a room to himself; he was dapper, with white striped teeth and black-striped trousers, a disciplinarian. 'Richardson should make less noise,' was often remarked. I charmed him not with thimbles and soap but with clean nibs and ink. I did make a deal of noise.

Like most boys of my age I had high spirits, and at the same time I happened to have something of a head for heights. I was always climbing things. Mr Lines, coming into the main office, found me unaccountably crouched on the top of a bookcase next to the ceiling.

I remember when I was at school I bet someone that I would climb all round the school on the ledge that surrounded the building. The Brother Superior's room was back-centre facing the garden first floor with pillars and balcony. I disappeared from view on the ledge, going well in progress to the back of the school. I never reappeared to claim my bet. When I reached the balcony between the pillars I could look right into the Brother Superior's study. Unalarmed at my quite considerable height from the ground, I was chilled on looking within to observe that person sitting at his desk writing. He continued to write, then he looked up and saw me. I do not know if he was chilled, but he opened the window, grasped me by the neck and drew me into the room. 'Come in, little boy,' he said, 'come in.' The interview that followed lost subtlety and concluded in a primitive manner.

This painful experience did nothing to cure me of my love for climbing. There is a ledge that can be seen today around the office building on the corner of High and New Street, Brighton—they were our offices. I thought one day when I was at work that it would be amusing to traverse this ledge above the heads of the populace below. Perhaps I wanted to show off, perhaps it was the purer inspiration of adventure—the Alpine climber's audience is sparse.

Past experience at school had taught me caution in achieving an exploit. The passage on the ledge had, like the Brother Superior's, to pass the sacred room. I chose my time; I waited until the Boss was out. In happy security I achieved the meridian of my airy course right in the window of the Boss's room. I had chosen an ill moment: Mr Barry returned, the door of the office opened and in he walked. He did not say

'Come in, little boy, come in.' He said nothing. His hand poised as it was raised to take off his hat, a confused expression passed over his handsome face. I smiled at him from outside, I waved to him, I put my head in through the top of the window. 'Mr Barry, Sir,' I said, affably, 'a pigeon.'

Mr Barry never commented on my odd behaviour but I think he must have underlined in red ink a note that he had already in his mind: 'Richardson is not reliable.'

Vera Bell and Cyril Shaw gave me much delightful friendship, helping me in my work, adding my postbook for me—covering up my mistakes as well as helping me in the production of my magazine. One of my tasks in the office was to operate the duplicating machine. We used to send out lists of quotations of some sort to all our sub-agents in the South of England. I enjoyed my printer's day—Thursdays—when I did this work. Then the idea came to me to turn out a little magazine of my own. This I circulated among friends and relations, starting with something like a dozen copies, but sales of the magazine quite rapidly rose to something like fifty, to people I did not actually know.

It is on my conscience that I did not treat the insurance company well. I was unable to interest myself in their service, but I stayed on with them, developing an interest of my own. All day long my thoughts were on my magazine, and I seduced my friends in the office to further that interest, though I don't think their work suffered in consequence. I wrote for my magazine in office hours; so did Cyril; so did Vera. Vera cut stencils for my magazine on her Remington.

I did not have the cheek to reproduce the paper in office hours, I stayed late for that. But I was snaky—there is no doubt of that. The duplicating machine had been in the office for a long time—it never occurred to me that it was not good enough to produce the lists that the company required; but in time I considered it not good enough to produce my magazine. In a shop in Brighton I had seen a beautiful Roneo printing machine. Like a beastly serpent—as a matter of fact I am very fond of serpents—like a beastly young man I suggested to Mr Lyons that it was in the interest of the dignity of his office that a better printing machine should be purchased, and I led him to the kill: he bought it.

My grandmother died at Newcastle upon Tyne. She had a large family, seven children of her own, and four of these had families of their own; nevertheless when making her will she was kind enough to remember me—of whom she had seen very little. She left me £500 for my education. My mother and I were staggered by this vast sum and we spent much excited time thinking how we should apply the gift. I thought 'it would be nice' to be a painter. I did not feel my needle of direction point very strongly to the idea—I was at that time unconscious of the possession of any such guiding instrument—and although I knew I must do some work I had no particular aim. At last it was decided that I should go to the Brighton School of Art. I thought then, and I still hold the opinion, that the most delightful life one could live would be to be a painter. I thought if I went to an art school I might find out if I had sufficient talent.

My plans laid, I knocked one day on Mr Barry's door. 'Mr Barry, sir,' I said to him, 'I am afraid I have bad news for you.' Mr Barry blanched. No doubt he thought that one more cheque had been posted to the wrong address.

'Well, Richardson, what it it?' he said with manly steadiness.

'I have come, sir,' I told him, 'into the possession of a very large fortune and I am sorry to have to tell you that I wish to give you notice.' Mr Barry rose from his desk. He came over and clasped me by the hand. 'My goodness, Richardson, how glad I am to hear you say that,' he said. 'I was going to give you the sack on Saturday and I hated to have to do it!'

I still possess a few drawings and water-colours that were part of my studies at the Brighton School of Art. They are not very good; they show neither vitality nor originality. Other students were showing much more ability. I was not encouraged by my masters. I did not find much courage in myself. Copying the big casts from the antique and making water-colours of bottle and drapery still-life bored me. Many years later, when I began to paint for my own enjoyment, I realised I had learnt something, and now I paint with pleasure.

There was an old lady student at the school. She was very eccentric in appearance, covered in all kinds of rings and chains and beads and chatelaines. She was well over seventy and very good-natured. She had been a student at one art school or another all her life, but she was still where I was—in the bottom class. Often we found ourselves alone in the big schoolroom during the morning sessions. The art school got busy in the evenings but this lady and myself took the day course.

Being kind by nature, she sought to start up some subject of conversation that might amuse me and one day she asked me if I read a great deal. I told her that my favourite author was Rider Haggard. She said she was very fond of Dickens and did I know him. I said I did not, and that night I inquired of my mother if she liked Dickens. 'No, no,' my mother said, 'I don't care for Dickens—the print is too small.' The next day the old lady brought me a copy of *Oliver Twist*.

That little action changed the whole pattern of my inward life. *Oliver Twist* fairly exploded inside me; it set up a chain reaction that is still going on. My first excitement was tremendous. What were those still white antique Discobolus and Hercules to me in interest beside Fagin, Sykes? The poor lady may have regretted her friendly action in lending me *Oliver Twist*; her gentle water-colour peace must have been shattered by my descriptions to her of what she had given me to read. I talked to her incessantly.

Later she lent me *Plutarch's Lives*, no doubt with the hope that it might prove a sedative.

I fell upon literature like a starved and hungry waif. I gobbled up the whole of Dickens within a few months of starting *Oliver Twist*. I read every single play of Shakespeare. While at school I had rejected what they forced down my throat; now at the school of art I eagerly devoured it.

Shaw was still publishing plays and prefaces. Aldous Huxley had just published *Crome Yellow*—I felt I had 'discovered' him.

In 1920, when I was eighteen years old, H. G. Wells published *The Outline of History*. This was dizzy stuff for me. My mother had brought me up as a firm Roman Catholic; Shaw and Wells wrote about evolution and the 'science of life', all new to me; also they exposed certain weaknesses, discrepancies and, indeed, crimes within the Roman Catholic church.

So, off like a shot with my new-found literary friends, I decided that the whole of my religious belief must be stuff and nonsense, and in consequence must be scrapped. This was a pity, because for a long time I added to my ignorance by going about with a silly cocksure know-all attitude which limited the horizon of my thought and reduced its elasticity. Of course the positive religious ideas I had held I had not acquired for myself; they had been injected into me in infancy and the fact that they had never been masticated or digested was perhaps responsible for my so violently throwing them up.

I made little progress with my drawing and the thought came to me that I was unlikely to make a living from reading books, although in a way it was to turn out that I was able to do this very thing; for it could be said of an actor's work that it is to read the author's script and then to vivify it in action—as it were, to whistle the tune.

The Brighton school, like most others of its kind, taught Crafts as well as Arts. One of these crafts was bookbinding. I was drawn to the bookbinding department because my fondness for reading had made the volumes themselves attractive to me. I liked the feel of leather and the smell of glue; perhaps it was in my blood from my leather-tanning family. There was a pleasant bustle in the place, with white-coated people banging about with their hammers and breathtaking gold-leaf.

I took up bookbinding and it was the first thing I had studied that did not bore me. Mr North taught the subject; he was a fine craftsman. My work was not outstanding, but I worked pretty hard both at the school and in a bookbinder's shop in the town, and I had a press in my bedroom at home. There I gave my old tutor, Ernest de la Grave, lessons in bookbinding for a shilling an hour—it really was quite reasonable, because I did know the elements of the job.

Now I thought it was possible that bookbinding might turn out to be a job in life for me, and I got my family in Newcastle to write to Mr Zaehnsdorf, who was a customer for their book leathers, to ask him to see me. He was one of the very best binders of our time and had a beautiful shop in Shaftesbury Avenue. Old Mr Zaehnsdorf was nice to me but was discouraging. He said the bookbinding business was falling to pieces; fine bindings were very expensive, people weren't spending their money that way. It was a long apprenticeship to learn the trade: young people weren't coming in at a rate to keep the shop running.

He said he had sons of his own but he wasn't putting them into the business and the best advice he could give me was to have nothing to do with it.

Meanwhile my £500 wasn't growing any fatter, and I couldn't think what to do. It was not a very satisfactory time for me, but it did not last very long, for suddenly my needle of direction swung over very strongly indeed. I decided to try to become an actor. I had for many years vaguely thought I would like to 'go on the stage', but it seemed an impossibly remote and difficult thing to do. My mother and I had never met an actor in our lives.

I used to go to the Theatre Royal, Brighton, and had seen quite a few plays, but used perhaps to enjoy the Hippodrome, the variety, best. There I saw all the wonderful comedians of that rich time—Little Tich, Marie Lloyd, G. H. Elliott, George Robey, Harry Tate and Vesta Tilley.

Yet it was not one of these giants of the music hall, or even one of the very greatest actors in the theatre, that produced for me the momentous and decisive moment that moved my compass. It was Sir Frank Benson as Hamlet. Benson had brought his company to the Theatre Royal; they had six or seven plays in the bill, and I went more than once, in the gallery. The moment that so impressed and triggered me off was the night they played *Hamlet* with Sir Frank as Hamlet—I knew the play quite well but I had never seen it on the stage. When the Ghost said to Hamlet: 'Revenge my foul and most unnatural murder,' Hamlet drew his sword—or rather, I think he had already drawn it but in response to the line scraped it, rubbed it, sharpened it as it were on the ground (he was kneeling); this produced a wonderful noise. I have heard that the 'business' was first invented by Henry Irving.

18

I don't suppose I reasoned it all out in one moment, but thinking about it I felt that that 'business' was something wonderful. A piece of mime, a sound not in the text, something that never interfered with the text but in a wonderful way illuminated it, like a book of illustrations, yet something that could be done nowhere else but upon the stage.

I suddenly realised what acting was and I thought: By jove, that's the job for me: read plays, not books, and illustrate not by drawing or painting, but by acting!

I lost no time in pursuit of my new idea. Not far from where I lived in Brighton there was a little theatre, half-professional, half-amateur, run by Mr F. R. Growcott. Though the next day was Sunday I went down to the theatre. I succeeded in getting the address of Mr Growcott, in the Port Hall Road. I knocked at his door and he answered it himself.

I gazed at the very first actor I had ever seen 'off the stage'. He wasn't very tall. He had on a dark brown, woolly kind of tweed. He had a hooked nose and pleasant blue eyes, neat tie and shirt, and was clean-shaven. By a remarkable coincidence he was a pocket edition of Sir Frank Benson (who was tall) on whom he liked to model himself, and in whose company he had once been.

I explained to Mr Growcott that I would like to become a member of his acting company. There was a silence. Growcott leaned against the door and looked me over.

'What acting have you done?' he asked me. I told him none.

'Then I don't see how, as an actor, you would be very useful to me,' he said pleasantly. This was an impasse.

'Mr Growcott,' I said cautiously, 'I might be able to pay you a small premium.' He stood bolt upright. 'Come inside,' he said.

We had a long chat. I said I felt it was possible that I might have a little talent. He said we would soon find out about that. But as a complete beginner, I inquired, how long did he think it might take to make a useful sort of actor out of me? Growcott thought it might take some time; he thought it might take three months. In this calculation Growcott was far out—it took, in fact, nearly fifteen years before I could be said to be a useful sort of actor. However, based on Growcott's time, I made a suggestion. We would make an agreement for six months. For the first three months I would pay him 10s. a week to work in his theatre, for the following three months he would pay me 10s. a week for working for him.

Growcott pondered this proposition in the manner of Napoleon. Growcott was the most 'born' actor I have ever met; he acted every single moment of his life. The only time he was for an instant natural was when he was on the stage. There he was uncertain, because he never knew the lines of the character he was playing. Both aspects of his nature—the artificial and the real—contained a great deal of charm. Then Growcott said:

'Would you pay a month's premium in advance?' I thought I could do this. 'Well, then, meet me at 11.30 tomorrow at the theatre and I'll hear you recite something. We'll soon see if you have got anything in you.'

My mother, like the good sport and affectionate helper she had ever been to me, provided me with the £2 for the advance of premium.

The piece I chose to deliver to Mr Growcott was Falstaff's description of his being thrown into the Thames from *The Merry Wives of Windsor*. On the Monday morning I set out clutching Shakespeare and £2, crossing my fingers in the hope of good luck for the audition.

At 11.30 there was no Growcott, . . . at 12.30 there was none. I grew impatient, and when, at 12.45, he strolled in as if nothing had happened, I said crossly, 'Mr Growcott, you have kept me a long time waiting.' His reply, the first words uttered to me in the theatre, was both sapient and prophetic:

'Young man, if you are going to get on in the theatre, you'll have to learn to wait.'

I recited my piece. Growcott's expression was good-humoured. 'That is quite awful,' he said. 'It is shapeless, senseless, badly spoken, you don't even know it very well, and I can't think why you chose the piece you did, because you could never, never be any good as Falstaff.'

I did not say anything. Sadly I took up the copy of Shakespeare into which I had so hopefully folded mother's £2. I looked round for my hat.

'By the way,' said Growcott easily, 'did you remember to bring that little premium? If you have, we might go and have a spot to celebrate, before getting down to work.'

Without knowing it, I carried Growcott's remarks about my reading for long in my memory. More than twenty-five years later, when we were discussing a new season's play for the Old Vic, Laurence Olivier said: 'Why don't we do the two parts of *Henry IV* and let Ralph play Falstaff?' I at once said 'I'd never, never be any good as Falstaff.'

'I think that's rather silly of you, Ralph,' said Laurence. 'I don't see that it's more difficult than any other part.'

I stayed happily with Frank Growcott, not quite long enough for the whole of our six months' plan to mature, but for most of it. He was my first manager, he taught me a number of things, and I owe a lot to him.

The play in which he was immediately engaged was a wartime comedy he had written himself, and was to be played that very night. I was told that I was to be the noises off. I was to make the sound of a Zeppelin air-raid which was an important part of the play. I was given two petrol tins on the end of a leather strap which, with practice, can make quite a good din. I practised, but I was told to shut up, it interfered with rehearsal.

Growcott's theatre was a small, modest, fit-up affair. It was converted from a bacon factory, and it needed no sharp wit to make up jokes at our expense about the place continuing to turn out 'ham'. The little stage Growcott had built himself. He did practically everything himself, always the leading man, with his wife, Blanche, the leading lady, his sister-in-law, one or two actors who lived in Brighton, and who were glad to 'fill in' between better engagements, and one or two students like myself.

At last the time came when I was briefed for my part in the play. I was shown a small space underneath the stage, and I was told to crawl down there with my petrol tins. I was instructed that upon the signal from Growcott on the stage above I was to give the tins all I had got. I went below. Growcott signalled by tapping his toe on the boards.

'Can you hear me?' he said. I could hear very well; the thin and flimsy boards were an inch above my head, their cracks even provided me with enough light to see by.

Now Growcott was quite a short man; he was rather sensitive about this, and when he acted he used to build himself up with very high heels. When this, my first play, commenced that night, great confusion took place when Growcott entered the stage above me on his high heels. I took his step for tap signals, and went into action with my petrol tins. I was not an overnight success in my new job. Later on, I was able to be quite useful. Growcott taught me electric wiring, scene construction and scene painting, all in a very elementary style, but it pleased me greatly.

Growcott's personality commanded respect. He was proud and arrogant (he always pronounced that word as 'ag-arr-ant'); adventurous but undisciplined, he possessed magnetism and panache on the stage and off.

Growcott was very abstemious in drinking and he never used a 'bad word'. It could be said that he was affected, because he was always acting, but the part he chose to act in his private life was an heroic character that Martin Harvey might have played on the stage, so that the 'effect' was to the good. He was good-humoured, but he could not match the sardonic humour of his wife. I think she was a bit older than Frank. She looked as if life had not been all roses for her, she wore a tragic air, and she was splendid on the stage as Nancy in *Oliver Twist*, or Madame Defarge. She was wonderfully humane and charitable, but with a sharp, ironic humour. I had never met anyone like her and she fascinated me.

The Growcotts took me back to their flat in Port Hall Road. I spent many happy hours there. They drank cocoa; and during the five months I was with them I drank all the cocoa I needed for the rest of my life.

Among other things, I made myself useful to my manager as a chauffeur of a kind; all my life I have been fascinated by things one could drive on or in. At eighteen all I possessed was a pushbike. I spent hours cleaning and polishing it, and most evenings before the show I would call for Growcott, who would get up on the step behind me, and I would whizz him down the hill.

This fondness for driving things about was later to do me a good turn.

My usefulness in the theatre had a poor start, but it improved; it could hardly have done otherwise. Like Caliban I emerged from my cave underneath the stage to the elegance of scene painting, property and wardrobe departments, and it was not too long before I stepped upon the stage itself as an actor in a red and blue uniform, a gendarme in *The Bishop's Candlesticks*, by Honoré de Balzac, adapted and translated by F. R. Growcott.

I played, among a number of parts, Bill Sikes, Malvolio, Henry IV and, unique, I think, I doubled Banquo and Macduff. I hadn't the slightest idea what I was doing as an actor. I was splashing about in the shallow end of a swimming bath, not even knowing what the correct action of swimming was like; and in the shallow end because our little theatre was so small that however I spoke my lines they could never be inaudible.

One did not even enter into a state of self-criticism, there was no time for that. One did a play, made the scenery and made or collected the props for the next, and played the part in the same state of mind as one screwed the hinges on the door of the set.

When the first three months of my 'contract' were over, I did not more than once in the moon see the ten shillings a week we had agreed on. Each Saturday night there was an argument which sometimes led to blows. My first manager is the only one so far that I have actually struck. No bones were broken, nor feelings hurt, for that matter, and I still remained on good terms with the family. Calmer reflection told me they had not got the money, and they tolerantly put down my excitement to the impetuosity of youth.

Sipping my cocoa, laughing round the supper table in the Port Hall Road, I was happy to be with such pleasant companions and proud to think I was a humble member of the great theatrical profession.

The tin of cocoa upon the table bore a yellow label and printed on it was the name 'FRY'. There was a sign to me. Before she married, my grandmother Catherine had been a Fry of that same cocoa family, and now it was from her wealth that I drew my daily bread, through her benefit that I sat in this company; and I had no right whatsoever to consider myself as a professional actor; Grandmama's funds were running low. The yellow signal soon must turn to red.

Now I wrote certain letters. There were many good repertory companies touring the country in those days. There were Benson and Martin Harvey. There were Ben Greet and Charles Doran. I had seen them and a lot of others at Brighton. I wrote to all four. I obtained an interview with Ben Greet on the Palace Pier Theatre. He was nice to me but had no vacancy. Charles Doran was the only one who replied to my letter and told me to come and see him at Eastbourne, where he was to play in a week or two.

I arrived before the matinée and inquired for my appointment. Everyone was polite to me, and I admired the lofty ease of those actors I saw preparing for the matinée—it was *The Merchant of Venice*. Mr Doran's dresser came to tell me the guvnor would see me in his room directly after the matinée.

I was too nervous to go in front and see the play, and, anyway, I had seen Doran as Shylock before. I cycled round the Devonshire Park muttering over the piece I had prepared to recite to him, should he require it. Perhaps we would never get so far.

The audience came out of the theatre, the time had come. I stood outside Charles Doran's dressing-room. I straightened my tie and oh, goodness, only just noticed in time that I still had on my bicycle clips.

When I went in, Doran was sitting framed in light at his make-up table, wiping off his Shylock with a towel with red edges; at such times one can be very observant. He had on a vest and his stage tights. He regarded me through the mirror in front of him, not at all piercingly.

'Sit down, Richardson,' he said, 'and tell me what you have been doing.'

Doran had a very charming voice with a little Irish accent. He was heavy and formidable in build. As I talked to him I was fascinated to see, so close to me, hanging on the wall, Shylock's costume that I had last seen from the gallery in the Brighton theatre, and I was a little startled out of my imagination to see next to it the grey flannel waistcoat and jacket that no doubt he was going home in. Perhaps I imagined he never wore less than a toga. What I failed to observe was that the trousers of the flannel suit had fallen from the hanger and lay upon the floor.

Doran was very affable and seemed interested in what I told him, and after a while he asked me if I could speak a little something for him. As I rose, I gave myself a cunning smile. Not again would I make the mistake of that dreadful Falstaff! I started off with simple, plain

Friends, Romans, Countrymen . . .

I thought I was getting along fairly well until I came to the line

Doran exploded: 'Stop it, man, stop it!' he roared. I was shattered. 'I'm sorry, Mr Doran,' I said, 'wasn't it any good?'

'It's all right, it's all right,' he said, 'but you are trampling on my trousers!'

The trousers restored, good humour returned, but Doran asked for no more oratory. 'I'm willing to take you on,' he said. 'What are your terms for a tour with me?'

'Mr Doran, Sir,' I said, 'if I am to join your company, I am afraid you will have to pay me 30s. a week.'

'I'll give you a contract for £3,' said Doran, 'go and fix it up with my manager.'

Joyfully I pounded my pedals back to Brighton. Now, with an Esher contract in my pocket, I fancied I must be a professional qualified actor. I had not yet come upon Keats' observation that fancy is a deceiving elf.

Doran held his rehearsals in London in August. I had hardly ever been to London proper, only passing through a couple of times on a visit to Newcastle, or for the day; I had never spent a night in London or seen a play there. On recommendation from an actor in Growcott's company, I had a room in a boarding house over the Waterloo Road where the Festival Hall now stands. For the first time I was on my own in the world and all my worldly goods were in a small wicker basket. Actors were supposed to provide a part of their costume in those days and, according to instructions I received, in the basket were:

> 2 wigs—1 juvenile, 1 scratch character.
> 2 court shoes—1 russet, 1 black.
> 2 tights.
> 2 ballet shirts.

It was like a list for school. In a way Doran's company was a school. It wasn't a school run for the purpose of teaching you anything—why should it, since it paid you—but it worked on a method of acting, and I found I had many hard lessons to learn there.

As a new boy I found this school very, very confusing. At full strength there were ten plays in the repertory. In the first three-weeks' rehearsal in London, we prepared six or seven of them. The majority of the company had been in the plays before, but some had now been given new parts, and there were a small number of new actors in the company, though none as inexperienced as I. I had a small part in each play, and the job of second worm or assistant props. Abraham Sofaer, who had already toured with the company, was 'first worm'.

Doran had a good company: in it were Edith Sharp, Barbara Everest,

Hilton Edwards, Earle Grey, Donald Wolfit, Norman Shelley, Cecil Parker, Arthur Young and Muriel Hewitt.

It was not rehearsing seven plays at the same time that so confused me so much as adapting myself to the method of acting practised. Now it came to me that I had been acting without any method at all, and in so small a manner and in such a little theatre that my work would be useless in a proper playhouse.

The Doran company worked to a plan. They were an orchestra. With Growcott, I realised, we had all been soloists with no conductor in charge.

Doran's company were mostly young people: he alone was experienced. His main asset was his beautiful voice, but it was not particularly powerful. His orchestra was planned to make the maximum of sound, bustle and vitality so as to leave calm, quiet passages for his playing. This was not a new method even in those days, but it got the best out of the company and its star, and it was a definite plan, which is very valuable in the theatre.

Doran must have wondered if in me he had bought a pig in a poke. My Mark Antony passed muster in a dressing-room, but my Lorenzo wasn't much good in our room of rehearsal. He and the company did not regard me with great favour. Lorenzo was the most important of the first set of parts I was given. The most distressing thing was that it seemed I was so feeble. I had no strength; no energy, no voice, no lungs. I commanded no attention.

'Keep it up, Richardson, keep it up,' said Doran every time I spoke. Bewildered, I shouted, I screamed and rushed about the stage as if it had been on fire. I banged Salanio and Salerio on the back as if they were choking. I spoke so fast I felt my tongue must gabble out of my head. I laughed like a tipsy hyena, but 'Oh, Richardson, do keep it up' was all the response I got.

I possessed, indeed, more than enough strength and voice for the purpose. When I was young I am unabashed to say I had a good voice, and I was tall, I was active and energetic, but I did not know how to apply my forces. Actually it requires very little force to speak quite forcefully on the stage, but the delivery requires timing. Alas, I had no coaching. When I took a breath, I burst myself. I did not know that a breath correctly taken gives a relaxed and almost empty feeling to the chest. I batted my eyes all over the stage, giving out so many confusing signals that when I really needed to send out some message with my eyes, no one was interested in the sender.

Had I played tennis I might have noted how fatal it is to wait until the ball is upon you before raising the racket. It is equally fatal for swift, smooth, polished speech to wait till the idea of the line comes before taking the breath. The first breath process is often the natural one, but art must improve on nature. With these and many, many other faults I seemed to have got away to some extent on the tiny stage at Brighton, but it is a hard fact that a big stage and good lighting show up rather than cover faults.

'Keep it up, Richardson, oh do keep it up,' rang dismally in my ears, as each night, when rehearsal ended, I walked over the old Waterloo Bridge to my lodgings—it all seemed hopeless: had Brighton not made me a good swimmer, I felt I could have jumped into the river.

For the failure of the early scenes of Lorenzo, and for the other minor characters I had been given to play, I had only myself to blame. But for the last act of Lorenzo, I can acquit myself—it is one of the most fiendishly difficult assignments an actor can take on. The great trial scene in the play is over, the dramatic tension is completely exhausted— enter Lorenzo with one of the most beautiful, but at the same time, one of the most complex, poetic speeches:

Look how the floor of heaven is thick inlaid with patines of bright gold.

The musical equivalent of these passages could be likened to some passages of Mozart over which Heifetz might crease a frown. I do not blame myself, with five months' experience, for making a mess of them. It could be said I should never have been allowed to play the part, but that is the way provincial companies who gave chances to young people were able to work. Perhaps because they worked that way they exist no more. Those who suffer are the young people who do not now have the chances I had.

We opened our tour at Lowestoft. I let it down at Lowestoft, I did not 'keep it up'. The week over, I stood on the empty stage at night packing my props into their baskets. My patines of bright gold on the floor of heaven did not seem to be shaping well: I looked on the floor at my feet, saw the thick hard boards of the stage dented with the left-overs of plays, musicals and variety shows, and scattered among them was a constellation of bright screws, tacks and nails. Here was my floor of heaven and I was treading it.

Yet the worst was over, and as the tour went on, I began to find my feet. 'Doran hardly rages at me at all,' I find in a diary. I stayed with Charles Doran for three years. I had a good time. I travelled about all over the country and in Ireland; all was newly fascinating.

We had a few weeks' holiday a year, not many, and these we could enjoy as we were sure of re-engagement. During my holidays I stayed with my mother, and now I could afford to change my push-bike for a motor-bike. It was a Rudge, a powerful machine with no clutch or gearbox, only an expanding pulley on a rubber driving belt; but to start up you had to give a running push. You opened up, she was off like a rocket, you leapt into the air and landed on the saddle—or else.

When we rehearsed in London I was now relaxed enough in the evenings to visit the London theatre. There was Charles Hawtrey, I think the best actor I've ever seen, and Mrs Patrick Campbell who knocked me flat. When, as Hedda Gabler, she burnt her lover Lovborg's poems in the stove, I nearly passed out. She took up the packet of poems and moved across the stage with the awful symmetry of Blake's own tiger. With a clang she opened the top of the stove, and, creating therein an inferno, with a glance, she spoke like some terrible trumpet:

'My child and Lovborg's? I'll singe your baby locks!' As she threw the love-letters into the fire, she was a devil incarnate.

As each tour took place I got better and better parts, two or three new ones each time, and in the end I was playing Orlando, Mark Antony, Macduff, Bottom and a lot of others. When you inherited a new part in the company, it was expected that you played it as near to the performance of its previous owner as you could. This was the real traditional theatre, and for young people it was a practice that had many advantages, provided the original moulds were good. I was lucky with some of mine; for instance, I stepped into the shoes of Arthur Young, who was a jolly good Bottom. I don't know if he invented the characterisation, or where it came from, but it was the basis of several performances of the part I later gave which were quite successful, so I am very grateful to him.

Three years seems a long time when you are young. I was just twenty, and as we played nothing but Shakespeare I thought it would be best if I could get a change from tights and togas for my working dress, and put on a pair of trousers. But I felt it was a plunge to chuck up my job and seek new work from the London agents whom I did not know.

There were many companies on tour in those days; most successful London plays sent out one or two provincial reproductions, so there was plenty of work, but there were also plenty of actors. Perhaps not more in the profession than there are at present, but few films were made in England, and there was no radio or television, so the whole pack were after the theatre. I took a room in London and did the round of the agents. I have been so lucky that I have not often had to do that—I did not find it very pleasant. They were not very courteous to one who was unknown. One day, after weeks of the round, I went into Miss Connie's Agency. It was crammed with people and Miss Connie was busy and bouncing, and I thought she would have no time for me; but when she came out she saw me sitting there and hauled me straight into her office.

'Now,' she said to her staff, 'here is a likely looking lad.' I was tremendously cheered by this. Subsequently, when I came to make films, I did much happy traffic with Connie's office.

At last I got a part with No. 1 Company of Sutton Vane's *Outward Bound*. This was a well-written modern play, very much suited to give the new experience I was after. But I was not quite equipped for this experience, and to begin with I found myself back in trouble. There were about eight equal parts which had to carry the play between them. Then I realised how I had been nursed so far by always playing in a company led by a powerful leading actor who had pulled the train along.

Next, I did not find the trousers nearly so easy to wear as I had imagined. I had found a certain air with which to wear a toga, but this wouldn't do at all. I felt naked. I hadn't the slightest idea what to do with my hands. Before, they might rest on a dagger or sword or caress a plumed hat—what could I do now? I couldn't always keep them in my trouser pockets!

Another thing, which was worse, was that I had been used to the bustle and variety of repertory. We never played the same play twice in a week: now I couldn't keep my mind steadily in one direction, my performance varied from night to night. If the manager came on an 'off night', which he always seemed to do, there were painful interviews after the show.

The great actor Lucien Guitry is reported to have said: 'Acting is a trick,' and to have said no more on the subject. If it is true, it might be added that it is a trick with three cards. The first card, or trick, is the plan, the blueprint of the performance. The second trick is printing or performing the blueprint with complete accuracy as many times as, and at the time that, it is required—be it however many times, late or early, hot or cold, feeling elated or miserable, bored or excited.

The third trick is to force the audience to accept this blueprint, be they few or many, bored or excited, hot or cold: and to be able, should acceptance not prove delicious to them, to resort to forcible feeding. Tricks two and three may be learnt by patient practice, but trick one, the making of the plan, the blueprint, is something about which I would very much like to have Guitry's advice. No doubt he was wise to be silent, for it is foolish to analyse acting and, if there is any truth in what I have added to Guitry's famous remark, that truth is as evasive and as deceitful as is 'the Lady' herself when the three-card trick is played on the racecourse. For example: card one can only be played after card three.

I toured next in *The Way of the World* as produced by Nigel Playfair, but it was not so much in the way of the world or in the way of my work that I gained at that time, as in my own private way of life.

I mentioned, as being among Charles Doran's company, the name of Muriel Hewitt, known to us as Kit. Kit and I had long been friends, and when I left the company we missed each other. Then Kit left Doran and on the tour of *The Way of the World* we were married. She was sixteen, and I was twenty-one.

Muriel Hewitt was the perfect example of the natural actress. Nothing was any trouble for her, everything she did was right. Graceful in movement, with perfect diction and a serenity unruffled under any stage conditions. Kit was small in stature but large in courage. Returning home a few minutes before me one night, she surprised a burglar in the house. This man no doubt owed his life to his agility in scrambling over the wall in the back garden whence she had chased him. When I came in I found Kit like a wild cat just deprived of a mouse.

Her career on the stage was brilliant but brief, and her courage was terribly tested, for after a few years of work she fell under some rare nervous attack, perhaps akin to polio, and some years later she died.

But there were no clouds in the first years of our married life; for we both had the good fortune to join Sir Barry Jackson's company, first for a year on tour in *The Farmer's Wife*, in which Kit and I had a beautifully written scene together, then for a year at the Birmingham Repertory Theatre under the fine direction of H. K. Ayliff. Then for the first time I was able to create a few original characters instead of reproducing other actors'. Barry Jackson gave me my first chance to play in London in *Yellow Sands* at the Theatre Royal, Haymarket, in 1926. Kit was the juvenile lead in this play, but she had already played the modern-dress Hamlet in London. There was a big difference in those days between the provincial and the London actor and this was great promotion for me.

Yellow Sands ran for two years with 613 performances and I learnt a great deal from the experience. I had a small part which was extremely tedious to play, I was on the stage for long periods of time with little to do but attend to others. We played three matinées a week. I nearly went raving mad with boredom, but it was the making of me. Those years of grind formed the first thread of nervous tissue connecting what I had in my mind and what I was doing with my body.

I was surrounded by the best actors I had so far been in contact with. Cedric Hardwicke was the character lead, and 'Dear Old'—as all who knew and remember him instinctively call him—Frank Vosper. Rebellious, petulant, furious with himself, wonderfully funny 'Dear Old' Frank Vosper!

During the long scene of the reading of the will in *Yellow Sands*, I sat next to the solicitor on the stage played by H. O. Nicholson. I learned a lot listening to him. Most of us were rather rough lads from the Rep.

Company, but Nicholson was a real 'London actor', one of the best of the old school. Superb, diamond-sharp diction, never a finger out of place and pervading over all a gentle, sweet humorousness.

Now Kit and I had our own flat, actually furniture of our own, and we had a car as well. This was the first model of the Austin 7 h.p. I was tremendously proud of this machine. I had a rich semi-cousin who lived near Wolverhampton, and I paid him a visit. With every spoke of those spidery wire wheels polished, I swept the Austin up his drive. With a gesture I invited his admiration: 'Yes, yes, Ralph,' he said, 'how exciting. They are beautiful little cars—we are giving them this year for Christmas!'

Cedric Hardwicke was wonderfully kind to Kit and me. He was the big leading man of the Birmingham Company. He never had a trace of 'side'. He possessed beautiful cars which he knew I envied. A Vauxhall 14 h.p. and then a front-wheel-drive Alvis which could far outpace my little Austin.

'You know, Ralph,' he would often say to me, 'do you know what that car of mine wants? It wants a good, long, fast run. Could you spare the time over the weekend to take her out for me?'

Many years later I possessed a twelve-cylinder Rolls. Cedric was here on a visit from America and I was mad to show it to him. We got into Regent's Park. 'Now Cedric,' I said, 'you drive.' We changed places. 'Before you start off,' I said, 'I want you to listen to the engine— pretty quiet for all that power, eh?' I have never seen anyone so impressed. Cedric put his head right down. 'Amazing,' he said, 'can't hear a thing.' I smiled indulgently. 'Now drive off,' I said. We did not budge —I had stalled the engine!

Cedric Hardwicke is a great character actor. His comic old men were wonderful and Uncle Dick, in *Yellow Sands*, one of his best. He used to be easy-going about his work, everything seemed effortless to him. We had a Green Room in the Haymarket in those days. Some people were asking Cedric where he 'found' the character of his Uncle Dick. 'Surely,' they said to him, 'you must have put in endless work in search of such a man.' I knew Cedric never went about things that way and, sure enough, he answered:

'As a matter of fact, Uncle Dick is Bill, the stage doorkeeper here. I spotted him as I walked in for the first rehearsal.' And, of course, Bill was the twin brother of Uncle Dick, only we had never noticed.

Theatrical managers are a rare breed and they have become rarer still in my time. I hope this diminution will not continue, but only one of my acquaintances, Sir Bronson Albery, has a son in the business.

I have been associated with a selection. Clayton and Waller, Maurice

Browne, C. B. Cochran and Lilian Baylis, now in heaven. Gilbert Miller, Stephen Mitchell, J. B. Priestley, Mitchell Hill, Alex Rea and Guthrie McLintock, Robert Whitehead of the U.S.A., Slazengers of South Africa and Garnett Caroll of Australia. And Hugh Beaumont, for whom I have been working on and off for the last twenty-five years.

As I said much earlier, I have come to blows with only one of these, a pity, for he was the smallest. Had I struck Garnett Caroll, the largest, I have no doubt he would have knocked me out—happily I never had any desire to do anything of the sort; indeed, there is not one manager I have worked for I am not delighted to see whenever we meet.

Few people are adapted for the profession of theatrical manager. Obviously you must have access to large sums of money which you must be prepared to spend with alarming lavishness, yet must somehow get back into the kitty.

The manager must possess a nerve that is expected of a bomb-disposal expert, for the artists he handles are crammed with T.N.T. and will go off and smash everything if mishandled.

He must be able to make those artists feel that he loves acting and likes them—for, given choice, any artist would rather sell his product to someone who appreciates it, for he then puts his best into it.

Though the manager may be fond of acting he must never—and this is hard on him—indulge in it himself. In a well-run theatre all the acting is confined to the stage and never gets into the office.

A manager once told me he had a part for me and then he went off to India for a holiday. When this manager returned he sent for me to sign the contract. While in India he had had his ears pierced and he sported gold earrings. The pen froze in my hand. 'Never, never,' I told myself, 'have a manager with earrings.' However, I did sign and all went off happily.

I would not look to the theatrical manager for light comic entertainment—but Garnett Caroll can be very funny.

After the play one night in Sydney, Garnett said to my wife and me: 'Let's have supper together tonight—I'll go on to the restaurant and fix it up.' But when we came out of the stage door, to our surprise, there he was standing among a small knot of people, who were waiting to see the actors come out. Our car was waiting for us, and as we passed Garnett he swept off his hat and almost prostrated himself at our feet—'Thank you, thank you,' he uttered in strangled tones, and as we drove off he roared down the street after us: 'Great artists—great artists—great artists.'

In the twenty-five years I have known Hugh Beaumont I have never once seen him 'show off'. Corrupting power has never made him vain. In business he has a remarkable faculty for dividing his mind into watertight compartments, and he never lets one play flow into another. He keeps away from rehearsals until the very end, and then, for me, his full value comes out, for with a fresh eye he is able to apply his long experience and astute intelligence.

After Binkie Beaumont, my next longest association with a manager was with Sir Alexander Korda, in films. I had a contract with him from 1935 until 1956, when he died.

Alex had a genuine respect for acting—he could be rough and impatient with technicians and directors or writers, but he was gentle with actors: to me he was ever a prince. For me there was something magical and hypnotic in his quicksilver personality. Theory has it that one cannot be hypnotised to do anything against one's will; Korda used rougher magic in the film business: he mesmerised me into doing many things I did not think I wanted to do, but with him they always turned out to be to my advantage.

If I made a little list of the actresses whom I have had the honour of playing with, I think all but one would agree that I was luckiest to have played with Madge Titheradge. All who knew her loved her. She applied the forces of her art not so much in the creation of character as in the depiction of beauty and dazzling English womanhood. Perhaps she was in the school of Ellen Terry, of whose peal of bells I caught but an echo. In the play we acted together she was a Frenchwoman, but Madge swept that aside. This play was *Promise*, by Henry Bernstein. Madge had to be hard and cynical. She had treated her husband— whom I played—abominably for years. Then, coming home one night, she saw her husband sitting by the fire. She opens the door, and in a second the remorse of a lifetime of selfishness overcomes her. 'Emil,' is all she says.

Madge made this moment superb. Her great eyes swelled with tears, the audience was breathless. I was on the stage alone before she entered for her magic moment. Now I have always been very sensitive about noises off-stage—and there was Madge off-stage, chattering, giggling, practically dancing. I would remonstrate afterwards. 'Oh, you poor lamb,' she would say, 'I'm so sorry, I'll be like a mouse.' She was a mouse for the next night and the next, and then her gaiety and irrepressible high-jinks would simply bubble up and burst in a Vesuvius of laughter. It was useless to repress her, and she never failed her 'moment'.

At the Theatre Royal, Haymarket, I played in *The Amazing Dr Clitterhouse*, and, as it turned out later, this was the best run of luck of all for me, because I played for the first time with Meriel Forbes; and later we were married. Then came the Goetzes' *The Heiress*, Hunter's

Day by the Sea, and Bolt's *Flowering Cherry*, all at the Haymarket, so that I have happily inhabited the playhouse for more than seven years.

As well as providing as good a frame as a play can have the Theatre Royal is grand to speak in. It does not give itself away for nothing, it needs an attack, but I am afraid that rather suits me—'Keep it up, Richardson.'

There is much wood panelling in this theatre, which I believe helps tone. The best theatre I ever spoke in is in Ghent; it seems to be made of wood altogether, and it is like a violin. I don't like the small theatres where you can spit in the eye of the man in the circle. Distance, for me, lends the audience enchantment. I like the Opera House, Manchester, which is not pretty and is vast.

I hope Leon Quartermaine does not read what I am saying. He would assassinate me. He says large theatres destroy acting. I will risk the Quartermaine stiletto; I would rather be killed than climb into a coffin. I must except the little Duchess Theatre, where I played in *Eden End*, a glorious piece, and *Cornelius*. That little Duchess is a member of the Theatre Royal family.

Among actors, my oldest and best friends have been Cedric Hardwicke and Laurence Olivier, going back to the days of the Birmingham Repertory; and from the days of Harcourt Williams and the Old Vic I have had the friendship and the help in my work of John Gielgud.

Thanks to Barry Jackson I got my first part in London, but I owe thanks to Sir John Gielgud for taking an even greater risk in giving me my first leading part when he directed Somerset Maugham's *Sheppey*, in 1933.

John Gielgud is younger than I am, but he knows things about acting that I do not. When he first played Prospero at the Old Vic I was struggling with the part of Caliban. One day he suggested I might like to stay after rehearsal and run over our scenes together. Then he gave me some wonderful advice. Unfortunately I cannot recall a word of what he said.

Johnny G. does not employ the precision of the range rifle when expressing himself, he goes off like a catherine wheel; but one would indeed be a dullard not to catch a spark of enlightenment from his discourse. Since *Sheppey*, I have been lucky to have been produced in several plays by John Gielgud, and I have always found, maybe after small experiment, that I have ended up in a good position for my best speech and have faded mysteriously out of focus when not wanted, and I ask no more.

I also worked for the Lords of the Admiralty, and they, too, knew how to get the best that could be given out of the humble and obedient servant I had the honour to remain to them for five years.

The way the Navy got the best out of one was by giving trust. Given a job, no one snooped around to see how you were getting on with it. They assumed you were doing your . . . the place for the Nelson touch.

The job I got with the Navy I owed to my fondness for machines to drive about on or in. This had developed in 1935 to the purchase of a Gipsy Moth. When the war came I had more than 200 hours' flying time on my log. They were cautious hours. I did not fly in bad weather and I did not fly on my instruments. The Fleet Air Arm was then short of pilots and they took me on. I was glad to think I had a job in the air, but I was terrified of the Naval service—I had been unhappy at school and I thought this would be much worse. As it turned out, I had a splendid time and everyone was kind to me.

It took time to shake down. On my very first morning at the Naval Station, the Commander sent for me. Looking very grave, he said:

'Ah! Richardson, I have a mission for you.' A mission! My heart went into my boots, or rather into my shoes, for my flying boots had not yet been issued to me. A mission! I thought he was going to send me into Germany dam-busting. Should I tell him how little flying I had done? I remained silent—but pale.

The Commander's face grew grimmer still as he pushed some papers over to me.

'Take a look at these, Richardson,' he said. 'These are the butchers' bills, I want you to go down and see that man; I think we're overcharged.'

When at last my first mission did come it certainly gave me a fright—through the very fact that it was so simple. I was told to fly a wireless telegraphist two hundred miles straight up a North course, make one turn, and come straight back—they wanted a test on his signals.

When I had flown in my own craft I had been very cautious. Every quarter of an hour or so, I'd take a turn to look round about me. When I went on this 200-mile course, and made my one turn—it was about 4 o'clock on a winter's afternoon—the sun was dead low, all was haze—I could not see a thing. I nearly ate my map with fright—of course, had I remained calm the old Blackburn Shark that I was flying would no doubt have nosed her own way back to her stable; which indeed she did and my passenger at the back was safe and sound. He little knew what I thought of his chances when I first made that turn. Later I learned a certain detachment.

Altogether mine was a 'cushy' war and I suffered little worse from it than some spells of boredom. I made more than one friend during that time. I discovered a friendship in Anthony Quayle, and I found a friend in L. A. Hart, who was then a solicitor and now is a banker in the City. Hart and I were in the same flying squadron at Eastleigh.

34

One day he and I were requested by the captain to take charge of the secret books. I can imagine why Hart, the solicitor, was chosen for the job but I don't know why the captain picked on me, though I was pleased at the prospect of this work. Secret books sounded exciting, romantic, perhaps they might even be a little naughty!

Every ship and every Naval station under the Admiralty is issued with this little library. The books at Eastleigh were kept in a safe in the captain's office where at all times someone was on duty. In addition to being guarded it was required that the books should be kept up to date as alterations or replacements were sent from the Admiralty, and at set times an inventory of all had to be made. These cares were to be our charge.

On examination the secret books proved to be completely devoid of entertainment value. A railway timetable is, in comparison, a thriller. They were, however, terribly complicated. I doubt if the captain understood them; he certainly never made use of them.

Hart, however, as my partner, was a godsend to me; with his trained legal orderliness, he deciphered and mastered their intricacies. I simply dusted the books, or staggered round the office under their weight—for many were bound in lead covers so that in emergency they might be cast overboard—and placed them at Hart's direction in proper order. However, the duty of secret book-keeper gave one a certain position on the station; for, if detailed to some unpleasing duty, one could occasionally say that one was sorry but the secret books needed attention at that very time. Asked the nature of that attention one could look embarrassed and say: 'As a matter of fact—secret—sir.' One was excused.

When war times became troubled the Admiralty sent out signals to make ready to throw secret books overboard. At Eastleigh we interpreted these instructions by taking our books out of the office and piling them into a brick incinerator we had constructed near by for the purpose. This was the time when the threat of invasion was in the air and everyone everywhere, especially on the south coast, was agog with uncertainty. Our little community at Eastleigh station regarded our activities at the incinerator with acute interest. We were like the little couple on the Swiss barometer, popping in and out to indicate 'wet' or 'fine'.

One morning Hart and Richardson could be seen lurching towards their incinerator, grim-faced, laden with volumes. 'Here we go, boys—' the sailors would mutter, 'clear decks for action'. A few hours later H. and R. could be seen taking all the books out of the furnace with fatuous grins, and Eastleigh station would know the alarm had passed.

We performed this task many times but never burnt a page. At the time it was my belief that the best way to confuse and baffle the enemy to the point perhaps of putting them right off the war would have been to have given them our secret books to read.

I think through my influence, Hart took up painting, which was a wonderful hobby for me at that time. Now Hart has a studio off Harley Street and there, every now and then, we joyfully repair. The spirit of turpentine is conducive to companionship.

The most remarkable instance of 'making friends and influencing people' was the way I discovered a friendship with Anthony Quayle. Before the war I had been at the Old Vic with him, and though I liked him well enough we neither of us had the time to spare to become particularly well acquainted.

When the war came, Quayle joined the Army and I heard vaguely that he had been sent abroad. At Eastleigh I received first one, and then several more letters from him. These letters were remarkable—I wish I had kept them, they were very long, beautifully written and most revealing.

In the letters, which came from Malta, he questioned and answered himself on his whole philosophy. He told me of his past and of what he aspired to in the future. He explained his fears and wherein he found comfort. First I was astonished to receive these communications, then I was touched. Last I felt flattered. That Quayle, so far away, should spend so much time to write to me—to think of me! I had no idea that Anthony Quayle held me in such special regard. There must, I decided, be something a great deal more magnetic about my personality than I had previously suspected.

A while later, I got a little leave and went up to London and there, in Scott's Restaurant, just home from Malta, was Anthony Quayle. We sat down at the counter and had some oysters. Now I regarded Quayle in a different light. I felt I knew him much better. I pressed him to tell me about himself.

'I used,' he said, 'to write long letters, reams of them, you know, and when they were written I'd put them in an envelope and post them off to the first name that came into my head.' Obviously he had quite forgotten that I had been a recipient.

But through this accident, and the accident of seeing him later in Gibraltar, I did discover a real friendship in Quayle, and later, when he was in charge there, he asked me to play at Stratford-on-Avon. I was indeed grieved to repay the faith of a friend and of a manager with such work as I did there. Everything turned out badly. I played Prospero, Macbeth and Volpone. I don't know which was the worst. I had always wished to play Macbeth, but when it came to the point, I couldn't do it for nuts—not for a second did I believe in the airdrawn dagger, and if I couldn't, no wonder no one else did.

Acting is make-believe. To make the audience believe in acting all the time, the actor must believe in that acting at least some of the time. *Hamlet, Lear, Macbeth* and *Othello* are the four glorious peaks of dramatic literature, and to ascend their majestic height must be the ambition of every actor who sets his foot upon the stage. From the point of view of the playgoer, it is, perhaps, as well that all do not succeed in doing this, as it might prove monotonous for them.

But to the actor who has been given the chance, who has been equipped, as it were, with rope and axe for the ascent, his course mapped and studied, the glint of the peak in his eye; it is a sad and sorry experience for that actor to find himself bathed in sweat from exertion in the effort, after all is over, still so very near the ground. This was the position in which I found myself with *Macbeth*.

I had played plenty of Shakespeare but I had little experience in the particular demands that these four parts make. Actors who attempt these great parts may be placed into three divisions—those who succeed the first time they play them; those who are doomed never to succeed however many times they try; and those who could succeed with practice.

Clearly I don't belong to the first division. It could be that my place is in doomed second; I have been told in *The Sunday Times*, by the great James Agate, that it is in that second division I belong. Agate was speaking of the only other experience I have had in these parts, when in 1938 I played Othello. The notice was headed *Othello without the Moor*. Agate marked how far off I had missed the part and said I was 'like a chauffeur at the starting-handle wrenching his arm off but getting no spark because the engine was cold'.

As a motorist I condemn James Agate's metaphor as nonsense, but as the actor on the spot I concur that this description is perfectly just and relevant. Neither as Othello nor as Macbeth did my imagination fire. Both were cold. Perhaps that should be the end of it. After two attempts, both with fine directors and with fine actors around me, one should simply call it a day and settle for the second division.

Is it, on the other hand, quite so proved? Is there not still a chance of coming in with the third division—those who could 'succeed with practice?'

It is very annoying, very frustrating, not to be able to play these parts as one would wish. It puts one on bad terms with oneself. Did I not realise this, I imagine that this is the kind of thing that could cause an inhibition; one might become upset by it, would finally have to go to a psychologist, and then, perhaps after many weeks, he might say: 'Richardson, at last I have discovered the cause of your neurosis. You were bad as Macbeth.'

But truly I imagine that if one were to attain proficiency in these great exercises, the result would be to render to all one's other work an ease, a facility, and a strength. It is for this reason that I envy those who have succeeded.

Of course, the 'fattest' part in Shakespeare, in more ways than one, is Falstaff. I did play Falstaff once, and that did not come off so badly. This was at the Old Vic in 1945, when, as I have mentioned, the two parts of *Henry IV* were played consecutively. This is not an easy thing for a theatre to do, as there are so many important parts involved, but we had a strong company with Laurence Olivier, Sybil Thorndike, Margaret Leighton, Joyce Redman, Nicholas Hannen, George Relph and Michael Warre, to name only a few.

I started off with a great advantage as Falstaff. I looked the part. I owed my appearance to Miss Alex Stone, a talented artist we had in the wardrobe department. Many actors who play this part are obliged to muffle themselves up with heavy clothing and high boots to achieve the size of the man. Miss Stone, with great skill, sculptured for me in silk quilting an exact and vast anatomy: legs, stomachs, chests. First putting on a casing of towelling, for it was warm within, I climbed into these flexible cases; then over them I was able to wear light, revealing costume, so that there could be seen

The limbs, the thewes, the stature, bulk and big assemblance of the man.

Perhaps the part of Falstaff is as richly drawn in character as any in dramatic literature. He is, in words he himself uses—'Apprehensive, quick forgetive, full of nimble, fiery and delectable shapes.'

Now the player of Falstaff is relieved of the special technical difficulties that surround the tragic four; unlike them, he is permitted to retain and enjoy his basic character without terrible 'translation'. Unlike them, he is not projected at breathless speed to his doom. Falstaff proceeds through the plays at his own chosen pace, like a gorgeous ceremonial Indian elephant.

Not so often now, but in times past, one was offered little books with the request to fill in answers to questions such as:

'What is your favourite colour?'

'What is your favourite flower?'

With nib wobbling with annoyance you think to write 'Daffodil'. But then—'Why?' Why on earth, by omittance, infer a slight to the violet? Perhaps say—'No favourite flower', or 'Don't like flowers'. It does not seem right to be asked to think about things in such a silly way.

Sometimes I am asked: 'What is your favourite part?' Then I try to evade reply, for I feel I want to say: 'Don't like parts'. Now, however, to my own question, I will say: 'My favourite part is "Peer Gynt",' for now I shall be able to qualify my answer a little.

As well as a liking for the character of Peer Gynt the shape and structure of the plot appeal to me. In character, Peer is a little mad, which in his case keeps him jolly; he is rather naughty, which gives him edge; he is childish, which gives him charm. He is placed in an amazing variety of situations, and wherever he finds himself he always imagines he is somewhere else. He is like a wicked Don Quixote.

For all its variety, the fairy-tale is very simple, and it is at the end, I find, touchingly charming. At the beginning of the play, in one or two delicate scenes, Peer woos Solveig, who goes to live with him in his hut in the forest, in Norway. Then Peer, feeling Solveig too good for him, allows himself to be lured by the trolls and she is heartlessly abandoned.

At the end of the play Peer, after a long life of adventure in many countries, returns, an old man, to the forest of his boyhood. There he is met by the Button Moulder, who tells him that his end is near, and that the Master, regretting to see that Peer has made such poor use of his life, has commanded the Moulder to melt him down in his ladle, as he is waste material.

Peer is aghast. 'Me, melted down?' he says with incredulous indignation. 'With any Tom, Dick or Harry! You must be mad!' 'I'm sorry,' says the Moulder, 'I don't see why you make such a fuss. What difference can it make to you, if, when you die, you disappear, because you never yet have been yourself. You really are nothing good or bad.' Peer, of course, is a great egoist, he imagines himself a tremendous person. 'You make me laugh,' he says to the Moulder. 'Perhaps I've not been so very pious, I won't make much claim to that, but as for being nothing! As a matter of fact I'm a Sinner, a most tremendous Sinner— why in my time . . .' Then a light shines in the window of Solveig's hut in the forest, and she comes out. Peer, seeing her now, perhaps after fifty years, calls: 'Cry out, cry out my sins aloud!' 'You have sinned in nothing, my own dear lad,' is her answer. 'Then I am lost, lost unless you can answer a riddle.'

'What is it?'

'It is said I am nothing; it is said I am lost—where has Peer been since he saw you last?' And then Solveig says:

'In my faith, in my hope and in my love,' and she takes him to the hut, away from the Button Moulder. She takes the old man in her arms and sings:

'I will rock you to sleep and guard you.
Sleep and dream, my own dear boy.'

And so we feel that although Peer has made nothing of his own life, he has, at least, a chance in that he has made love for Solveig. The play is so broad that it contains the final scene without any strain of sentiment. I like the scene with the Button Moulder, a morality play character. Our drama is based on the morality play and it is a pity we have rather lost touch with such effective themes.

If I may say so with all imaginable respect, God is a very good part on the stage. He has in the past been very often on the boards, and the thick, dense, but penetrating illusion that the theatre can produce is capable of holding an idea of 'The Master'. The monks in the old days knew that very well. But a character like the Button Moulder would not appear in a Shakespearian play; perhaps 'Everyman' was too recent to him, and there was a revolution of thought?

Much as I like Peer Gynt, I must qualify my 'favourite' to 'a favourite', because, after all, it must be spoken in translation, and it seems that Norwegian, especially Ibsen's idiom, is difficult to render in English.

I have been favoured by much beautifully-written English to speak on the stage, and perhaps my favourite is the dialogue of J. B. Priestley: his seemingly simple diction is rich in melody. The best shorter part I have ever had was that in *Eden End*. There I was given wonderful jokes all set to music—what more could one ask? But of all the long parts I have played Peer is the only one I would like to turn back to, or I will say half turn back to, not half heartedly but half partedly. I am now too old to be able to play the youthful Peer, but I have thought that it might be very pleasant should my son Charles not outgrow his present kink of looking a little like me and should he later on become an actor. Then he might play the young Peer in the first half of the play and I could dodder along in the second act.

A near-favourite play of mine that I very nearly played in, but did not, is *Waiting for Godot*. The reason I did not act in this play was from a stupidity on my part. When the play was sent to me by Mr Donald Albery, I was enthusiastic about it. There were, however, some things I did not understand. I asked if I could meet the author who would, no doubt, clear my mind of difficulty. At first there seemed to be uncertainty that I could meet him, but then he very kindly came to visit me at the Theatre Royal. I suppose I had done a silly thing. I had prepared a little list of my problems and when I produced my piece of paper I sensed disapproval when I asked especially about Pozzo: 'Who is Pozzo?' was number one on my laundry list.

Then I had an impression I had rubbed Mr Beckett the wrong way. He told me my questions could not be answered. He had written the play as it had come to him, and he could not enter into explanations of things that could not be explained in that way. Stupidly I was damped. I felt I could not hope to make a play clear to the audience if I did not understand it myself. I turned the piece aside, and did something else. Now this was silly, because, had Mr Beckett been inaccessible, with my original enthusiasm I should have pushed ahead and myself overcome the difficulties.

Although for me there were great beauties in the script of *Godot*, especially in the appearance of the child in a marvellous little scene towards the end, when he brings the news that Godot may not be coming for a while; on the other hand, there were things I found obscure. I am sadly literal-minded, and don't like obscurity anywhere— but in the theatre I could not work with it for a second. The trouble is that the word 'obscure' is itself wrapped in obscurity—it has a different meaning for every one of us. For instance, I do not think I find the later Turner paintings obscure though there are, perhaps, some who still do, but I find obscurity in many valued modern painters. I do not have to have them in the house: but in the playhouse it is awkward when only some of the audience know what is going on, for a theatre audience works well only when it comes together as a unit.

I suppose Mr Beckett would say that that is too bad, and that the standard of intelligence of the audience as a unit should go up. With a painter, an obscurity stands only between the artist and the beholder of the work, but in the theatre things would become muddled if a director were to endeavour to explain something he does not understand to an actor who then plays that mystery to an audience.

There exists, between the word 'obscurity' and the word 'mysterious', an immense difference. We know at once what that difference is when we say that in Shakespeare there is no single obscurity; but that Shakespeare, seldom obscure, is drenched in mystery.

The ability to convey a sense of mystery is one of the most powerful assets possessed by the theatre. The cinema, which is a shadow, and we speak of mysterious shadows, is, surprisingly, unable to contain mystery to the same degree. The theatre, which is a solid, can convey mystery, revealing mystery. *Peter Pan*, which is a minor mystery play, could scarcely be effective on the screen. It is wonderful and mysterious to fly across the stage; it is uninteresting on film.

For me, the child in *Waiting for Godot* was mysterious, but Pozzo was baffling and obscure.

I do not know if it is generally known, or, indeed, if it is general among actors, but I for one do not always all the time play upon stage the part that is advertised on the bill. What I really mean is that, like most other people in most other jobs, one finds oneself, while acting, thinking many stray odd thoughts, not necessarily connected with what one is doing, but employing such thought as an aid to keep the mind lively

It did so happen that while playing in Mr Graham Greene's *Complaisant Lover* I found myself often thinking of Mr Beckett's *Godot*. It seemed somehow to haunt me—what connection there could be between the two plays I could not possibly say. Perhaps it is best not to go into this very far, for if it were to come to be generally known that actors did this sort of thing the Authors' Society might go into the question of royalty. However, if Mr Beckett were ever to forgive me and offer me another part; and if, in his service, I were to run out of ideas, I might steal a few in recompense from the fertile store of Mr Graham Greene.

Jean Anouilh, James Bridie, Henry Bernstein, Robert Bolt, Clemence Dane, Graham Greene, N. C. Hunter, Barry Linden, Somerset Maugham, Eden Phillpotts, Bernard Shaw, R. C. Sherriff and H. G. Wells are among many authors I have jockeyed for, and now and then I have had the privilege of riding a winner. But J. B. Priestley has been to me the most indulgent of all, both as an author and as a friend. (Among many good things Jack has put me on to is the game of squash. I played no games as a boy, but since he did me that good turn I have racqueted about happily.)

Laurence Olivier's warm friendship has been a great joy and solace to me over many years, and especially over the early years, which in one respect were cloudy. Laurence had a wonderful gaiety, and I do not think I have ever laughed so much with anyone as I have done with him. To say that we fell about laughing is the literal truth. When we were both young we were foolish. But there was a difference in our natures.

One day Laurence drove me over the crossroads at the junction of the Croydon by-pass and the Purley road at what seemed like seventy miles an hour. I said to him:

'If I live to be hundreds and hundreds of years old, Laurence, I shall never forgive you for that.' He said:

'Old man, what are you fussing about? When you come to a point of danger, pass over it as quickly as you can.' Later he brought a car back from America, and in trying it out I drove him down Piccadilly at eighty-three miles an hour. Laurence never said a word.

That great master of all actors, William Shakespeare, I have served altogether for six years. He has denied me partnership in his most splendid glories, although I have several times asked to be taken in.

Looking back, I observe the pattern of the track left behind wanders sometimes uncertainly. Down dale now and then, and never on hill so very high. Never mind—I'll beg only to keep high hopes and remember what Growcott first said to me:

'If you want to get on in the theatre, you'll have to learn to wait.'

From *The Sunday Times*, 1960.

42

Basil Boothroyd (b. 1910 and in fact christened John Basil, hence the J.B. which sometimes turns up in the byline of his earlier writing) is one of an alas rapidly vanishing breed of massively elegant and innately stylish literary humorists. The official biographer of the Duke of Edinburgh, and a Punch contributor since 1938, he has been a familiar radio voice for many years but had kept somewhat silent about his pre-war theatrical connections until he divulged all at my request in 1975.

The Hell of the Greasepaint, the Bore of the Crowd

TAXED WITH it, I'd have said I'd never trod the boards of the Scala Theatre in *Night Must Fall*, as one of the Thalian Repertory Players, under the patronage of Baroness de Goldsmid da Palmeira, all proceeds to the Polish refugees. You forget these things.

But here's the programme, and there am I. Twice. Lord Chief Justice in the prologue and Inspector Belsize in the play. More, I have an asterisk and a footnote: 'By permission of St Pancras People's Theatre'. So my career on the amateur stage was well beyond its budding.

Further down the cast list, playing Mrs Bramson's comical cook, was Daisy Nichols. She's changed it to Dandy now, and you'd know her better as Mrs Alf Garnett. There's a picture of us. Her in her fur tippet, me in my cascading inspector's moustache, in case the audience thought I was still the Lord Chief, doing a bit of ultra vires and heading the police inquiries.

All proceeds didn't, in fact, go to the luckless Poles. My watch, cigarette case and wallet went to persons unknown, nipping in from Charlotte Street while I was on stage passing sentence of death. Portraying, as I was, both executive and judicial arms of the Law, I now remember being narked at this. Cheeky. I ran about backstage in full-bottomed wig and underpants threatening to sue the manager. He might have said, and possibly did, that my inspector, so astute in bringing Mr Emlyn Williams's anti-hero to the gallows, should strictly have made short work of a petty pilferer working the make-up tables.

It was a lesson in distinguishing Theatre from Life, something I was having difficulty with at the time.

To have forgotten the engagement is pardonable. The run was short, occurring on February 6, 1939. It was not my London début as a man of the theatre. That had been in the previous September, at the Phoenix, Charing Cross Road. I suppose Munich was happening around then, but I took no notice. When you're young, and writing the music for a Chinese play (under the patronage of H.E. the Chinese Ambassador) you need all your concentration for what matters. So I was only in the orchestra pit for that one, and conducted from the piano, much relied on for clever chords representing gongs. Gwen Ffrangcon-Davies did most of the singing, in a surprisingly sweet soprano which was a great relief to me on the opening, i.e., the closing night. I wasn't used to the self-conserving professional approach, and she had rehearsed in a husky mutter, through billowing cigarette smoke and powerful pince-nez.

There was a further piece of professionalism from another member of the cast, who liked the score so much that he took it to America and lost it. I shrugged. It was tough on the world of the arts, deprived of a second *Chu Chin Chow* like that, but for me, what of it? Plenty more where that came from. I was already at grips with my 1938 *Dick Whittington*. Again the orchestra pit. The piano pit, rather. John Furness played the other piano. Now a TV producer. Hi, John, any jobs going? As for the cast, I fancy Margery Mason was in it, and probably Cecile Chevreaux. I know that Princess April Shower was in the capable hands of a Miss Joy Adamson, only later to ask such pointed public questions as 'Can you eat it?'

This was at the St Pancras People's Theatre, a rum, rum repertory set-up that was ruling my life around then, until Hitler's voice, with its harsh insistence on costly blackout materials, penetrated even there, and closed us down for good. Resources were bound to be slender, with unreserved seats curiously fixed at sevenpence, and the best in the house at half-a-crown. The wardrobe was sparse, but infinitely adjustable under ingenious needles. A few feet of gold piping on Dad's suit from *Love on the Dole*, and you'd got General Robert E. Lee shooting up Harper's Ferry in *Gallows Glorious*. Trollope crinolines from *The Small House at Allington* were next week's full-sleeved Russian pyjamas for *Tovarich*. Wigs were a desperate scramble. You could get lumbered with the least favourite, known to all as Little Nitty.

I often wondered, myself, stuck with it, whether it had once been worn by Maurice Evans, André Morell, Michael Hordern and others who got their first heady whiff of grease-paint at St P. and went on to lose their amateur status. The grail of professionalism danced before us all, but out of a company of about a hundred I don't suppose more than a dozen got their hands on it. My own exit was somewhat blocked by fond parents having put me into a bank, thus realising their proudest hopes. Clean, safe, reputable work. Pension at sixty. A postcard saying that I'd quit, and was doing ASM at Horsham Rep for two quid a week would have been brutal. True, it was a bank recently quitted by T. S. Eliot. Did he knock off *The Waste Land* on some ledger desk, as I did *Dick Whittington*? Wodehouse had been a banker, and got out. I lacked his stern resolution.

Most part-time Thespians, or Thalians if you prefer, manage one production a year: perhaps two, in rare organisations free of the temperamental in-fighting that folds up most amateur groups like deck chairs and has whole villages not speaking to each other. At St Pancras we did one a week. Temperaments were frowned on. Discipline was fierce. Miss a rehearsal and you were out. When the cast-lists went up in the green room there were cries of agony and bliss. The agonised, unselected this week, were fit to take their lives. The blissful left at a run for French's, in Southampton Street, to get a copy of the play, and avidly count their lines at the bus-stop, standing the while in the actor's stance, weight on the right leg, the left a half pace forward and bent, surprising the rest of the queue with sudden, outflung gestures, or tentative mouthings of telling repartee.

Don't think, by the way, that I walked straight into the London theatre, drawing the sevenpenny audience, without distinguished provincial successes behind me. My *Our Miss Gibbs* ran for three nights at Brigg, and toured for another at Sleaford. The *Horncastle News* described my performance in *Are You a Mason?* as 'effective', and noted that the Act II curtain rose on my solo rendering of 'I Love the Moon' for alto saxophone. By hindsight, I worry about that. We weren't much concerned with interpreting the author's intention in those days. He didn't see the production, being luckily dead. How, I wonder, did I dispose of the instrument and slip smoothly back into the character, a man whose musicianship wasn't even hinted at in the text?

Actors' biographies tend to leapfrog the years 1939–45. 'After seeing service in North Africa . . .' In my case, this would be to conceal a significant period of my career. I saw my own service in North Lancashire, at a remote RAF station with no aeroplanes, where time hung heavy and no bomb fell. Morale could have sagged dangerously, even despite the dedication of a few bold spirits among us who did our best for it with an unremitting stream of cabaret and variety. I hadn't been up there long before it was accepted that the gymnasium was used for nothing else. My monologue on the state of the East Camp ablutions, which got two sergeants posted to Iceland, is still, I think, remembered, especially by them. This was fearless stuff, for an acting corporal. Was it enough? We knew about the war from the radio. It seemed remote. What was needed to bring it home was our production of *Journey's End*, which ran for years, off and on, and was toured round the bomber and fighter stations to show the crews what the real thing was like.

I went through hell as Captain Stanhope, and never had a qualm about pinning up his MC ribbon for the second act. To endure the offstage explosions—we must have shot off more ordnance than the whole Eighth Army—called for nerves of steel. Realism was all. We bashed dents into our mint-fresh tin hats with revolver butts, and wondered, every time the sensational dugout collapse came round, if we hadn't overdone it and enfeebled their protective standards.

My finest hour, though, had come in the early days of the project. With only non-commissioned status, but fired with artistic integrity, I pulled my stage captain's rank on a genuine flight-lieutenant in the cast, playing Mason, a mere private, who thought himself entitled to the best breeches in the costume basket. It meant going over his head to the CO, but I got them, all right.

It was a long time, back again in the palmy days of peace and village dramatics, before I had to give anyone a piece of my mind on that scale. That was when my own bank manager—I'd at last graduated to the customer's side of the counter—crouched over the sound-effects tape of *Love From a Stranger*, brought up the national anthem loud and clear in the middle of Act One. I was alone on stage at the time. It takes skilled ad-libbing to get round a thing like that, especially when some other fool, triggered like a Pavlov dog, drops the curtain on you just as you're getting the situation mastered. I told him, I remember, that I had a damned good mind to take my account elsewhere. If he'd had the figures handy he wouldn't have paled and trembled as he did.

One thing about the amateur drama, it makes you 'feel it here, dear', as a lady producer at St P., rumoured to have been three years in *The Garden of Allah*, used to say.

And what you feel, inanely, childishly enough, is that nothing else matters. If for that reason alone, I'm sorry to have quit the amateur boards (though I was offered a Second Wise Man in a nativity play last year—didn't they realise I'd once played no less than Herod?).

Just now, what with one thing and another, it might be restful to slip back into something more real than real life.

From *Punch*, 9 July 1975.

One of my three godfathers (the other two will be found later in this collec-
tion as will my father: I am nothing if not family-conscious) Peter Bull
(b. 1912) started out as an actor and producer and ran the only repertory
company in the world (Perranporth, to be precise) where the meals for the
company came in hampers from Fortnum and Mason. After a distinguished
war in the Navy he returned to the theatre but also took to writing books
*and published a sequence (*To Sea in a Sieve, Bulls in the Meadows *and* I
know the face but . . ., *from which last this extract is taken) dealing in*
some detail and considerable hilarity with his memories of life as, respec-
tively, a sailor, a child, and an actor. More recently he has taken to shop-
keeping and runs an immensely successful Zodiac emporium in Notting Hill
Gate; addicts of his acting may however still be able to find him playing
John Bull in a television commercial for butter.

Do I believe in Godot?

IT ALL began during that lovely, lovely summer of 1955; I was minding
my own business and quietly enjoying the sun at the Oasis and Serpen-
tine swimming-pools, when a phone call came from the Arts Theatre. A
Mr Peter Hall wanted me to read a play called *Waiting for Godot*. He
was away in Spain at the time, but had left word that he hoped for a
speedy decision. Whatever the play was like, it needed time to consider
the pros and cons, because although I was in my usual parlous state of
penury, the prospect of a few weeks' work at the Club theatre didn't
exhilarate me. You are (or were) paid twelve pounds a week and nothing
at all for rehearsals (four weeks), though you were presented with a sheaf
of tickets with which to purchase luncheon at the snack bar. An additional
liability is that friends wishing to see the piece invariably have to get you
to get them tickets, as you have been made an Honorary Member. If you
are in a very popular play they rally round like flies and if you aren't
frightfully good, forget to come round after the performance and pay
for their seats. This is a double disappointment.

But, and it is a big But, some of the productions there have enormous
prestige value and do one a lot of good professionally; for example, *The
Lady's Not For Burning*, which only played for two and a half weeks at
the Arts Theatre but was to provide me with the best part of two years'

work. Contrariwise I have also played there in a sensational flop called *Second Best Bed*, which was the Coronation offering of the little theatre. A gentle satire on W. Shakespeare's courtship of the late Miss Hathaway, it incurred the wrath of critics and audience alike. We did appalling business with it although, just before one Saturday matinée, I popped my head inside the box-office and asked for eighty-four seven and sixpenny seats for that performance (meant as a joke actually) and the lady said: 'I'm sorry, Mr Bull, we're sold out for the matinée.'

I was frankly incredulous until she told me that the British Drama League had arranged for a section of its membership to come, and had booked the seats before the notices. Very rarely have I played to an angrier audience, who practically hissed their disapproval, and it was quite a relief at the evening perf to play to our usual half-empty house, mainly composed of non-paying customers, or members of the Arts Theatre Club who could find no armchairs available in the lounge.

So on receiving the script of *Waiting for Godot*, I had one hit and one miss as precedent. I also found myself totally incapable of making any sort of decision after reading the play for the first time, which was in itself an extraordinary experience. I thought either the author or I must be potty, and yet even at first reading there was a hypnotic quality about the dialogue which could not be lightly dismissed. But I could not begin to understand what my proposed role (Pozzo) meant, and in consequence decided to turn it down, as I considered it pointless to contemplate playing a part through which I could see no daylight. I had hardly turned it down before I received a charming letter from Peter Hall asking me to reconsider the play and diabolically suggesting that I was ideal for the part. It was so cleverly phrased that I was completely won over to the idea, though even when I had agreed to have a shot at it, I stipulated that, if I felt unhappy in the part after a few days' rehearsal, I could leave. The fact that I felt unhappy months after playing it has nothing to do with this point. We were to start practising the first week of July and I looked forward to it with alarm and despondency.

The original cast was composed of Paul Daneman, Timothy Bateson, Peter Woodthorpe and myself. The only one I knew nothing about was P. Woodthorpe, who was a discovery from the Cambridge Footlights Company and drove us all barking mad at the beginning. It was infuriating in my case (my silver wedding with the theatre had just been celebrated) to find an amateur actor with more talent than oneself, acting one off the stage, and his seeming confidence and technique struck an impertinent note. It was also a bit galling to discover that he hadn't yet made up his mind as to whether to go back to the University for his final year or continue to play with us. He was at any rate a 'natural', and I've rarely seen such incredible promise. Timothy Bateson was fairly new to me, though vastly more experienced, and I remember him playing very old gents and young things at the Old Victoria Music Hall and with Sir Laurence and Lady O, in all those *Cleopatras*. As we were to remain tied to each other throughout the engagement, it was essential that we should remain on friendly terms, and in this we succeeded admirably and I found his acidity and wit helped me enormously throughout a depressing run.

Paul Daneman played Vladimir (one of the two tramps) only at the Arts and gave a wonderful performance, tinged with great compassion and simplicity. He was a tower of strength and a joy to work with. To complete the cast was a small boy, and the young actor playing this part had to be constantly whisked out of the theatre, when the 'Dirty' bits were being spoken. He also had to be changed periodically, owing to the L.C.C. laws regarding stage children. The result of this was a caterpillar of young gents of varying talent and disposition. One with the face of an angel could be heard from one end of the theatre to the other hurling very adult epithets at his mother. Rehearsals started soberly, and I took an instant liking to the young director Peter Hall, who made no bones about the play.

'Haven't really the foggiest idea what some of it means,' he announced cheerfully, 'but if we stop and discuss every line we'll never open. I think it may be dramatically effective but there's no hope of finding out till the first night.'

There was certainly no assistance coming from the author Mr Samuel Beckett, and looking back on the production, I'm rather glad he didn't put in an appearance till quite late in the run. The rehearsals were the most gruelling that I've ever experienced in all my puff. The lines were baffling enough, but the props that I was required to carry about my person made life intolerable. Aspiring actors are hereby warned against parts that entail them being tied to another artiste, as they will find it restricts their movements. As well as this handicap I had to carry an overcoat, a giant watch, a pipe, lorgnettes and heaven knows what else. The rope had to be adjusted continuously, so that I could pull it taut round my slave's neck, if possible not throttling Mr Bateson (Lucky was the name of the character). Fortunately there were long duologues between the tramps, so while they rehearsed on the stage proper, Master Bateson and I could have a bash in the Oak Room of the Arts Club, until complaints came up, via the head-waiter from the restaurant below, about the noise and general banging about. It was wonderful weather (always is during rehearsals), and at lunch time I used to grab a sandwich or eight and dart off to the Oasis swimming-pool. This brought back sanity with the chlorine and I was able to get through the afternoon. They were dreary days and evenings, as none of us, I think, dared to go out at night owing to the necessity of getting the lines into our noddles. One of the main troubles was that an identical cue kept recurring every few pages of the script, so that it was remarkably easy to leave out whole chunks of the play. (We did, in fact, skip four pages on the actual first night at the Arts but, like fools, went back instead of pressing on.) In the second act I had to say 'Help' about twenty times, a cue which didn't in fact help my fellow actors.

I found it frightfully difficult to get any sense out of my intended characterisation, until the last week of rehearsals, when I suddenly decided to cheat and pretend Miss Margaret Rutherford was playing the role, which had the immediate and blessed effect of stopping embarrassing myself. It is a platitude to say that when an actor embarrasses himself, he is bound to embarrass the audience. I had noticed that my friends were clearly mortified at having to hear my lines, and Bob Morley had thrown the script from one end of his garden to the other, when I had unwisely asked him to take me through the part. The dress rehearsals were gloomy affairs and not relieved for yours truly by the physical discomforts of wearing a wig constructed of rubber, in the middle of a heat-wave. Owing to the author's eccentricity it was necessary for Pozzo to take his bowler-hat off at one stage of the piece and reveal a completely naked head. This was symbolic (the only explanation for the nightly torture given to me) and then he put his titfer on again. It was only for a second or two, but proved to be one of my major miseries. A firm of wig makers, Wig Creations Ltd, had constructed for me what amounted to a bathing-cap, which had to be encased in rubber solution. This caused an *impasse* when dry, owing to lack of air in the hair, and by the end of any performance there were several pints of not madly attractive sweat accumulated in the rubber wig, which made one feel as if one's head had burst. Later in the run I contracted a series of skin diseases as a result and had to issue a *pronunciamento*. The consequence was that a new type of bathing-cap was dished out, not so chic, as it had a few wisps of hair at the back, which meant that I did not have to seal off my head completely. The whole thing was pretty preposterous because, as Mr R. Morley kindly pointed out, the wig-join was clearly visible from Row K in the stalls. Make-up has never been my *forte*, and in this case the earlier I came in to do it, the more frightening seemed to be the result. I used to arrive some two hours before my first entrace in *Godot*, and by the time I reached the stage, the rubber started to come unstuck, which resulted in *ditto* for my performance. If I ever got held up by necessity or accident and got into the theatre late, I was always able to put on a superb make-up in ten minutes flat!

The first night was, I think, my most alarming experience on the stage (so far). I have a habit of comforting myself on first nights by trying to think of appalling experiences during the war, when terror struck from all sides, but the windiness felt on the Italian beach-heads and elsewhere was nothing to compare with one's panic on that evening of August 3rd, 1955, and why the cast were not given medals for gallantry in the face of the enemy is inexplicable. Waves of hostility came whirling over the footlights, and the mass exodus, which was to form such a feature of the run of the piece, started quite soon after the curtain had risen. The audible groans were also fairly disconcerting. By the time I had to make my first entrance (twenty minutes after the rise of the curtain) I realised that I was in for a sticky evening and I'm not referring to my rubber wig. The laughs had been few and far between and there was a general air of restlessness and insecurity around. I lost my head quite early on by inserting the rope, to which Mr Bateson was attached to me, INSIDE my coat sleeve. Knowing what I do now and how the audience were never surprised by anything that happened during *Godot*, I should have just said, 'Pig, put my coat on properly, pig', which was the endearing form of address that I habitually used to my slave.

As it was, I spent the next quarter of an hour in a semi-hysterical condition, knowing that if I hadn't actually strangled Mr Bateson by the time he got to his big speech, it was highly probable that he would have to make it in pitch darkness owing to non-arrival at the position on which his spotlight was trained. As it was Mr Bateson's big moment, I hazarded a guess that he might not be best pleased. I gradually eased the rope up my sleeve in order to reduce the danger, but at the expense of my performance, which had by now been reduced to a question of survival without having heart failure. I was blowing the audience out of the auditorium with the volume of my shrill voice—(quote Kenneth Tynan) 'over-vocalisation' (unquote) which was the understatement of the year. But T. Bateson got his light, declaimed his gibberish and brought the house down with terrifying accuracy.

After this the audience were a little more attentive, and though an occasional groan or rudely upturned seat rang through the building, we got through without disaster. I pulled myself together in the second act and the Messrs Daneman and Woodthorpe were very moving indeed in the last scene of all. The curtain fell to mild applause, we took a scant three calls and a depression and sense of anti-climax descended on us all. Very few people came round, and most of those who did were in a high state of intoxication and made even less sense than the play. I slipped quietly away with the Scofields and Maurice Kaufmann, who had all promised to pick up the bits.

The notices next day were almost uniformly unfavourable, confused and unprovocative. We played to poor houses, but on the Sunday following our opening the whole picture was to change. We quite suddenly became the rage of London, a phenomenon entirely due to the articles written by the Messrs Tynan and Hobson in the *Observer* and *Sunday Times* respectively. One phrase quoted from each doyen of criticism was enough to send all London running to the Arts and subsequently the Criterion Theatres. Mr Hobson said, 'Something that will securely lodge in a corner of your mind as long as you live', and Mr Tynan told his readers that 'it will be a conversational necessity for many years to have seen *Waiting for Godot*.' With no mock humility I have to report that Mr H. also said, 'This Bull's bellow troubles the memory like the swansong of humanity.' but I fancy Mr Derek Granger in the *Financial Times* was nearer the mark when he said I looked like a 'vast obscene baby'.

That Sunday night we played to near capacity and the whole trend of audience behaviour was to alter for the remainder of the run at the Arts. Gusts of laughter and tense silences greeted our efforts, and people started to come round to tell us what They thought the play meant. There were rumours even of a transfer, but in the meantime our run was extended. Mr Hobson mentioned the play every week in his columns, and we were suddenly informed that Mr Donald Albery, who owned the rights of *Godot* anyhow, had arranged with his father Sir Bronson Albery to take us to the Criterion Theatre. This was a real turn-up for the book, as this delicious little house is a dream emporium for the actor's wares from every angle. It has what is known as a marvellous 'passing' trade, is easily accessible and a wonderful theatre to play in. The only disadvantage lies in conditions backstage, which is nobody's fault, but at first sight one might easily be in the sewers of Paris. It is chronically airless and there are mixed pongs coming from the restaurants and kitchens above. Owing to the smallness of the cast we were able to have a largish dressing-room to ourselves, and after a slight argument with Mr Albery about billing, I signed the contract.

I hoped it would sound a bit grand, that last bit about billing I mean. It wasn't actually and I merely happened to ask my agent to arrange that I should be billed after Hugh Burden, who was taking over the part of Vladimir from Paul Daneman who was about to go into the ill-fated *Punch Revue* at the Duke of York's. I didn't ask for neon lights or red letters eight foot high or anything, but Mr Albery said there was no question of order of billing, as he exercised the right to have the names of actors in the bills or NOT. He was absolutely correct and in order, but I did point out (through my agent) that there would be not much point, having performed anonymously at the Arts Theatre, in doing *ditto* at Piccadilly Circus, the Centre of the World. We came to a midget *impasse* and I decided not to rehearse for a few days until things were settled. I popped off to the Oasis swimming-pool, while he made up his mind whether to replace me. Fortunately for me he decided against that and I returned browner, and I fear smugger, to rehearse.

We opened in the second week of September and were to run continuously till the end of the following March. It was the oddest theatrical experience of my life and had a nightmarish quality that is difficult to recapture in words. Both physically and mentally it was a disturbing play with which to be associated. The bleakness and sordidity of the set and the clothes, the spitting and drooling that formed part of the pattern, had a most depressing effect on me and I came to dread going to the theatre. I also found, as time went on, that I started to disbelieve in the merits of the play and to become more and more intolerant of the praise and importance that were bestowed on it in certain quarters. I got wildly bored by the endless banging-on at parties, in the street and particularly in my dressing-room. But of course it was all this *brouhaha* that helped to pay my rent for so long.

The High Teas on Saturdays helped a great deal. For me one of the nicest traits of Mr Donald Albery's character is his care of his actor's stomachs, and with a twice-nightly carry-on every Saturday (5.30 and 8.30 perfs.), he has instituted a splendid idea in his theatres, whereby a kind lady comes in and serves delicious cold-cuts and coffee between the two shows at enormous expense to Mr A. The actors can then lollop away to their dressing-rooms with a plate and make pigs of themselves. It was a bit tricky when friends came round between shows, but one could usually find a bone to toss to them. In any case I kept a widows' cruse of brandy handy, not only for myself, but for those customers stalwart enough to stay the course.

It must be admitted that a lot of people didn't, and it was a remarkable thing to come on in the first act and feel a bungful house, only to return in the second to find a certain percentage of gaps in the theatre and the audience shrunk in size. Not that it was a great surprise, because those who had left did not attempt to cover up their movements. It was not just the banging of seats and slamming of exit doors, but quite often they would take the trouble to come right down to the footlights, glare at the actors and make their egress into outer space, snorting the while. Incidents were numerous and cries of 'Rubbish', 'It's a disgrace', 'Take it off', 'Disgusting', and I regret to say on one occasion 'Balls', floated through the auditorium. There was one unforgettable night when, during the second act, the two tramps are alone on the stage cogitating about life as they were apt to do and one says: 'I'm happy', to which the other replies, 'I am happy too', after which a gent in Row F shouted: 'Well, I'm bloody well not.'

At this point there was a certain amount of shushing, but the man would not be shushed and stood up and yelled at the audience: 'And nor are you. You've been hoaxed like me.'

A free fight ensued (well, fairly free; 15s. 6d. a head actually) and during a lull Hugh Burden observed quietly:

'I think it's Godot,' which brought the house down and enabled our attendants to get rid of the angry middle-aged man.

But perhaps the drollest night was when I got my comeuppance. It had been reported to me by the stage manager that a party of eight had arrived rather late, and had made a good deal of noise sitting down in the front row. They were all in full evening dress with a fine display of jewels and/or carnations. By the time I'd been on for a bit I realised that they didn't seem best pleased by me or my performance. The muttering and whispering grew to a crescendo, until in a loud clear voice the dowager lady seated in the middle of the party said:

'I do wish the fat one would go.'

I took a hurried look round at my fellow actors and decided that I had never seen a thinner bunch and guessed that she must be referring to me. I was a fraction shocked as, after a long and not terribly notable career in the service of the theatre, I have never actually been insulted DURING a performance. People have attacked me in the streets or in public transport, but never while I was actually doing it. I seethed inwardly with rage, but apart from glaring at the lady I was unable to make a come-back; luckily my beloved slave made handsome amends. As we were about to leave the stage, I shortened the rope which bound me to T. Bateson and he made as if to leap into the lady's lap, a threat which caused the entire party to leave hurriedly. Afterwards we were all filled with intense compassion and the milk of h.k., as it turned out that the party had arrived expecting to see a revue called *Intimacy at 8.30* which had vacated the Criterion Theatre a few weeks previously. Putting one and five together and realising the storm of criticism that would assail her at the end of the evening, the hostess had wisely decided to cut her losses.

Of course a lot of people were blackmailed into coming to *Godot* by the quotes in the Press plastered outside the theatre and in the newspaper columns. It was no good expecting to find 'one of the funniest plays in London' if two tramps wrangling for a couple of hours on a stage, naked except for a leafless tree, wasn't your idea of a gay evening out. Then there were those who thought they wouldn't be asked out ANYWHERE if they hadn't seen it, thanks to Mr Tynan's pronouncement about it being a 'conversational necessity'. Sometimes I longed to stop prospective customers streaming up to the box-office and try and divert them to *Dry Rot* at the Whitehall Theatre, though I fancy a lot of them thought they had been seeing the latter anyhow.

But theatrical London did flock to it, and in consequence the piece did one's reputation a great deal of good, though a lot of members of the profession were not strong enough to stay the course. Early in the run my phone rang one morning and it was Mr R. Morley on the other end.

'Guess who was in front last night?' he asked.

'Boris Karloff,' I replied correctly.

'AND me,' he said, hurt. 'At least, for the first act,' he added. 'But I told the people I was with that there was no point in staying for the second, as it was exactly the same apart from you being dumb in it.'

I told him coldly that I was blind in the second act, and that I had troubled Mr Harold Hobson's memory 'like the swansong of humanity', but Mr Morley could not be tempted to return, and indeed his memory was so troubled that he used to ring me up periodically and mutter on the phone:

'I've been brooding in my bath, and it is my considered opinion that the success of *Waiting for Godot* is the end of the theatre as we know it.'

Constance Lorne, a brilliant Perranporth graduate, came by herself one evening, and in the interval her neighbour turned to her and asked:

'What do you make of it?'

Constance, temporarily floored, opined that it made a change from all those ice-shows, at which the lady burst into floods of tears.

'It's my last night in London,' she sobbed, 'and they told me I HAD to see this.'

Miss Lorne comforted her and packed her off to the Prince of Wales revue round the corner. During Motor Show Week we did sensational business, but the rush to the exit doors could not have been conducted faster than if it had been the twenty-four hours' race at Le Mans. One night after the curtain had fallen to no applause, a lady motorist rose to her feet and shouted to the world in general:

'You bloody suckers.'

Not all of the criticism was vocal, and a lot of our unfan-mail came in with a twopenny-halfpenny stamp on it and sometimes with no stamp on it at all. There was a gentleman who wrote in to say that he didn't pay fifteen shillings and sixpence to smell Peter Woodthorpe's feet from Row S, and a lady who pointed out that her pipes were frozen, her drains refused to function, and that she'd come up with her daughter to take their minds off things and would we send her twenty-seven shillings by return.

Of course not everybody felt like this. Hordes of people thought that it was 'absolutely wonderful', 'a great treat', 'gloriously funny', 'heart-breakingly noble', 'took one out of oneself', or 'it was just like life'. I thought them 'absolutely wonderful' too, because it meant that I was paid for several months longer than I had ever dared to hope. But even

55

this type of customer could be alarming, because they either sat spell-bound in respectful silence or laughed their heads off in such a sinister way that the actors thought that they must have forgotten to adjust their costumes. And it was worse when they came round to the dressing-rooms after the play to tell us what the play meant. It was far too late for that sort of thing anyhow, and it didn't help me at this stage in my portrayal to learn that Pozzo represented Facism, Communism, Lord Beaverbrook, Randolph Hearst, Mussolini, James Joyce, or rather surprisingly, Humpty Dumpty.

It was all a very great strain and preyed on our nerves, and it is easy to understand why one of the actors who played my part on the Continent went barking mad and had to be locked up for a bit. Considering everything, it was amazing that I only contracted laryngitis, colitis, dermatitis, and found my friends saying that they had noticed a CHANGE in me, not, I gathered, for the better. I do realise now that I was very irritable and nervy for many months and that this state was entirely induced by 'my work'.

The author left his Montparnasse lair and visited us round about the hundredth performance and proved to be shy, modest and not fright-fully helpful about the meaning of his play. We got the impression that he didn't care for the London production a great deal. He gave us a party, where we were all rather rude to him, but he took it in good part, and left for France after telling us that he didn't think the pauses quite long enough. We told him that if they were any longer, not a customer would be left in the building. Our Christmas arrangements (usually a cheerful sight to the actor when posted outside the theatre) were announced, and included just the ten performances in Christmas week. It wasn't, we felt, a madly Christmassy or festive play, or indeed, absolutely the attraction that the kiddy-winks would insist on being taken to, but it was no good arguing with the bosses on this subject. It was suddenly broken to us, however, that we were going to have a relatively new production incorporating a lot of Beckett's ideas.

The news came to us by a carrier pigeon and we could not believe that there was a vestige of truth in the rumour. But a rehearsal call went up on the board, and we were instructed to report every day during the week before Christmas which didn't quite fit in with our Christmas arrangements. It was then that I saw red, which (let's face it) never suits an actor of my nomenclature, and I suggested that it might be wiser, before embarking on a series of rehearsals, to engage an understudy for Mr Burden and Mr Bateson. Their current one, Mr Roderick Cook, was about to leave our establishment in order to play in *Listen to the Wind* at the Arts Theatre. Both the Mr B.s were a bit peaky in health round about this time, and it seemed ludicrous to us that they were not what is technically known as 'covered', with a cast of only four men and a boy.

However, nothing constructive was done about it, though it is fair to say that auditions were held, but no one was apparently suitable, and on Christmas Eve the inevitable occurred. T. Bateson had an impacted wisdom tooth, and his poor dear face was swollen up to balloon size. He played several perfs in great pain and discomfort, but it was out of the question for him to play any longer. And so there we were, up the creek without an understudy. It was an impossible part to learn in a day or indeed weeks, but by a freak chance, the Arts decided not to give a performance on Christmas Eve, and Roderick Cook was released to play Lucky, and very good he was, too.

But far worse was to follow. I was having a sensational tuck-in on Boxing Day when the Stage Director phoned to say that Hugh Burden had been taken away in an ambulance, and he would be obliged if I would come to the theatre as soon as poss. I got there, I regret to say, rather ebullient and be-wined, and learnt that the stage Director would be READING the part for the two performances that evening. The role of Vladimir in *Waiting for Godot* could hardly be described as a 'cough and a spit', as he never, in fact, leaves the stage (except once to urinate, the dear old-fashioned thing), and bangs on fairly continuously for two hours. I could not imagine the customers at the two performances being best pleased, particularly as, Boxing Night being what it is, they'd all booked months previously.

It was a nightmarish evening, and the two audiences were stunned. The curious thing is that fewer people than usual crashed out, mainly, I imagine, because they could not believe their peepers. The poor Stage Director, dressed as a tramp, was careering over the stage at whim, reading from what seemed to us a not absolutely up to date script. A strong note of hysteria swept through the actors, and poor Peter Wood-thorpe took a terrible beating. As this was his first professional job, he found it even more of a nerve-racking ordeal than we did. During the interval, it seemed unlikely that he would resume his stage career, having locked himself in his dressing-room and, despite everyone's efforts, re-fused to emerge. Eventually, I winkled him out by telling him that he would be suspended by Equity if he didn't re-appear. I am happy to say that at no period in the evening did I use the nauseating phrase, 'The show must go on', because this was a typical occasion when the show 'mustn't go on', and everyone should have been given their money back.

Donald Albery, who wisely kept away from the theatre during the crisis, had sent two bottles of champagne for the company to wish them a Happy Christmas. I whipped through them at lightning speed as nobody else fancied them, and, in consequence, didn't fare too badly.

Timothy was still in great pain, and I am bound to say, I rather hoped in my secret heart that he would be too ill to play the following day, because then they would have had to close the building, unless the lady stage manager was sent on to READ Mr Bateson's role, which would have given a novel twist to the play, and anyhow, I suppose I would have had to call her 'Sow' throughout.

The next night's performances were even more nerve-racking than the previous two owing, in my case, to there being an absence of champagne, but we got through somehow, with glazed faces and terror and hate in our hearts. Egged on by Timothy Bateson, I rang up Mr Donald Albery and said that we would prefer that this sort of thing didn't occur again. I have to point out that I was not in a fearfully strong position at the time, as I had blackmailed him into letting me play the Ugly Duchess in a TV production of *Alice in Wonderland*. He had refused several times, and my agent could get nowhere with him. I was determined not to give up without a struggle, as the number of times a man is asked to play the Ugly D. are strictly limited, and as innumerable kind friends pointed out, there would be no need to put on anything other than a straight make-up.

But it was scheduled to be televised on the Sunday following Christmas and Mr Albery thought that it would be too much of a strain after the ten performances of *Godot* in Christmas Week, and how right he was. At a party a few weeks previously I launched into a tiny guerrilla warfare. I started on Mr Albery early in the evening.

'Am I playing the Ugly Duchess?' I asked naïvely.

'No, you aren't, actually,' he replied, with the ghost of a smile.

I popped up at regular intervals throughout the evening, and finally cornered him after a record number of negative encounters.

'You did say I could play the Ugly Duchess in *Alice in Wonderland*, didn't you, Mr Albery?' He muttered his assent in a series of expletives, and I went happily back to the lobster canapés.

So that was that. I was to regret his decision by the time I actually got to the B.B.C. Television Studios in Lime Grove. However, I am anticipating, and I must get back to the Great Godot Crisis. An actor had taken away a script over the Christmas week-end, with a view to understudying, and announced on Wednesday that he was willing to have a bash at Vladimir on Wednesday night. He was called Richard Dare, and was nothing short of a miracle. He got through superbly and we were in the clear again. But by that time, William Squire had been signed to open in the part in three weeks' time, and Paul Daneman had been asked to resume his original role until Squire was ready. It so happened that Paul Daneman had a few weeks off between a film and embarking on the John Clements season at the Saville Theatre.

So we now had just the three Vladimirs in the offing, which was an advance on minus one. But this was to bring fresh difficulties and embarrassment. So successful was Richard Dare in the part that Paul Daneman, after a few rehearsals, was told he wouldn't be required, and I think Mr Albery would have quite happily got out of his contract with Mr Squire if he could have managed it. But Richard Dare deservedly got his break for his bravery, because directly William Squire joined our cast he disappeared to the New Theatre, also under Mr Albery's management, to take over the lead from Nigel Patrick in *The Remarkable Mr Pennypacker*. This left us without an understudy again for quite a time, and plunged us into a helpless rage once more.

It meant a great deal of rehearsing, and the ensuing weeks after Christmas were an appalling strain. The Saturday before *Alice in Wonderland*, I was attacked by a severe bout of laryngitis, and could hardly get through the two performances. I made the unfortunate Stage Director alter his secret report, which read, 'Mr Bull hardly able to speak', to 'Mr Bull seemed to be suffering from a slight cold'. I did not want Mr Albery to stop my Ugly Duchessing at the last moment, and it was likely to affect all our chances of outside work for the remainder of the run. Discretion to let actors in West-End runs do broadcasts, TV, or open the Hanging Gardens at Derry & Tom's, is entirely in the hands of the management, and a strict employer can lose one a lot of side money.

My performance as the Ugly D. was pretty macabre, and must have frightened the bejesus out of the kiddy-winks. An ugly croak came out, and that was about all. But I got through, and really rather enjoyed the production. Gradually my voice came back during the following week, and apart from a severe rash which I got from my rubber wig, *Waiting for Godot* did not have any other startling effect until, in March, the last weeks of the run were announced, when we were all pretty near the end of our tethers, particularly those actually attached to one in the production.

We rang down on March 24th, 1956, after last-minute attempts at a transfer had failed. We had run eight months, and 'Done it' nearly three hundred times. I packed my rubber wig away for the last time (or so I thought), and heaved a gigantic sigh of relief. I thought of thanking Mr Donald Albery publicly by taking a small column in *The Stage*, and announcing: 'Mr Peter Bull thanks Mr Donald Albery for a lucrative but not frightfully enjoyable engagement', but decided wisely against it. In fairness to Mr A. he did pop my salary up by five pounds a week, quite unexpectedly, and off his own bat, which made me feel half a heel when I went whirling up on my weekly visits to the British Actors' Equity Association to report, as deputy, on general conditions.

No one seemed madly anxious to employ me, and instead of going away, I hung about London trying to get a move on with my second book. My first, *To Sea in a Sieve*, had come out on February 27th, and to my amazement was bringing in some splendid dividends. It was then that a new vista opened. Perhaps I'd be able, in a few years' time, to retire from the stage to a lovely cottage in Kent with roses and paper backs littering the place, and a lot of old photographs of scenes from *Waiting for Godot*. But it was not to be yet. Suddenly, a Mr Michael Wide rang me up to ask if I would consider going out on a tour of *Waiting for Godot*. I told him he must be out of his tiny mind, and he said, oh no, he hoped to make a lot of money. He added then that Timothy Bateson and Peter Woodthorpe had said they'd do it if I did. I was frankly flabbergasted by the whole project, but suddenly thinking that it might be the funniest tour ever organised, I said I would. I asked for a percentage (knowing that the 'returns' would ensure one good laugh per evening and certainly per matinée) and an armed guard to and from the Stage Door at the Grand Theatre, Blackpool, a wise precaution as you will see.

It was to be an eight weeks' tour, and at the end of the sixth I could give notice to quit. Three of the dates were in the London suburbs, so topographically it could not be so ghastly. It would also enable me to save a bit against my holiday which I was determined to take that year. Robert Eddison (with whom I hadn't acted since the disastrous *Boy David*), was to play Vladimir and Richard Scott was to direct. Rehearsals were held in the Chelsea Community Centre (handy for me, living just down the road), and I fear nice Mr Scott, who had hoped to give the play an entirely new production, was a bit disappointed to find that the gallant survivors not only wouldn't but couldn't alter their performance. It was a case of '*sauve qui peut*', and I was only concerned for Robert who had the heavy end to carry. But he rose triumphantly to the occasion and went confidently and quietly about his business.

We opened at the Coliseum Theatre, Harrow, on May 21st, 1956, a house of entertainment we practically closed down. A few weeks later it was reconstructed into apartment houses. It was not an auspicious opening date, as the theatre resembled a tunnel, and back-stage conditions were bleak. There was no doorkeeper, no call-boy and no audience to speak of or even speak back. But we were able to get back to our respective homes in the evening and there was a frequent train service. I don't think any of the Harrovians slipped out of their dorms to 'get the message', and it was only during this week that we discovered to our huge delight that Michael Wide's principal backer was none other than Miss Winifred Atwell, the ebullient and talented coloured boogie-woogie pianist. So this made it all right somehow. Her husband, who was also her business manager, used to ring up every evening at Harrow to ascertain the figures, and it was fortunate that the phone was between Master Bateson's and my dressing-room, so there was a rush to give them to him. Actually the first twice (if you know what I mean) he could not believe them at all, and when on the Friday we'd nosedived into the fifties, he thought there must be an error and we meant £250 odd. It was lucky that his wife was playing to around the £1,000 mark EVERY performance at that time in the Palladium.

We played to £499 12s. 10½d., so the cast did not get very much extra that week, but the Monday following we opened at the Arts Theatre, Cambridge, which was to be quite a different pair of tramps. You would have thought by the laughter, bookings and general behaviour that we had brought the great Laughing Success of the Century to their doors and we played to virtual capacity. The running time went up by fifteen minutes in order to give the audience a chance to get over their apoplectic fits, and dons showed us round their collections of precious glass and things. We were patronised by the local theatre groups, who kindly interrupted their activities for a second to tell us what THEY were doing NEXT season, and Peter Woodthorpe (ex-Footlights star) had a great personal triumph on the stage, in the Press, and all over the street, which plunged Timothy and me in an orgy of beastliness to him. He took it in fairly good part and we pressed on to Blackpool.

Miss Atwell and her husband, to say nothing of Mr Wide, had been perked up considerably after the Cambridge week, only to be plunged into gloom by our sensational visit to the Lancashire seaside resort. It was to provide us with some unforgettable memories, and what possessed the management to book us in must be shrouded for ever in mystery. But even this cardinal error was eclipsed by their invitation to the Blackpool Old Age Pensioners to view *Waiting for Godot* at 1s. a head on the Monday night. It was soon apparent that this gesture was not far short of insanity. The O.A.P.s were very angry indeed, after the first few minutes, at not only having to witness *Waiting for Godot*, but also having to pay twelve pennies for the privilege. They determined to have their say, which meant that during the second act we couldn't have ours, so there was a bit of an *impasse*. Bedlam reigned, what with the banging of seats, yells of derision and one or two pertinent remarks when the tramps suggested hanging themselves. We started off with 700 persons in the Grand Theatre, and finished up with under 100. We took one quick curtain and there were rumours of the police being called out for 'our special safety' as it says on some fire curtains. The awful thing is that I rather enjoyed the evening, as I had not needed a clairvoyant to tell me that Blackpool was not going to be one long triumph.

We were to do every penny of £444 on the week and we had a fairly alarming mid-week matinée. The Blackpudlians eyed us more than curiously in the streets and one felt one should ring a leper's bell on approaching Boots the Cash Chemists to change one's library book. Mark you, the local Press went to town about the whole affair (it was slightly out of season anyhow) and rallied to our support. We were front-page news for the entire week. '*Godot* went through without interruption' or 'There were two curtain-calls last night at the Grand Theatre' were typical sub-headlines and there was even a 'leader' saying Blackpool didn't DESERVE to be sent shows like us and the Carl Rosa Opera Company, if they were going to behave like this. The truth of the matter was that poor Blackpool didn't deserve *Waiting for Godot*. In a city almost entirely devoted to sex-shows, oysters, plastic macs and the pursuit of pleasure, it was an anachronism to present such a piece there.

By the end of the week we were all a bit nervy and I couldn't wait to get out of the town. Even 'Sex-drugged girls tell all' had turned out to be two giggly nudes; I had had one bad shrimp and been sick on the pier, so I decided to go to London that week-end, whatever the cost. Now to leave Blackpool on a Saturday night is a tricky assignment, as the only chance is to catch the 10.39 out of Preston, a city which lies about 15 miles out of Blackpool. Well, as the curtain of *Waiting for Godot* in theory didn't come down till 10.15, it was going to be a close shave, to put it mildly. But Master Bateson, who was taking part in the expedition, and I were by now desperate men and we were not going to be defeated by such a little obstacle as Time. We went to the Messrs Eddison and Woodthorpe, our tramp confederates, and asked them if they would be so kind as to leave out ALL the pauses in the play at the second house on Saturday. Those of you who saw the play will remember that the pauses occupied most of the play. But even the artistes were staggered by the results. We whipped through the play and cut just the twenty minutes out of the play that night, and it was, I think, My Most Enjoyable Evening In the Theatre. It was, oddly enough, the only performance that seemed to go remotely well in Blackpool and, needless to say, we were on the verge of maniacal laughter throughout. Pozzo and his slave made every entrance and exit as if they were Belita and Chataway at the height of their powers, and after their disappearance in the first act one tramp had to comment in the course of the play:

'Well, that passed the time.'

'It would have passed in any case,' is the reply.

'Yes, but not quite so rapidly,' says the first tramp, which on this occasion was said with such meaning that they both started to go off into paroxysms, only stopped by the Messrs Bateson and Bull making threatening gestures from the wings.

We had a car waiting for us and, with most of our make-up still on, tore through the night only to find that we had ten minutes to spare at Preston station.

After this, the Pavilion Theatre, Bournemouth, was the Department of Anti-Climax, and we sent most of the inhabitants off into a deep sleep. Very comfortable seats and the sea air took away the unpleasantness and, as usual, I stayed at the Seamoor Commercial Hotel and Café (prop. J. Gourlay) which costs, or did, under four pounds all in for actors. The Gourlays are sweet and kind, and though there was a permanent TV show through the supper (until mercifully kibitzered by Mr Bateson's naughty feet getting entangled in the wires), it was also what is known as A Good Pull-Up for Carmen, which meant that one had a CHOICE in the evenings, which made a splendid change from ordinary digs where the plate is plonked in front of you william-nilliam. Also we had the use of their bathing-hut, which helped us through the week, during which we jolly nearly touched four figures.

Then gently down the coast to Brighton, where we were back to banging of seats and a certain amount of confusion. There was a night when a retired military gent could be heard inexplicably shouting above the turmoil: 'No wonder we lose the colonies if they put on drivel like this', but we passed the £1,000 mark and the Headmaster of Lancing liked it (or so he said).

The next two weeks we were to play in the suburban theatres of London. It was delightful living at home again, and this comfort easily compensated for the appalling business we did at the gigantic Streatham Hill Theatre, where they threw pennies on the stage on the first night, but never into the box-office during the week. It was nice to move on to Golders Green the following week, where people seemed to enjoy the play for a change, and I had a dressing-room with a star on the door. This week we all started speaking to each other again, after losing our heads to such an extent in the purlieus of Streatham that notes were being left at the stage door.

Our lady patron, Miss Winifred Atwell, came to the matinée at Golders Green and seemed delighted with her property, though she carped a bit at the interval music. She thought it would be more in keeping with the mood of the piece to play some serious stuff (Schubert's 'Valse Triste' was a suggestion), but I did point out that the audience at most suburban and provincial theatres, to say nothing of the orchestras concerned, would leave in a body if The Desert Song and The Student Prince didn't pop up in the repertoire at least once a month.

I gave in my notice at Golders Green, but said I would play the extra week at Birmingham which had been tacked onto the end of the tour by this time. We were all beginning to feel the strain by now, and even Robert Eddison said he could not go on for more than a week after we all left. We played at the Birmingham Repertory Theatre, which is a charming bandbox of a theatre and I would love to be there in happier circs. There is also a table-tennis set in the wardrobe which makes it perfect. The resident company were away on a foreign tour and we were to fill the gap for two weeks. The booking was tremendous (the theatre only held about 600) and we were listened to in reverence and fairly stunned silence. In a way it was almost more maddening than hate and interruptions, but I was by now in a psychological state about the whole thing. We all found ourselves unable to speak to each other much off the stage, and the words came out automatically with even less meaning than they had had originally. I found the fortnight lying very heavily on my hands and could not wait for the final night of all.

Timothy and I caught the night train out of Birmingham, after having enjoyed one of the most expensive but happy dinners imaginable. It was July 28th, 1956, a year almost to the day since we started at the Arts. We felt so relaxed and relieved that we could only smile stupidly at each other as we bundled out in the dawn of Euston Station. Yet although we were able to throw off the physical side of *Waiting For Godot*, in my case certainly it was to haunt my memory for many a long month, as indeed Mr Hobson had prophesied.

In a casual assessment I would say that being in it did me far more good than any other performance I have ever given, and only a few weeks ago I was asked to do a Shell-Mex advertising film for TV and use my *Godot* voice, whatever that meant. I was asked to speak on the play to the British Drama League, an invitation which I fear they regretted, owing to the subsequent gibberish that poured out of my mouth.

I hadn't been back a week before dear Mr Donald Albery, who must have watched our meanderings round with the keenest enjoyment, was on the blower asking my reactions to a six weeks' season at the Comedy Theatre to lure the American tourists. I said that I would want £1,000 a week and two TRAINED nurses in attendance, and he didn't seem to think it was worth all THAT.

And although this is the end of that particular little section of my life, I have a lurking suspicion way back in my noddle that I shall end my days playing Pozzo in some of the less accessible repertory theatres of England. But heaven and the theatre-goers of Britain forbid!

From *I know the face but . . .*, 1959.

The only drama critic in history allowed to publish his autobiography over nine entire egotistical volumes, and therefore much to be envied and admired even if the feat was accomplished at a time when paper costs were considerably lower, James Agate (1877–1947) reached the Manchester Guardian *in 1907 and wrote the* Sunday Times *theatre column from 1923 until his death. The first journalist to achieve real power as a modern theatre critic, he was immensely readable, immensely prolific and often immensely wrong. The following, however, written in 1916 about an actress who was then 71 and seven years away from her death, is about the best description I know of the older Bernhardt in action.*

Bernhardt

IN FRONT of her glass, physically exhausted but ever so mentally alert, sits the great workwoman. Disdainful of subterfuge, she gives you the full face of which the lineaments belong to a nation, confronting you unshrinkingly that you may read according to your wit and imagination that mask on which a thousand passions of the scene have left their trace. She stretches out the fine hand of the ageing artist, which so many of the scene's tragic kings have 'lipped and trembled kissing'. The voice is hoarse now, but in the restless eyes the old fires smoulder. The nostrils are still a-quiver, as who should say a horse scenting peril. The spirit is dauntless, defiant of age and natural shock. 'Jusqu'au bout!' the war play's last word of exhortation to France, might well be the device of the actress in the long and stern fight against latter-day misfortune. 'Quand-même!' her actual device, is the watchword of the steel conscious of the fraying scabbard.

'Les critiques ne savent rien!' was a half-serious thrust I made no attempt to parry. We may, however, note that Mme Bernhardt is no stranger to that transcendent theory of the art of acting by virtue of which the actor imposes a single personality on all his parts. In this school such contrary folk as Hamlet and Richard Gloster are one, Iagos confound with Othellos, Shylock disputes with Lear as to which shall most resemble the player as he lives. The passion of a Phèdre, the story of a Joan of Arc, the glamour of a Marguerite Gautier are all merged in a single effulgence. But this canonisation of personality is not without its handicap. The actor is debarred by his very flamboyance from all but the greatest creations, and may no longer cope with the insignificant. When Mme Bernhardt essays the dying stripling of her war play she does it not for our conviction but for her own interest. It amuses her to tear to ribbons the sleeves of the shirt under the tunic. 'Il faut être réaliste!' she declares lightheartedly. Beneath the ostentatious splash of life-blood she paints for her own edification a realistic little wound. This affords an almost child-like gratification. 'Ca ç'amuse!' No theory of acting here, only an echo of the gaiety that surrounds her genius. But the performance has not been without some of the real stuff of acting. The wistful fingering of the standard, the reverence of the disciple for the relic, the delirium of the mystic and the visionary, the ecstasy of the martyr and purged innocence of the saint—these things are as wonderful as ever. They are part of the supremest workmanship of our time. Let us beware of attributing the fervour of these war performances to patriotism rather than to the actor's art. Not even these latter days can give to 'Porte-drapeau, mon camarade!' a greater exultation than was to be found in L'Aiglon in the days of profound peace. One is not quite sure whether, curiously enough, actual war has not taken some of the edge off this fine frenzy of patriotism that is Mme Bernhardt's—to an infinitesimal degree but still perceptibly. Her art has always been at its greatest in contact with the abstract and the ideal. The present flame is kindled by a big war, the biggest of all wars if you like, but a particular war after all, with local gratifications and the recovery of an actual Alsace. When, as in L'Aiglon, our minds were not tuned to immediate advantage, her art seemed to soar on a freer wing. The little play has to its credit half a dozen lines on the function of the artist, significantly declaimed by Mme Bernhardt. 'The sword of the soldier pierces the flesh, the word of the poet is still to dominate the spirit.' To fight is not more noble than to inspire.

As one leaves the theatre one's mind goes back to the first rising on one's youthful horizon of this now mellowing star. The theatre was the Prince's Theatre, Manchester, and the play that hectic, flushed masterpiece of the hothouse, La Dame aux Camélias. From some untravelled end of the earth, on her way to Paris, came the great actress, the wings of genius touching us lightly as she passed. It was all very wonderful and incomprehensible. One thing only did one realise clearly, and that was the imminence of eclipse which must always threaten radiance more than mortal. The flame of Rachel's genius, people said, had burned too fiercely for the frail body, and here was just such another fire. . . . This early enthusiasm, wonderful though it was, wonderful as are all first acceptances of greatness dimly seen and insecurely grasped, was at the time little more than the eager response of youth to the exotic and the incredible. One looks back, oh! ever so leniently, upon all that half-discerning enthusiasm which has deepened so immeasurably. The quality of our appreciation has changed; this art, which in its heyday lit up a firmament, moves towards its setting in infinite serenity. We find a reason now for the old unreasoning emotion; incalculable glamour begins to fade. There has succeeded a lasting reverence for the supreme and unfailing conscientiousness of the artist, an enduring recognition of her great spirit.

From the *Manchester Guardian*, 1916.

*Geared like all drama critics to a three- or four-hour maximum attention
span in the theatre, I find even away from the stalls a curious inability to
sustain interest in books which take much more than an evening and a night
to read. This has ruled out for me vast areas of Victorian and indeed
modern Russian fiction and has cut me off from most of Charles Dickens
(1812–70) whom I'm still inclined to think of first and foremost not as a
novelist but as a pioneer of the one-man show. Barnstorming America in
1867–68 with his own readings, he prepared the way and the Americans for
that succession of other authors from Oscar Wilde through to Dylan
Thomas and Brendan Behan who later criss-crossed the States in search of
fame or fortune or alcohol or a combination of all three. Of all his novels,
however, Nicholas Nickleby (written 1838–39) has lived best in my
memory, mainly for the character of the travelling actor-manager Vincent
Crummles, father of the Infant Phenomenon and surely worthy of a book
all to himself. Played in the 1947 film by Stanley Holloway, Crummles
has never really been done justice elsewhere and perhaps now that Robert
Newton, W. C. Fields, Robert Atkins and Donald Wolfit are no longer
with us he never will be; here however he is in his full glory, from
Chapter 23.*

Treats of the Company of Mr Vincent Crummles, and of his Affairs, Domestic and Theatrical

As Mr Crummles had a strange four-legged animal in the inn stables,
which he called a pony, and a vehicle of unknown design, on which he
bestowed the appellation of a four-wheeled phaeton, Nicholas proceeded
on his journey next morning with greater ease than he had expected: the
manager and himself occupying the front seat: and the Master Crummleses and Smike being packed together behind, in company with a wicker
basket defended from wet by a stout oilskin, in which were the broad-
swords, pistols, pigtails, nautical costumes, and other professional
necessaries of the aforesaid young gentlemen.

The pony took his time upon the road, and—possibly in consequence
of his theatrical education—evinced, every now and then, a strong

inclination to lie down. However, Mr Vincent Crummles kept him up pretty well, by jerking the rein, and plying the whip; and when these means failed, and the animal came to a stand, the elder Master Crummles got out and kicked him. By dint of these encouragements, he was persuaded to move from time to time, and they jogged on (as Mr Crummles truly observed) very comfortably for all parties.

'He's a good pony at bottom,' said Mr Crummles, turning to Nicholas.

He might have been at bottom, but he certainly was not at top, seeing that his coat was of the roughest and most ill-favoured kind. So Nicholas merely observed that he shouldn't wonder if he was.

'Many and many is the circuit this pony has gone,' said Mr Crummles, flicking him skilfully on the eyelid for old acquaintance' sake. 'He is quite one of us. His mother was on the stage.'

'Was she?' rejoined Nicholas.

'She ate apple-pie at a circus for upwards of fourteen years,' said the manager; 'fired pistols, and went to bed in a nightcap; and, in short, took the low comedy entirely. His father was a dancer.'

'Was he at all distinguished?'

'Not very,' said the manager. 'He was rather a low sort of pony. The fact is, he had been originally jobbed out by the day, and he never quite got over his old habits. He was clever in melodrama too, but too broad—too broad. When the mother died, he took the port-wine business.'

'The port-wine business!' cried Nicholas.

'Drinking port-wine with the clown,' said the manager; 'but he was greedy, and one night bit off the bowl of the glass, and choked himself, so his vulgarity was the death of him at last.'

The descendant of this ill-starred animal requiring increased attention from Mr Crummles as he progressed in his day's work, that gentleman had very little time for conversation, Nicholas was thus left at leisure to entertain himself with his own thoughts, until they arrived at the drawbridge at Portsmouth, when Mr Crummles pulled up.

'We'll get down here,' said the manager, 'and the boys will take him round to the stable, and call at my lodgings with the luggage. You had better let yours be taken there, for the present.'

Thanking Mr Vincent Crummles for his obliging offer, Nicholas jumped out, and, giving Smike his arm, accompanied the manager up High Street on their way to the theatre; feeling nervous and uncomfortable enough at the prospect of an immediate introduction to a scene so new to him.

They passed a great many bills, pasted against the walls and displayed in windows, wherein the names of Mr Vincent Crummles, Mrs Vincent Crummles, Master Crummles, Master P. Crummles, and Miss Crummles, were printed in very large letters, and everything else in very small ones; and, turning at length into an entry, in which was a strong smell of orange-pee l and lamp-oil, with an undercurrent of saw-dust, groped their way through a dark passage, and, descending a step or two, threaded a little maze of canvas screens and paint-pots and emerged upon the stage of the Portsmouth Theatre.

'Here we are,' said Mr Crummles.

It was not very light, but Nicholas found himself close to the first entrance on the prompt side, among bare walls, dusty scenes, mildewed clouds, heavily daubed draperies, and dirty floors. He looked about him; ceiling, pit, boxes, gallery, orchestra, fittings, and decorations of every kind,—all looked coarse, cold, gloomy, and wretched.

'Is this a theatre?' whispered Smike, in amazement; 'I thought it was a blaze of light and finery.'

'Why, so it is,' replied Nicholas, hardly less surprised; 'but not by day, Smike—not by day.'

The manager's voice recalled him from a more careful inspection of the building, to the opposite side of the proscenium, where, at a small mahogany table with rickety legs and of an oblong shape, sat a stout, portly female, apparently between forty and fifty, in a tarnished silk cloak, with her bonnet dangling by the strings in her hand, and her hair (of which she had a great quantity) braided in a large festoon over each temple.

'Mr Johnson,' said the manager (for Nicholas had given the name which Newman Noggs had bestowed upon him in his conversation with Mrs Kenwigs), 'let me introduce Mrs Vincent Crummles.'

'I am glad to see you, sir,' said Mrs Vincent Crummles in a sepulchral voice. 'I am very glad to see you, and still more happy to hail you as a promising member of our corps.'

The lady shook Nicholas by the hand as she addressed him in these terms; he saw it was a large one, but had not expected quite such an iron grip as that with which she honoured him.

'And this,' said the lady, crossing to Smike, as tragic actresses cross when they obey a stage direction, 'and this is the other. You too, are welcome, sir.'

'He'll do, I think, my dear?' said the manager, taking a pinch of snuff.

'He is admirable,' replied the lady. 'An acquisition, indeed.'

As Mrs Vincent Crummles recrossed back to the table, there bounded on to the stage from some mysterious inlet, a little girl in a dirty white frock with tucks up to the knees, short trousers, sandaled shoes, white spencer, pink gauze bonnet, green veil and curl-papers; who turned a pirouette, cut twice in the air, turned another pirouette, then, looking off at the opposite wing, shrieked, bounded forward to within six inches of the footlights, and fell into a beautiful attitude of terror, as a shabby gentleman in an old pair of buff slippers came in at one powerful slide, and chattering his teeth, fiercely brandished a walking-stick.

'They are going through the Indian Savage and the Maiden,' said Mrs Crummles.

'Oh!' said the manager, 'the little ballet interlude. Very good, go on. A little this way, if you please, Mr Johnson. That'll do. Now!'

The manager clapped his hands as a signal to proceed, and the savage, becoming ferocious, made a slide towards the maiden; but the maiden avoided him in six twirls, and came down, at the end of the last one, upon the very points of her toes. This seemed to make some impression upon the savage; for, after a little more ferocity and chasing of the maiden into corners, he began to relent, and stroked his face several times with his right thumb and four fingers, thereby intimating that he was struck with admiration of the maiden's beauty. Acting upon the impulse of this passion, he (the savage) began to hit himself severe thumps in the chest, and to exhibit other indications of being desperately in love, which being rather a prosy proceeding, was very likely the cause of the maiden's falling asleep; whether it was or no, asleep she did fall, sound as a church, on a sloping bank, and the savage perceiving it, leant his left ear on his left hand, and nodded sideways, to intimate to all whom it might concern that she *was* asleep, and no shamming. Being left to himself, the savage had a dance, all alone. Just as he left off, the maiden woke up, rubbed her eyes, got off the bank, and had a dance all alone too—such a dance that the savage looked on in ecstasy all the while, and when it was done, plucked from a neighbouring tree some botanical curiosity, resembling a small pickled cabbage, and offered it to the maiden, who at first wouldn't have it, but on the savage shedding tears relented. Then the savage jumped for joy; then the maiden jumped for rapture at the sweet smell of the pickled cabbage. Then the savage and the maiden danced violently together, and, finally, the savage dropped down on one knee, and the maiden stood on one leg upon his other knee; thus concluding the ballet, and leaving the spectators in a state of pleasing uncertainty, whether she would ultimately marry the savage, or return to her friends.

'Very well indeed,' said Mr Crummles: 'bravo!'

'Bravo!' cried Nicholas, resolved to make the best of everything. 'Beautiful!'

'This, sir,' said Mr Vincent Crummles, bringing the maiden forward, 'this is the infant phenomenon—Miss Ninetta Crummles.'

'Your daughter?' inquired Nicholas.

'My daughter—my daughter,' replied Mr Vincent Crummles; 'the idol of every place we go into, sir. We have had complimentary letters about this girl, sir, from the nobility and gentry of almost every town in England.'

'I am not surprised at that,' said Nicholas; 'she must be quite a natural genius.'

'Quite a——!' Mr Crummles stopped: language was not powerful enough to describe the infant phenomenon. 'I'll tell you what, sir,' he said; 'the talent of this child is not to be imagined. She must be seen, sir —seen—to be ever so faintly appreciated. There; go to your mother, my dear.'

'May I ask how old she is?' inquired Nicholas.

'You may, sir,' replied Mr Crummles, looking steadily in his questioner's face, as some men do when they have doubts about being implicitly believed in what they are going to say. 'She is ten years of age, sir.'

'Not more?'

'Not a day.'

'Dear me!' said Nicholas, 'it's extraordinary.'

It was; for the infant phenomenon, though of short stature, had a comparatively aged countenance, and had moreover been precisely the same age—not perhaps to the full extent of the memory of the oldest inhabitant, but certainly for five good years. But she had been kept up late every night, and put upon an unlimited allowance of gin-and-water from infancy, to prevent her growing tall, and perhaps this system of training had produced in the infant phenomenon these additional phenomena.

While this short dialogue was going on, the gentleman who had enacted the savage came up, with his walking shoes on his feet, and his slippers in his hand, to within a few paces, as if desirous to join in the conversation. Deeming this a good opportunity, he put in his word.

'Talent there, sir!' said the savage, nodding towards Miss Crummles. Nicholas assented.

'Ah!' said the actor, setting his teeth together, and drawing in his breath with a hissing sound, 'she oughtn't to be in the provinces, she oughtn't.'

'What do you mean?' asked the manager.

'I mean to say,' replied the other, warmly, 'that she is too good for country boards, and that she ought to be in one of the large houses in London, or nowhere; and I tell you more, without mincing the matter, that if it wasn't for envy and jealousy in some quarter that you know of, she would be. Perhaps you'll introduce me here, Mr Crummles.'

'Mr Folair,' said the manager, presenting him to Nicholas.

'Happy to know you, sir.' Mr Folair touched the brim of his hat with his forefinger, and then shook hands. 'A recruit, sir, I understand?'

'An unworthy one,' replied Nicholas.

'Did you ever see such a set-out as that?' whispered the actor, drawing him away, as Crummles left them to speak to his wife.

'As what?'

Mr Folair made a funny face from his pantomine collection, and pointed over his shoulder.

'You don't mean the infant phenomenon?'

'Infant humbug, sir,' replied Mr Folair. 'There isn't a female child of common sharpness in a charity school, that couldn't do better than that. She may thank her stars she was born a manager's daughter.'

'You seem to take it to heart,' observed Nicholas, with a smile.

'Yes, by Jove, and well I may,' said Mr Folair, drawing his arm through his, and walking him up and down the stage. 'Isn't it enough to make a man crusty to see that little sprawler put up in the best business every night, and actually keeping money out of the house, by being forced down the people's throats, while other people are passed over? Isn't it extraordinary to see a man's confounded family conceit blinding him, even to his own interest? Why I *know* of fifteen and sixpence that came to Southampton one night last month, to see me dance the Highland Fling; and what's the consequence? I've never been put up in it since—never once—while the 'infant phenomenon' has been grinning through artificial flowers at five people and a baby in the pit, and two boys in the gallery, every night.'

'If I may judge from what I have seen of you,' said Nicholas, 'you must be a valuable member of the company.'

'Oh!' replied Mr Folair, beating his slippers together, to knock the dust out; 'I *can* come it pretty well—nobody better, perhaps, in my own line—but having such business as one gets here, is like putting lead on one's feet instead of chalk, and dancing in fetters without the credit of it. Holloa, old fellow, how are you?'

The gentleman addressed in these latter words, was a dark-complexioned man, inclining indeed to sallow, with long thick black hair, and very evident indications (although he was close shaved) of a stiff beard, and whiskers of the same deep shade. His age did not appear to exceed thirty, though many at first sight would have considered him much older, as his face was long, and very pale, from the constant application of stage paint. He wore a checked shirt, an old green coat with new gilt buttons, a neckerchief of broad red and green stripes, and full blue trousers; he carried, too, a common ash walking-stick, apparently more for show than use, as he flourished it about, with the hooked end downwards, except when he raised it for a few seconds, and throwing himself into a fencing attitude, made a pass or two at the side-scenes, or at any other object, animate or inanimate, that chanced to afford him a pretty good mark at the moment.

'Well, Tommy,' said this gentleman, making a thrust at his friend, who parried it dexterously with his slipper, 'what's the news?'

'A new appearance, that's all,' replied Mr Folair, looking at Nicholas.

'Do the honours, Tommy, do the honours,' said the other gentleman, tapping him reproachfully on the crown of the hat with his stick.

'This is Mr Lenville, who does our first tragedy, Mr Johnson,' said the pantomimist.

'Except when old bricks and mortar takes it into his head to do it himself, you should add, Tommy,' remarked Mr Lenville. 'You know who bricks and mortar is, I suppose, sir?'

'I do not, indeed,' replied Nicholas.

'We call Crummles that, because his style of acting is rather in the heavy and ponderous way,' said Mr Lenville. 'I mustn't be cracking jokes though, for I've got a part of twelve lengths here, which I must be up in tomorrow night, and I haven't had time to look at it yet; I'm a confounded quick study, that's one comfort.'

Consoling himself with this reflection, Mr Lenville drew from his coat-pocket a greasy and crumpled manuscript, and, having made another pass at his friend, proceeded to walk to and fro, conning it to himself and indulging occasionally in such appropriate action as his imagination and the text suggested.

A pretty general muster of the company had by this time taken place; for besides Mr Lenville and his friend Tommy, there were present, a slim young gentleman with weak eyes, who played the low-spirited lover and sang tenor songs, and who had come arm-in-arm with the comic countryman—a man with a turned-up nose, large mouth, broad face, and staring eyes. Making himself very amiable to the infant phenomenon, was an inebriated elderly gentleman in the last depths of shabbiness, who played the calm and virtuous old men; and paying especial court to Mrs Crummles was another elderly gentleman, a shade more respectable, who played the irascible old men—those funny fellows who had nephews in the army, and perpetually run about with thick sticks to compel them to marry heiresses. Besides these, there was a roving-looking person in a rough great-coat, who strode up and down in front of the lamps, flourishing a dress-cane, and rattling away, in an undertone, with great vivacity for the amusement of an ideal audience. He was not quite so young as he had been, and his figure was rather running to seed; but there was an air of exaggerated gentility about him, which bespoke the hero of swaggering comedy. There was, also, a little group of three or four young men, with lantern jaws and thick eyebrows, who were conversing in one corner; but they seemed to be of secondary importance, and laughed and talked together without attracting any attention.

The ladies were gathered in a little knot by themselves round the rickety table before mentioned. There was Miss Snevellicci—who could do anything, from a medley dance to Lady Macbeth, and also always played some part in blue silk knee-smalls at her benefit—glancing, from the depths of her coal-scuttle straw bonnet, at Nicholas, and affecting to be absorbed in the recital of a diverting story to her friend Miss Ledrook, who had brought her work, and was making up a ruff in the most natural manner possible. There was Miss Belvawney—who seldom aspired to speaking parts, and usually went on as a page in white silk hose, to stand with one leg bent, and contemplate the audience, or to go in and out after Mr Crummles in stately tragedy—twisting up the ringlets of the beautiful Miss Bravassa, who had once had her likeness taken 'in character' by an engraver's apprentice, whereof impressions were hung up for sale in the pastry-cook's window, and the greengrocer's, and at the circulating library, and the box-office, whenever the announce bills came out for her annual night. There was Mrs Lenville, in a very limp bonnet and veil, decidedly in that way in which she would wish to be if she truly loved Mr Lenville; there was Miss Gazingi, with an imitation ermine boa tied in a loose knot round her neck, flogging Mr Crummles, junior, with both ends, in fun. Lastly, there was Mrs Grudden in a brown cloth pelisse and a beaver bonnet, who assisted Mrs Crummles in her domestic affairs, and took money at the doors, and dressed the ladies, and swept the house, and held the prompt book when everybody else was on for the last scene, and acted any kind of part on any emergency without ever learning it, and was put down in the bills under any name or names whatever, that occurred to Mr Crummles as looking well in print.

Mr Folair having obligingly confided these particulars to Nicholas, left him to mingle with his fellows; the work of personal introduction was completed by Mr Vincent Crummles, who publicly heralded the new actor as a prodigy of genius and learning.

'I beg your pardon,' said Miss Snevellicci, sidling towards Nicholas, 'but did you ever play at Canterbury?'

'I never did,' replied Nicholas.

'I recollect meeting a gentleman at Canterbury,' said Miss Snevellicci, 'only for a few moments, for I was leaving the company as he joined it, so like you that I felt almost certain it was the same.'

'I see you now, for the first time,' rejoined Nicholas with all due gallantry. 'I am sure I never saw you before; I couldn't have forgotten it.'

'Oh, I'm sure—it's very flattering of you to say so,' retorted Miss Snevellicci with a graceful bend. 'Now I look at you again, I see that the gentleman at Canterbury hadn't the same eyes as you—you'll think me very foolish for taking notice of such things, won't you?'

'Not at all,' said Nicholas. 'How can I feel otherwise than flattered by your notice in any way?'

'Oh! you men are such vain creatures!' cried Miss Snevellicci. Whereupon, she became charmingly confused, and, pulling out her pocket-handkerchief from a faded pink silk reticule with a gilt clasp, called to Miss Ledbrook—

'Led, my dear,' said Miss Snevellicci.

'Well, what is the matter?' said Miss Ledbrook.

'It's not the same.'

'Not the same what?'

'Canterbury—you know what I mean. Come here! I want to speak to you.'

But Miss Ledbrook wouldn't come to Miss Snevellicci, so Miss Snevellicci was obliged to go to Miss Ledbrook, which she did, in a skipping manner that was quite fascinating; and Miss Ledbrook evidently joked Miss Snevellicci about being struck with Nicholas; for, after some playful whispering, Miss Snevellicci hit Miss Ledbrook very hard on the backs of her hands, and retired up, in a state of pleasing confusion.

'Ladies and gentlemen,' said Mr Vincent Crummles, who had been writing on a piece of paper, 'we'll call the Mortal Struggle tomorrow at ten; everybody for the procession. Intrigue, and Ways and Means, you're all up in, so we shall only want one rehearsal. Everybody at ten, if you please.'

'Everybody at ten,' repeated Mrs Grudden, looking about her.

'On Monday morning we shall read a new piece,' said Mr Crummles; 'the names not known yet, but everybody will have a good part. Mr Johnson will take care of that.'

'Hallo!' said Nicholas, starting, 'I——'

'On Monday morning,' repeated Mr Crummles, raising his voice, to drown the unfortunate Mr Johnson's remonstrance; 'that'll do, ladies and gentlemen.'

The ladies and gentlemen required no second notice to quit; and, in a few minutes, the theatre was deserted, save by the Crummles family, Nicholas, and Smike.

'Upon my word,' said Nicholas, taking the manager aside, 'I don't think I can be ready by Monday.'

'Pooh, pooh,' replied Mr Crummles.

'But really I can't,' returned Nicholas; 'my invention is not accustomed to these demands, or possibly I might produce——'

'Invention! what the devil's that got to do with it!' cried the manager, hastily.

'Everything, my dear sir.'

'Nothing, my dear sir,' retorted the manager, with evident impatience. 'Do you understand French?'

'Perfectly well.'

'Very good,' said the manager, opening the table-drawer, and giving roll of paper from it to Nicholas. 'There! Just turn that into English, and put your name on the title-page. Damn me,' said Mr Crummles, angrily, 'if I haven't often said that I wouldn't have a man or woman in my company that wasn't master of the language, so that they might learn it from the original, and play it in English, and save all this trouble and expense.

Nicholas smiled and pocketed the play.

'What are you going to do about your lodgings?' said Mr Crummles.

Nicholas could not help thinking that, for the first week, it would be an uncommon convenience to have a turn-up bedstead in the pit, but he merely remarked that he had not turned his thoughts that way.

'Come home with me then,' said Mr Crummles, 'and my boys shall go with you after dinner, and show you the most likely place.'

The offer was not to be refused; Nicholas and Mr Crummles gave Mrs Crummles an arm each, and walked up the street in stately array. Smike, the boys, and the phenomenon, went home by a shorter cut, and Mrs Grudden remained behind to take some cold Irish stew and a pint of porter in the box-office.

Mrs Crummles trod the pavement as if she were going to immediate execution with an animating consciousness of innocence, and that heroic fortitude which virtue alone inspires. Mr Crummles, on the other hand, assumed the look and gait of a hardened despot; but they both attracted some notice from many of the passers-by, and when they heard a whisper of 'Mr and Mrs Crummles!' or saw a little boy run back to stare them in the face, the severe expression of their countenances relaxed, for they felt it was popularity.

Mr Crummles lived in Saint Thomas's Street, at the house of one Bulph, a pilot, who sported a boat-green door, with window-frames of the same colour, and had the little finger of a drowned man on his parlour mantel-shelf, with other maritime and natural curiosities. He displayed also a brass knocker, a brass plate, and a brass bell-handle, all very bright and shining; and had a mast, with a vane on the top of it, in his back yard.

'You are welcome,' said Mrs Crummles, turning round to Nicholas when they reached the bow-windowed front room on the first floor.

Nicholas bowed his acknowledgements, and was unfeignedly glad to see the cloth laid.

'We have but a shoulder of mutton with onion sauce,' said Mrs

Crummles, in the same charnel-house voice; 'but such as our dinner is, we beg you to partake of it.'

'You are very good,' replied Nicholas, 'I shall do it ample justice.'

'Vincent,' said Mrs Crummles, 'what is the hour?'

'Five minutes past dinner-time,' said Mr Crummles.

Mrs Crummles rang the bell. 'Let the mutton and onion sauce appear.'

The slave who attended upon Mr Bulph's lodgers disappeared, and after a short interval reappeared with the festive banquet. Nicholas and the infant phenomenon opposed each other at the pembroke-table, and Smike and the master Crummleses dined on the sofa bedstead.

'Are they very theatrical people here?' asked Nicholas.

'No,' replied Mr Crummles, shaking his head, 'far from it—far from it.'

'I pity them,' observed Mrs Crummles.

'So do I,' said Nicholas; 'if they have no relish for theatrical entertainments, properly conducted.'

'Then they have none, sir,' rejoined Mr Crummles. 'To the infant's benefit, last year, on which occasion she repeated three of her most popular characters, and also appeared in the Fairy Porcupine, as originally performed by her, there was a house of no more than four pound twelve.'

'Is it possible?' cried Nicholas.

'And two pound of that was trust, pa,' said the phenomenon.

'And two pound of that was trust,' repeated Mr Crummles. 'Mrs Crummles herself has played to mere handfuls.'

'But they are always a taking audience, Vincent,' said the manager's wife.

'Most audiences are, when they have good acting—real good acting—the regular thing,' replied Mr Crummles, forcibly.

'Do you give lessons, ma'am?' inquired Nicholas.

'I do,' said Mrs Crummles.

'There is no teaching here, I suppose?'

'There has been,' said Mrs Crummles. 'I have received pupils here. I imparted tuition to the daughter of a dealer in ships' provision; but it afterwards appeared that she was insane when she first came to me. It was very extraordinary that she should come, under such circumstances.'

Not feeling quite so sure of that, Nicholas thought it best to hold his peace.

'Let me see,' said the manager cogitating after dinner. 'Would you like some nice little part with the infant?'

'You are very good,' replied Nicholas hastily; 'but I think perhaps it would be better if I had somebody my own size at first, in case I should turn out awkward. I should feel more at home perhaps.'

'True,' said the manager. 'Perhaps you would. And you could play up to the infant, in time, you know.'

'Certainly,' replied Nicholas: devoutly hoping that it would be a very long time before he was honoured with this distinction.

'Then I'll tell you what we'll do,' said Mr Crummles. 'You shall study Romeo when you've done that piece—don't forget to throw the pump and tubs in by-the-by—Juliet Miss Snevellicci, old Grudden the nurse. —Yes, that'll do very well. Rover too;—you might get up Rover while you were about it, and Cassio, and Jeremy Diddler. You can easily knock them off; one part helps the other so much. Here they are, cues and all.'

With these hasty general directions Mr Crummles thrust a number of little books into the faltering hands of Nicholas, and bidding his eldest son go with him and show where lodgings were to be had, shook him by the hand, and wished him good night.

There is no lack of comfortable furnished apartments in Portsmouth, and no difficulty in finding some that are proportionate to very slender finances; but the former were too good, and the latter too bad, and they went into so many houses, and came out unsuited, that Nicholas seriously began to think he should be obliged to ask permission to spend the night in the theatre, after all.

Eventually, however, they stumbled upon two small rooms up three pair of stairs, or rather two pair and a ladder, at a tobacconist's shop, on the Common Hard: a dirty street leading down to the dockyard. These Nicholas engaged, only too happy to have escaped any request for payment of a week's rent beforehand.

'There! Lay down our personal property, Smike,' he said, after showing young Crummles downstairs. 'We have fallen upon strange times, and Heaven only knows the end of them; but I am tired with the events of these three days, and will postpone reflection till tomorrow— if I can.'

From *Nicholas Nickleby*, 1838–9.

Actors writing about other actors are inclined to be grudging or patronising or sycophantic or simply jealous : in article after article and book after book John Gielgud (b. 1904) has proved an exception to this rule and has indeed through his Terry family connections and an extraordinarily retentive memory supplied some of the century's most valuable theatre history, quite apart from the history he himself has made on its stages. Here, in a book called Distinguished Company, *he is writing about the legendary Mrs Patrick Campbell.*

Mrs Patrick Campbell

'STELLA—STELLA FOR STAR,' cried the heroine of Tennessee Williams's *Streetcar Named Desire*. And I thought at once of another star—Stella Beatrice, the great actress Mrs Patrick Campbell. Brilliant, impossible, cruel, fascinatingly self-destructive, witty (especially when she had a foeman worthy of her steel—Herbert Tree, Bernard Shaw, or Noël Coward), devastatingly unpredictable, she could be grandly snobbish one minute and generously simple the next. She despised people who were afraid of her, would patronise an audience if she felt them to be unsympathetic, and make fun of her fellow actors if they failed to provide her with inspiration. I once saw her walk through the whole of the first act of *John Gabriel Borkman*, ignoring the other players and taking every other line from the prompter, only to electrify the house in the next scene when she was partnered by an actor she admired. Her stage movements were expressive and unlike those of any other actress. I can see her now in *The Second Mrs Tanqueray* (late in her career, on tour at a theatre in Croydon), peeling muscat grapes with her fingers and cramming them into her mouth, 'I adore fruit, especially when it's expensive'; stabbing the hat on her lap with a furious hatpin as Mrs Cortelyon left the stage in the second act, and gazing at her face in a hand-mirror at the end of the play just before her final exit. I see her opening champagne in *Ghosts*, laying a table, cooing to a baby, and digging into a hamper of old clothes in *The Matriarch*, knitting in the last act of *Pygmalion* with a look of unutterable boredom on her face, airing her newly taught society accent in hollow, supercilious tones.

She was beginning to be fat when I met her first, and would make constant references to her fast-vanishing figure—'I look like a burst paper bag.' She nearly always wore sweeping black dresses and hats with shady brims (she once told me proudly that the hat she was wearing that day looked so much better since she had trimmed the edges of it with a pair of nail-scissors), and her flowing velvets were usually sprinkled with the white hairs of Moonbeam, her beloved Pekinese. But she still appeared majestic as she swept down in the hotel lift to enthrone herself in a New York taxi, where she would proceed to chat with the driver on a variety of topics—the stupidity of Hollywood, the Abdication of the Duke of Windsor ('Such a gesture has not been made since Antony gave up a Kingdom for Cleopatra') or the necessity of a halt to walk her dog. 'Who's responsible for this?' the man demanded as he discovered a puddle on the floor of his cab. 'I am,' replied Mrs Campbell, as she alighted calmly.

Everyone referred to her as Mrs Pat, but I always hated the familiarity, and took care always to address her by her full name until the day when she rewarded me by asking me to call her Stella. I had been introduced to her, in the early Twenties, at a luncheon party in Brighton in a private suite at the Metropole Hotel given by a Lord who loved the stage. She was playing Hedda Gabler at a theatre on one of the piers (why didn't I go to see her in it?) and someone told her the performance was a *tour de force*. 'I suppose that is why I am always forced to tour,' she replied mournfully. Her company dreaded her, except for the few worshippers who dared to stand up to her when she was in a bad mood. She loved rich and titled people and would allow them to give her presents and entertain her, but she was very proud with younger folk and generous both in advice and criticism. She could be wonderful company, though I think she was often cruel to men who fell in love with her—even Forbes-Robertson and Shaw—and sometimes even more unkind to her women friends, letting them fetch and carry for her for a time and then making fun of them or casting them aside. But somehow I was never afraid of her, though the only time I acted with her, as Oswald in *Ghosts* in 1929, she played some alarming tricks and made a fool of me at one performance. The dress-rehearsal had gone off without mishap, and Mrs Campbell was word perfect and sailing through her scenes. At the first performance, however, she seemed less at ease, though still charming to me at the fall of the curtain, when she graciously thanked me for having helped her through. I beamed with delight and thought I had passed my test. At the second performance I was sitting at a table smoking. No ash tray had been provided, and I looked helplessly round when the cue came for me to put out my cigar. Not daring to leave my chair, for fear of complicating the moves that had been arranged by the director, I stubbed it out on the chenille tablecloth and dropped the butt under the table and then, a few moments later, stupidly put my hands on the table before lifting them to cover my face. Mrs Campbell, turning upstage, shook with laughter for the rest of the scene, and pouted, 'Oh, you're such an amateur!' as the curtain fell. During the second interval my aunt, Mable Terry-Lewis, never famous for her tact, burst into my dressing-room. 'Tell her we can't hear a word she says,' she announced, 'the Charing Cross Road is being drilled outside!' This counsel I naturally preferred to ignore, though it hardly tended to improve my already shaken confidence. But worse was yet to come. At the end of the play Mrs Alving stands aghast, staring at her son as he mutters, 'Mother, give me the sun. The sun! The sun!' In her hand she still holds the box of pills which she does not dare to give him. Mrs Campbell had evidently decided suddenly that she must make the most of this important final moment. With a wild cry, she flung the pillbox into the footlights and threw herself across my knees with her entire weight. 'Oswald. Oswald!' she moaned. The armchair (borrowed by Mrs Campbell herself from a friend, because, as she said, 'the back is high enough to hide my chins') cracked ominously as she lay prone across my lap, and as I clutched the arms in desperation for fear they might disintegrate, she whispered fiercely, 'Keep down for the call. This play is worse than having a confinement.' Yet she had been of the greatest help during rehearsals and I always thought she could, if she had chosen, have been a fine director herself.

It was very difficult to judge the extent of her real talents in those later days. Of course I never saw her at the time of her early triumphs, when she was slim and elegant and Aubrey Beardsley drew her, willow-slender, for an exquisite study in black-and-white. I think she never took much exercise—the leading ladies of her day didn't deign to walk—and she was very fond of food. During the rehearsals of *Ghosts* we would lunch together, and she would sit in the Escargot Restaurant, devouring snails by the dozen. One day, while we were there, a striking-looking lady, with black hair parted in the middle and drawn back in a great knot at the nape of her neck, appeared in the doorway, attracting considerable attention from everyone in the room. 'Surely that is Madame Marguerite D'Alvarez, the famous singer,' I ventured to remark. Mrs Campbell lifted her eyes from her plate and murmured in tragic tones, 'Ah yes. Me in a spoon.'

I thought she did not much care for the Terry family, for my great-aunt Marion had been a famous rival of hers. She had played Mrs Erlynne on one occasion in Dublin to Mrs Campbell's Lady Winder-mere, and taken over her part at the last moment when Mrs Campbell quarrelled with Forbes-Robertson during the rehearsals of Henry

Arthur Jones' *Michael and his Lost Angel*, though Marion proved to be ill-suited and the play was a complete failure. They were to play together once more in the 1920 revival of *Pygmalion*, and I fancy that she and Mrs Campbell must have worked on this occasion with velvet gloves. But she always spoke to me of Ellen Terry with great admiration though she could not resist one crushing remark about my mother's family. I had been distressed to find her in New York (this was in 1936), living without a maid in a second-rate hotel room, clothes and papers strewn everywhere, laid up with influenza. She wrote afterwards to Shaw that my eyes had filled with tears when I arrived. 'All the Terrys cry so easily,' was her typical comment. But when I tried to send her a cheque as a Christmas present she refused to accept it and sent it back.

One afternoon, while I was playing *Hamlet* in New York, Mrs Campbell offered to take me to visit Edward Sheldon, the playwright. This remarkable man had been a youthful friend of John Barrymore, and had encouraged him to further his stage career by the brilliant series of classical revivals and romantic plays (*Richard III, Hamlet*, Tolstoy's *Living Corpse, The Jest*) in which Barrymore triumphed in the early Twenties. Sheldon was also the author of two sensationally successful melodramas, *Salvation Nell* for Mrs Fiske and *Romance* for Doris Keane, with whom he had been very much in love. He was now completely paralysed and blind as a result of some petrifying bone disease, but, despite his infirmity, he retained all his intellectual faculties, and continued his friendship with all the most brilliant players of the New York theatre, who went continually to see him and greatly valued his advice.

I realised, of course, that it was a great compliment to be given the opportunity of this meeting, and arrived punctually at the address in the East Sixties where he lived. Mrs Campbell was not yet there, and I was somewhat dismayed to be shown up to the penthouse, where I was ushered in to a big lofty room with many windows looking out on to a terrace. Flowers, photographs, and books were everywhere, and there was no feeling of a sickroom except for the great bed, covered with a dark brocade coverlet, on which Sheldon lay stretched out, with his head tilted back at what seemed a dreadfully low and uncomfortable angle. His smooth face was beautifully shaved and he wore a neat bow tie and a soft shirt, but his eyes were covered with a black mask, and his hands were invisible beneath the coverlet.

Of course I was very shy at first, but as soon as he began to talk (though with a grating tired voice) he managed immediately to put me at my ease, and by the time Mrs Campbell arrived we were chattering away as if we had known each other all our lives.

Books and newspapers were read to him every day, and he was

amazingly well-informed, especially about the theatre, and seemed to know everything that was going on. He asked me if I would come again one day and act some scenes from *Hamlet* for him, and of course I promised to do so. Again, he contrived to put me at my ease, and I never played to a more sensitive and appreciative audience.

In the years that followed he never forgot me, sending cables and messages even during the war years (he was destined to live longer than Mrs Campbell, who died in 1940) and when I was acting in Congreve's *Love for Love* in 1944 I received a telegram 'How I wish I could see you in Valentine's mad scene.'*

On that first afternoon, Mrs Campbell appeared ten minutes after I did. I fancy Sheldon had asked her to be late, so that he could break the ice with me alone. She was in one of her complaining moods, pouting and holding up her pekinese against Sheldon's face, sighing that nobody wanted her any more in the theatre now that she was old and fat. Sheldon suddenly grew very quiet, and I noted how quickly she changed her manner and began to behave and talk in the fascinating, brilliant way that showed her at her very best. When we went away I tried to tell her how much I appreciated her charming gesture in taking me to see Sheldon and how delightfully she had helped to entertain us both. 'Ah,' she said, with real sincerity, 'one has to be at one's best with Ned. After all, we are all he has left. Think of it. There he lies in that room up there which he will never leave, and here we are walking in the street in the sunshine.' I never loved her more than on that day.

In a lecture recital which she concocted in the early Thirties, I realised that she was a complete Pre-Raphaelite. Neither Shakespeare nor the Bible served to exhibit her to real advantage. She boomed too much, sometimes even verging upon absurdity. I once saw her attempt Lady Macbeth, appearing with the American actor James Hackett, and she evidently did not care for acting with him. She had one fine moment at the end of the banquet scene, when she wearily dragged the crown from her head and her black hair fell to her shoulders as she sat huddled on the throne. But on her first appearance, looking like the Queen of Hearts about to have the gardeners executed, she swept her eyes over the stalls, graciously bowed to acknowledge her reception—leading ladies always entered to applause in those days—and, solemnly unrolling a large scroll (which, as one critic remarked, it would have taken a whole monastery a month to illuminate!), she read out Macbeth's letter with stately emphasis but ill-concealed contempt. In her recital, however,

* The remarkable memories of the older well-educated generation are very striking. Mr Justice Frankfurter, a famous American High Court Judge, quoted verbatim the whole opening scene of *Love for Love* when I met him in Washington at supper after the performance.

the excerpts from Pinero, Shaw, and Ibsen were very fine, and I was especially impressed by her rendering of *The High Tide on the Lincolnshire Coast*, a Victorian poem by Jean Ingelow. Her success with this made me realise why she had been so greatly in demand at parties in the Nineties, when she would recite (no doubt for an enormous fee) 'Butterflies all White—Butterflies all Black', in competition with Sarah Bernhardt, who was also a fashionable diseuse at the smart houses in those days whenever she acted in London. The two stars became great cronies, and on one occasion they played *Pélleas and Mélisande* together in French. Mrs Campbell had played Mélisande before with Martin Harvey and Forbes-Robertson, and in her recital she used to give an excerpt from the play (in English naturally), delivering the speeches of both the lovers in two contrasting voices, but this was not a very happy experiment as it seemed to me. The two actresses were fond of exchanging long telegrams with one another. I think Stella was not, as Ellen Terry was, an inspired letter-writer, and her correspondence with Shaw compares very poorly with that of Ellen. But I well remember a small luncheon party which I gave in New York when Mrs Campbell read to us aloud an article she had written on Bernhardt for a theatre magazine. This was charmingly written and immensely moving, and of course drew more 'Terry tears' from me.

She had always been amused to shock people by her behaviour, though she was sometimes rather prudish too, and I took care never to make ambiguous jokes when I was with her. My mother told me that once at a dinner party, when Stella was first married, she made a sensation, as the ladies rose to leave the table, by seizing a handful of cigars as they were being passed to the gentlemen by a servant, and, sticking them boldly in her *décolletage* one by one, announced gaily, 'Poor Pat can't afford cigars.'

Her witticisms have become a legend. Of Noël Coward's dialogue, 'His characters talk like typewriting.' Of a leading lady she was acting with, 'Her eyes are so far apart that you want to take a taxi from one to the other.' 'Tell Mr Alexander (who was playing Tanqueray) I never laugh at him while we are on the stage together. I always wait till I get home.' Of Shaw, 'One day he will eat beefsteak, and then God help us poor women.' But Alexander Woollcott's famous remark after her Hollywood film débâcle a few years before she died, 'She is like a sinking ship firing on its rescuers,' was sadly to the point. She became impossibly difficult, insulted managers who made her offers, appeared in one or two absurdly bad plays, and made them worse by clowning in the serious scenes and assuming a tragic manner in the light ones. When she was appearing in a light comedy of Ivor Novello's in New York, for instance, she insisted on interpolating a speech from *Electra* in the middle of a most unsuitable context. But she never lost her sense of style or her regal bearing, and the deep voice, so often imitated, retained its thrilling range and power. James Agate still talked of 'the questing sweep of her throat' and her feet and ankles were slim and elegant to the last.

I read one of the lessons at her Memorial Service in 1941, on the morning following a first night at the Old Vic at which I had essayed King Lear. Coming out of the Church I heard someone say, 'It was an exciting occasion at the Old Vic last night,' and the answer, 'Yes, until the curtain went up,' was, I felt, one that Stella's shade would have surely relished. She might so easily have delivered it herself.

From *Distinguished Company*, 1972.

Alongside Paul Scofield (unrepresented here only because he has committed so very little of himself to print) Alec Guinness (b. 1914) hovers over the postwar history of the English theatre like some immensely rare and distinguished eagle, distanced from his co-workers and able to leave acres of space around himself on stage or screen. The life he refers to briefly here in an advertising agency had not been a great success, and indeed one morning in 1933 the Daily Mail *had appeared with a large blank space on its front page under which was printed the caption 'Reserved for Mullard's Valves' because the young Guinness had forgotten to order the photographic block in time for the ad to be made up. The school of dramatic art he refers to was the Fay Compton Studio, where his contemporaries included Richard Hearne and John le Mesurier: 'the mornings were devoted to musical comedy and tap dancing, and in the afternoons we had a little brush with Shakespeare'. The following fragment of autobiography was written by Sir Alec in 1956; the rest is still on his typewriter.*

The Gielgud Hat

'IF YOU are as hard up as you say you are perhaps we had better get off these tuppenny chairs and sit on the grass,' said the girl at my side. She said it with great sympathy, having listened through the whole bright July afternoon in Regent's Park to my egotistical tale of woe and ambition. The collector was approaching slowly, gathering coppers from sleepy bodies in deck chairs. I made a quick calculation as to the relative value of hurt pride and the seven shillings I had left in the world, and decided that fourpence was a minor fortune and the grass was pleasanter anyway. We left the chairs and shifted into the shade of a tree, where I sat gloomily watching the boats bumping each other on the lake, and elderly gentlemen exhibiting their skill at 'feathering'.

My companion drew on a cigarette with all the sophistication of an inexperienced smoker. She and I were both students at a school of dramatic art; the summer recess of 1934 had started, and that morning I had heard from my guardian (I was twenty at the time) that my allowance of twenty-five shillings a week, on which I lived, had ceased once and for all.

Work had to be found, and so far as I was concerned it had to be work in the theatre. For the last six months I had been a scholarship pupil, and previously to that had spent eighteen unfruitful months as a totally inadequate copywriter and layout man in an advertising agency.

After a long silence my companion stubbed her cigarette out and said, 'I don't think you should be sitting about on the grass. You should be *doing* something. Why not go and see if John Gielgud can help?'

I did not know Gielgud, but I felt it wasn't impossible to approach him. A few weeks before he had been one of the judges, together with Jessie Matthews, Fay Compton and Ronald Adam, at a public performance at which I had won a prize. Of course, he might have voted against me, but there I was, the possessor of a leather-bound copy of Shakespeare in tiny print and double columns, and presumably he would remember me if he saw me.

'I can lend you a pound,' the girl said, 'until something turns up.' She seemed to be a millionairess, living in great comfort in Golders Green. My pride was now really hurt, or that is how I chose to let my emotion appear.

'Thank you,' I replied, 'but I could have paid for those deck chairs over and over again, thank you all the same. How long will it take me to walk to Wyndham's Theatre?'

'Take a bus with the tuppence,' she suggested. I turned on my heel and walked.

I arrived at Wyndham's stage door and asked for Mr Gielgud. To my astonishment I was shown straight to his dressing-room. He had remembered my name though he looked somewhat surprised when he saw what I looked like. I was in rather dirty grey flannel trousers, a check shirt (to keep down the laundry bill) and skimpy sports jacket. Also I was very thin, large-eared and strange.

He sat making-up for the evening performance of *The Maitlands*, and I told him of the absolute necessity for my finding work. This was the first time I had seen a real live star actor applying his make-up; I believe I was even more fascinated by that than by being in the presence of a man I had hero-worshipped so long.

He was friendly and kind, but under the unpowdered grease-paint, which gives actors the look of china dolls, I couldn't tell whether he was really interested in my predicament and talents or not. He painted his eyebrows for a moment or two in silence and then became immensely practical.

People were telephoned and I was sent immediately to Sir Bronson Albery about a small part and understudy, which was soon to fall vacant.

As I left Gielgud's room he said: 'If you don't have any luck, come and see me again tomorrow.'

I didn't have any luck. This was the pattern of my life for the next few days: visits to Gielgud, who sent me after various jobs he heard of, and missing them by half an hour or so. The only exception was a brief audition I did at the Old Vic, where I didn't get further in Mercutio's Queen Mab speech than 'little atomies' before the producer told me I had no business in the theatre and wouldn't take me as a gift. (I have since been directed in a film by the same producer, and all was amicable).

I returned to Gielgud that evening and he was at the end of his resource-fulness, but by no means at the end of his generosity. All I had left was the proverbial half-crown. On the side of his make-up table was a neat pile of one-pound notes. 'The next time I do a play I'll give you a part,' he promised, 'but you are far too thin. Here's twenty pounds—for God's sake go and eat properly.' He frantically painted his eyebrows with embarrassment. I stared at the money. I had a vision of eating, buying clothes (particularly shoes), of spending fourpence a day on park chairs for twelve hundred days. Then I saw myself being thrown into gaol for debt. 'I am all right for money, thank you,' I said, so foolishly that it makes me blush even twenty-two years later, and walked out of his room.

Walking back to Westbourne Park Grove, rather light-headed, with only a green apple, a glass of milk and a bun inside me (which had been my daily diet for three days), I stopped to watch the bills for a new play go up outside the Piccadilly Theatre. Franklyn Dyall in *Queer Cargo*. Instead of going to the stage door for work my light-headedness led me to the box-office where my arrival coincided with the stage manager's.

I explained I was an actor, a piece of information which was received with kindly scepticism. 'But are you a *good* actor?' the stage manager asked me. With the desperation and arrogance of youth I replied 'Very good.' 'Then come and read three parts to me,' he said.

I read one part and he told me I had got the job. I played a Chinese coolie in Act I, a French pirate in Act II and a British sailor in Act III. And I understudied practically everyone, all for the princely sum of £3 a week. In my enthusiasm for appearing as a Chinese I shaved the top of my head; my hair never really recovered from the shock and now is lost for ever.

With my first week's salary I gave myself a huge but sensible meal, treated my Regent's Park friend to a celebration tea at Fuller's and bought myself a very cheap replica of the kind of hat Gielgud wore at the time, which gave me, I fondly imagined, a sort of elegance in the second class.

Gielgud was as good as his word. Three months later he gave me my first proper part and I received my first notice from a drama critic. Time has taught me that one good notice is not a whole career, and that talent, or success, or happiness, or indeed any quality, is not put on the head in the shape of someone else's hat.

From *The Sunday Times*, 1956.

My father (b. 1908) writing here about my grandmother (b. 1888) soon after her death in 1971. Up to the very end, Gladys Cooper believed like the Go-Between that the past was a foreign country and that they did things differently there; unlike the Go-Between, she also believed that one shouldn't be too ready to revisit it. The present and (especially) the future were what interested her, and the past she usually left to take care of itself; not because she hadn't often been very happy there, which she had, but because it seldom occurred to her that the view back over her shoulder might be more interesting than the one straight ahead.

She and her son-in-law, my father, were a generally devoted couple despite the fact that when Robert married my mother in 1940 press reports declined to mention his name, noting simply 'Gladys Cooper's daughter weds actor'. She was, then and to the last, a considerable star, though one not at first taken very seriously as an actress: 'Gladys Cooper surprised us' was, she reckoned, her best pre-war notice.

Her career started with a performance of Bluebell in Fairyland *at the Theatre Royal in Colchester on her birthday in 1905, and the First World War found her in France doing concert parties for the troops. By the 1920s, under her own management, she was at the Playhouse in the best of the Maugham plays (*The Letter, The Sacred Flame, The Painted Veil*) and by the end of the 1930s she was already in Hollywood starting on a film career which was to last the thirty years from* Rebecca *to* My Fair Lady.

At home, by the Thames in Henley in the 1960s, on those rare occasions when she wasn't either filming or playing, surrounded as she always then was by dogs and grandchildren and cats and great-grandchildren, it was still hard to think of her as a grandmother, certainly not the kind of grandmother who might need trays of tea taken up to bed. If there were trays to be carried round the house it was Gladys who carried them; but now, six years after her death, I begin to realise as I write her biography that really I hardly knew her at all. Robert, happily, knew her very well indeed.

ON THE last evening of her life, my splendid and courageous mother-in-law, Gladys Cooper, rose from her bed and making her way, not without considerable effort, to her dressing-table, proceeded to brush her hair and make up her celebrated face. Then, gazing into the mirror for what was to prove the very last time, she remarked to her nurse, 'If this is what virus pneumonia does to one, I really don't think I shall bother to have it again.' She got back into bed and presently died in her sleep. Her looks were something she habitually shrugged off. People used to tell me, as no doubt they told her, that it was in her bones. 'If your bones are right, you can't go wrong. Look at Katharine Hepburn.' I go along with them to a certain extent, but believe that bones, just as clothes, must be worn with panache. A lot of women have good bones. Very few of them looked like Gladys.

Among all the letters the family received when she died was one from the secretary of The Postcard Club of Great Britain, assuring us that their historian had every card which featured Miss Cooper and that her beauty was thus preserved for posterity.

Most mornings of her life, Gladys received at least one letter returning one of these celebrated postcards. Occasionally they came in dozens, wrapped up in brown paper, announcing that they were from the collection of a deceased relative of the sender, and towards the end of her life she became increasingly suspicious of them. Like the late Maurice Utrillo, she would question their authenticity.

'I don't think that's me at all,' she would tell us. 'I'm sure there was another woman who used to pose as me at times.'

'But,' we would ask, 'who but you, dear, would dress up as a shepherdess and clutch a rake, a hoe and a besom while being photographed in Mr Foulsham's or Mr Banfield's back garden?'

Nothing would surprise me less than to hear that those two gentlemen to whom my mother-in-law was in those days under exclusive contract, postcardwise, are alive and well and living in Leeds, producing that most favourite of all programmes, 'Stars on Sunday'. Anyone who has watched Anna Neagle or Louis Mountbatten undertake the chore, who has seen the choirs posed on the Elizabethan staircase, James Mason reading the bible by the fire blazing on a hot summer day, must acknowledge how much the incongruity of the proceedings owe to these early pioneers of the absurd. Was it, I wonder, Mr Banfield who worked the shutter and Mr Foulsham who dreamed up the setting, or vice versa? Perhaps they collaborated in procuring the golf sticks and the tennis racquets, the artificial snowballs and the genuine dead trout. What was the significance of the teacup which so often appeared, half raised in salute? Was one of them perhaps a teetotaller? There was always something going on. Not a lot, perhaps, but something.

At times there was just the very faintest hint, the slightest trace of the erotic. One of my favourites shows Gladys with her hair in plaits and dressed in a brown peignoir over a pink wrap over a blue night-dress, about to open a bedroom door. But perhaps erotic is hardly the word.

Saucy, that's what they were sometimes, saucy. When the children arrived, and Gladys insisted on supplying these herself, life sobered up a good deal. Only the hats remained coquettish. There is one photograph of her sitting beside her first husband in a motorcar. She hadn't as yet taken the wheel, apparently. The expression is as always non-committal. 'Here I am,' she seems to be saying, 'what next?' And on this occasion of course, 'Where to?'

What did they do with all these postcards, the great British public? And not only the British public. There must have been an enormous export market, hence the wording on the back: THIS IS A REAL PHOTO-GRAPH OF A BRITISH BEAUTY. HAND-PAINTED ON RAJAH BROMIDE CARD. The insistence that the photographs were genuine gives a clue perhaps to the awe in which the sitter was held at any rate in later life. But who bought them, and for what purpose? Certainly not to send through the post. Very few of the ones in my collection are actually written on. The exceptions have a fascination all their own. 'As promised, here is the pretty baby. Those flowers you sent Mother were lovely. Things are in such an unsettled state I don't know when I wrote you. Haven't forgotten the headsquare, and shall send the prayerbook.' There is a sad little note from Geo. to Flo. 'I was watching for the post all day. Just a line hoping you are in the pink and still enjoying yourself.' At any rate nowadays the lovesick are put out of their misery a good deal quicker. Nothing in the morning delivery and you've had it, chum.

A good many of the cards were bought by soldiers in the last war but one to carry into battle. You couldn't be accused of being yellow if you put a thick wad of postcards in your breast pocket just over your heart. It was just that you happened to be a great womaniser and of course like everyone else, a fan.

To start life as a picture postcard and end as a Dame of the British Empire. After such a start it seems only natural that my mother-in-law's first job should have been in 'Bluebell in Fairyland'. Indeed about the whole of her early career in the theatre there seems an element of make-believe. The whole story of her success was almost too good to be true if she wasn't in a sort of fairyland, or at any rate a book written for children. This beautiful girl who went on the stage and in an incredibly short time became a star with all London at her feet. How it was done, the formula for this extravagant success, the lightning fame and fortune which in these days seems only to come to property developers, remains for me a mystery.

She never discussed past triumphs and when you asked her, all she would ever tell you was that she learnt her acting from Hawtrey. It was not that she was wilfully reticent, but when she recalled the past at all, it was to tell of the things that had amused her, the quirks of her managers, the practical jokes she used to play on her leading men. What leading men they were—Seymour Hicks, Hawtrey, Gerald Du Maurier, Ivor Novello, Owen Nares, and the one she married, Philip Merivale, and whose presence lived on in her life always and whose family she adopted as she adopted us all.

Of all the performances I saw her give, my favourite was when she appeared in *The Indifferent Shepherd* and sat on the back of the sofa behind Francis Lister, or did he sit behind her? She had that unique gift of tugging at your heartstrings. Who can forget the curtain of *The Last of Mrs Cheyney*, or her standing on the staircase in *Cynara*, or the curtain again of *The Letter*?

The pleasure of watching her on the stage before I ever dreamt I would be her son-in-law, and then the pleasure of being her son-in-law. Since she died I have thought about her often, always with a chuckle and always realising how much there was about her that I never found out. I never even discovered what she thought of me. I never even discovered if she knew towards the end of her life how ill she was. She had the most beautiful manners and about some things she never let on.

She could be very sharp at times. She was not good at feeling sorry for people, perhaps because she never felt sorry for herself. If you were in trouble, you got out of it, with her help of course, but it was up to you in the end. If you got ill, you got better. She was in her way something of a health fiend. She didn't eat much. She worshipped the sun. When we stayed with her in her Californian home she would come back from the studios at dusk and start cooking our dinner and then, when everything was in hand, she would disappear and a moment later sweep across the patio, wrapped in towelling, for her evening swim. Ten minutes later she would be back and five minutes after that she would reappear in the sort of shift dress of which she was so fond, gold bangles on her arms, her hair and her make-up immaculate, to mix a final round of daquiris before she took the lamb from the spit.

How is it done? I used to ask myself. How can she be so elegant? If she was vain about anything it was about her cooking. Two things you were never allowed to criticise—her marmalade and her driving. Both, I always felt privately, left a good deal to chance. But about everything else she was eminently reasonable. How good an actress she thought herself to be, how seriously she took her profession, I was never sure. She acted like she did everything else, naturally. But of one thing I am very certain. She was immensely proud of the affection and gratitude of her public. She answered every letter, she acknowledged every compliment and no day was too cold or too wet for her to pause as she came out of her stage door, or in later years the supermarket in Henley, to have a chat to a faithful patron who wished to compliment her on some past performance in the theatre or on the screen or on television, or on just being Gladys Cooper.

Laurence Olivier recalled her as hurdling the various fashions of the theatre, and if sometimes she knocked one over or it collapsed beneath her, she never faltered or shortened her stride. She raced ahead, and those who expected that one day she'd come back to her field were wrong. She was still in front at the finish.

Perhaps I've dwelt too much on her comparatively early triumphs, not mentioned her later ones, her films, but here again even the best of them didn't compare with the splendour and wonder of watching her in *The Bohemian Girl*. She loved television, was very proud of having done *The Rogues*. Asked once what she regretted in her life, she said, 'I was very sorry when *The Rogues* finished and when I just missed being the first woman to loop the loop. I was in the cockpit when the pilot's wife arrived, and I gave way. I didn't want to break up the marriage, but I've always regretted it. One should go on with things.'

She had a passion for all animals, the wilder the better. Ducks, cats, dogs, monkeys, parrots shared her houses with her, and she relished any opportunity of acting with lions or tigers or leopards or bears. Nothing scared her. Once on a beach at Acapulco a rifle bullet pinged past us. I turned and ran into the sea. Gladys turned and walked towards the firing. 'What happened to you, then?' she asked when I rejoined her. 'I had a sudden absurd desire to paddle. Was there a shot?' 'The gardener,' she told me. 'The owners of the house are away and he's been left in charge. Natural, really, he couldn't have been more than ten.' Natural, it's the word I most associate with Gladys herself; she was a natural woman.

From *A Musing Morley, The Selected Writings of Robert Morley*, 1974.

James Thurber (1894–1961) writer and illustrator and creator of some of the greatest cartoon captions of all time (e.g. 'I knew their marriage was doomed when they called their honeymoon cottage The Qualms'; 'So if I rang the wrong number, why did you answer the phone?'; 'All right, have it your way, you heard a seal bark'; 'Why don't you get dressed, then, and go to pieces like a man?'; 'You wait here, and I'll bring the etchings down') and a man with a wonderful line in self-deprecation ('I myself have accomplished nothing of excellence except a remarkable and, to some of my friends, unaccountable expertness at hitting empty ginger ale bottles with small rocks at a distance of thirty paces'). Sadly he was not much involved with the theatre, though a play he wrote with Elliot Nugent, The Male Animal, *did well on Broadway in 1940 and, shortly before his death, his* Thurber Carnival *(from which this is taken) was converted into a Broadway and London revue with varying degrees of success.*

The Macbeth Murder Mystery

'IT WAS a stupid mistake to make,' said the American woman I had met at my hotel in the English lake country, 'but it was on the counter with the other Penguin books—the little sixpenny ones, you know, with the paper covers—and I supposed of course it was a detective story. All the others were detective stories. I'd read all the others, so I bought this one without really looking at it carefully. You can imagine how mad I was when I found it was Shakespeare.' I murmured something sympathetically. 'I don't see why the Penguin-books people had to get out Shakespeare plays in the same size and everything as the detective stories,' went on my companion. 'I think they have different-coloured jackets,' I said. 'Well, I didn't notice that,' she said. 'Anyway, I got real comfy in bed that night and all ready to read a good mystery story and here I had *The Tragedy of Macbeth*—a book for high-school students. Like *Ivanhoe*.' 'Or *Lorna Doone*,' I said. 'Exactly,' said the American lady. 'And I was just crazy for a good Agatha Christie, or something. Hercule Poirot is my favourite detective.' 'Is he the rabbity one?' I asked. 'Oh, no,' said my crime-fiction expert. 'He's the Belgian one. You're thinking of Mr Pinkerton, the one that helps Inspector Bull. He's good, too.'

Over her second cup of tea my companion began to tell the plot of a detective story that had fooled her completely—it seems it was the old family doctor all the time. But I cut in on her. 'Tell me,' I said. 'Did you read *Macbeth*?' 'I *had* to read it,' she said. 'There wasn't a scrap of anything else to read in the whole room.' 'Did you like it?' I asked. 'No, I did not,' she said decisively. 'In the first place, I don't think for a moment that Macbeth did it.' I looked at her blankly. 'Did what?' I asked. 'I don't think for a moment that he killed the King,' she said. 'I don't think the Macbeth woman was mixed up in it either. You suspect them the most, of course, but those are the ones that are never guilty—or shouldn't be, anyway.' 'I'm afraid,' I began, 'that I—' 'But don't you see?' said the American lady. 'It would spoil everything if you could figure out right away who did it. Shakespeare was too smart for that. I've read that people never *have* figured out *Hamlet,* so it isn't likely Shakespeare would have made *Macbeth* as simple as it seems.' I thought this over while I filled my pipe. 'Who do you suspect?' I asked, suddenly. 'Macduff,' she said, promptly. 'Good God!' I whispered, softly.

'Oh Macduff did it, all right,' said the murder specialist. 'Hercule Poirot would have got him easily.' 'How did you figure it out?' I demanded. 'Well,' she said, 'I didn't right away. At first I suspected Banquo. And then, of course, he was the second person killed. That was good right in there, that part. The person you suspect of the first murder should always be the second victim.' 'Is that so?' I murmured. 'Oh, yes,' said my informant. 'They have to keep surprising you. Well, after the second murder I didn't know *who* the killer was for a while.' 'How about Malcolm and Donalbain, the King's sons?' I asked. 'As I remember it, they fled right after the first murder. That looks suspicious.' 'Too suspicious,' said the American lady. 'Much too suspicious. When they flee, they're never guilty. You can count on that.' 'I believe,' I said, 'I'll have a brandy,' and I summoned the waiter. My companion leaned toward me, her eyes bright, her teacup quivering. 'Do you know who discovered Duncan's body?' she demanded. I said I was sorry, but I had forgotten. 'Macduff discovers it,' she said, slipping into the historical present. 'Then he comes running downstairs and shouts, "Confusion has broke open the Lord's anointed temple" and "Sacrilegious murder has made his masterpiece" and on and on like that.' The good lady tapped me on the knee. 'All that stuff was rehearsed,' she said. 'You wouldn't say a lot of stuff like that, offhand, would you—if you had found a body?' She fixed me with a glittering eye. 'I—' I began. 'You're right!' she said. 'You wouldn't! Unless you had practised it in advance. "My God, there's a body in here!" is what an innocent man would say.' She sat back with a confident glare.

I thought for a while. 'But what do you make of the Third Murderer?' I asked. 'You know, the Third Murderer has puzzled *Macbeth* scholars for three hundred years.' 'That's because they never thought of Macduff,' said the American lady. 'It was Macduff, I'm certain. You couldn't have one of the victims murdered by two ordinary thugs—the murderer always has to be somebody important.' 'But what about the banquet scene?' I asked, after a moment. 'How do you account for Macbeth's guilty actions there, when Banquo's ghost came in and sat in his chair?' The lady leaned forward and tapped me on the knee again. 'There wasn't any ghost,' she said. 'A big, strong man like that doesn't go around seeing ghosts—especially in a brightly lighted banquet hall with dozens of people around. Macbeth was *shielding somebody*!' 'Who was he shielding?' I asked. 'Mrs Macbeth, of course,' she said. 'He thought she did it and he was going to take the rap himself. The husband always does that when the wife is suspected.' 'But what,' I demanded, 'about the sleepwalking scene, then?' 'The same thing, only the other way around,' said my companion. 'That time *she* was shielding *him*. She wasn't asleep at all. Do you remember where it says, "Enter Lady Macbeth with a taper"?' 'Yes,' I said. 'Well, people who walk in their sleep *never carry lights*!' said my fellow-traveller. 'They have a second sight. Did you ever hear of a sleepwalker carrying a light?' 'No,' I said, 'I never did.' 'Well, then, she wasn't asleep. She was acting guilty to shield Macbeth.' 'I think,' I said, 'I'll have another brandy,' and I called the waiter. When he brought it, I drank it rapidly and rose to go. 'I believe,' I said, 'that you have got hold of something. Would you lend me that *Macbeth*? I'd like to look it over tonight. I don't feel, somehow, as if I'd ever really read it.' 'I'll get it for you,' she said. 'But you'll find that I am right.'

I read the play over carefully that night, and the next morning, after breakfast, I sought out the American woman. She was on the putting green, and I came up behind her silently and took her arm. She gave an exclamation. 'Could I see you alone?' I asked, in a low voice. She nodded cautiously and followed me to a secluded spot. 'You've found out something?' she breathed. 'I've found out,' I said, triumphantly, 'the name of the murderer!' 'You mean it wasn't Macduff?' she said. 'Macduff is as innocent of those murders,' I said, 'as Macbeth and the Macbeth woman.' I opened the copy of the play, which I had with me, and turned to Act II, Scene 2. 'Here,' I said, 'you will see where Lady Macbeth says, "I laid their daggers ready. He could not miss 'em. Had he not resembled my father as he slept, I had done it." Do you see?' 'No,' said the American woman, bluntly, 'I don't.' 'But it's simple!' I exclaimed. 'I wonder I didn't see it years ago. The reason Duncan resembled Lady Macbeth's father as he slept is that *it actually was her father*!' 'Good God!' breathed my companion, softly. 'Lady Macbeth's father killed the King,' I said, 'and, hearing someone coming, thrust the body under the bed and crawled into the bed himself.' 'But,' said the lady, 'you can't have a murderer who only appears in the story once. You can't have that.' 'I know that,' I said, and turned to Act II, Scene 4. 'It says here, "Enter Ross with an old Man." Now, that old man is never identified and it is my contention he was old Mr Macbeth, whose ambition it was to make his daughter Queen. There you have your motive.' 'But even then,' cried the American lady, 'he's still a minor character!' 'Not,' I said, gleefully, 'when you realise that he was also *one of the weird sisters in disguise!*' 'You mean one of the three witches?' 'Precisely,' I said. 'Listen to this speech of the old man's. "On Tuesday last, a falcon towering in her pride of place, was by a mousing owl hawk'd at and kill'd." Who does that sound like?' 'It sounds like the way the three witches talk,' said my companion, reluctantly. 'Precisely!' I said again. 'Well,' said the American woman, 'maybe you're right, but—' 'I'm sure I am,' I said. 'And do you know what I'm going to do now?' 'No,' she said. 'What?' 'Buy a copy of *Hamlet,*' I said, 'and solve *that!*' My companion's eye brightened. 'Then,' she said, 'you don't think Hamlet did it?' 'I am,' I said, 'absolutely positive he didn't.' 'But who,' she demanded, 'do you suspect?' I looked at her cryptically. 'Everybody,' I said, and disappeared into a small grove of trees as silently as I had come.

From *The Thurber Carnival*, 1945.

Like many lesser novelists than himself, Henry James (1843–1916) came disastrously unstuck as a playwright: he personally took to affirming that if London audiences were ignorant enough to applaud the plays of Oscar Wilde, who was doing rather better at the box-office in the 1890s, then they didn't deserve his plays anyway. They nevertheless got a good many of them before James returned to work on the novels, and by this time in his career he'd already established himself as a good if acid critic of his contemporaries. In 1881, the year he published Portrait of a Lady, *he also published (unsigned and in* Scribner's Monthly*) the extensive 'letter home' which follows. I know of no other comparably detailed or graphic description of the state of the London theatre and its plays and players at this time.*

The London Theatres

THE AUTHOR of these remarks was on the point of prefixing to them a different title from the one he has actually made use of, when it occurred to him that the latter would give a much better idea of his subject. 'The London Theatres' stands for something that may, more or less profitably, be talked about, but 'The English Stage' is a conception so purely intellectual, so confined to the region of theory, or reminiscence, or desire, that it eludes the most ingenious grasp. There are a great many theatres in London, enjoying various degrees of credit and prosperity; but there is nothing cynical in saying that there is no such thing in existence as an English stage. The stage is a collective organism, composed of the harmonious vitality diffused through a number of individual play-houses, which are nourished by a dramatic literature native to the country, and expressing its manners and feelings, and which work together to an effective end. When it substantially exists, it is usually summed up, typified to the world, in a theatre more distinguished than the rest, in which the education of the actor has reached its highest point, and in which it is the supreme ambition of the dramatic authors of the country to see their productions represented. There is a stage in France, of which the Comédie Française is the richest expression; and we are told that there is a very honourable stage in Germany, where two or three excellent theatres—literary theatres—

maintain the standard of finished and brilliant acting. It appears to be generally conceded that there was formerly a stage in England. In the last century, the English theatres went hand-in-hand with a literature which sprang substantially from the English mind itself, and which, though it has not proved of any value to posterity, ministered, for the time, to what we have called the vitality of the stage. At that time the actor's profession was looked upon as a hill of difficulty, not to be scaled at a bound, nor trodden by every comer. His art was not thought an easy one to master, and a long probation, an apprenticeship of humility, was the portion of even the most promising aspirants. The two great 'patented' houses, Drury Lane and Covent Garden, performed very much the same function that the Comédie Française has long been supposed to discharge (in spite of many lapses and errors) on the other side of the Channel. They protected the drama, and they had a high responsibility. They monopolised, in London, the right to play Shakespeare and the poetical repertory, and they formed the objective point of actors and authors alike. They recruited themselves from the training-school which the provincial theatres then supplied, and they rewarded merit, and consecrated reputations. All this is changed, as so many things are changed in literature and art. The conditions of production are immensely different from those of an age in which the demand for the things that make life agreeable had not become so immoderate as to create a standing quarrel between the quality and the quantity of the supply. The art of writing a play has apparently become a lost one with the English race, who are content to let their entertainment be made for them by a people whose whole view of life is, however ingenious, essentially different from their own. The comparatively simple and homogeneous character of the English stage has become a sort of musty tradition, and in its place we have several dozen small theatrical enterprises, some of which are very successful, and others not at all so, but all of which live entirely on what the French call 'expedients', and compass their degree of success by methods decidedly incongruous.

It is of the actual, however, that we pretend to speak, and not of the possible or impossible. Talking simply of the actual, the first thing to say of it is that the theatre is nowadays decidedly the fashion in London. People go to it a great deal, and are willing to pay high prices for the privilege; they talk of it, they write about it, and, in a great many of them, the taste for it takes the form of a desire to pass from the passive to the active side of the footlights. The number of stage-struck persons who are to be met with in the London world is remarkable, and the number of prosperous actors who are but lately escaped amateurs is equally striking. The older actors regard the invasion of this class with melancholy disapproval, and declare that the profession is going to the dogs. By amateurs we mean young men 'of the world' (for of the other sex, naturally, there is much less question) not of theatrical stock, who have gone upon the stage after being educated for something very different, and who have managed to achieve success without going through the old-fashioned processes. The old actors are probably right from their own point of view—the point of view from which a long course of histrionic gymnastics was thought indispensable, and from which the touchstone of accomplishment was the art of delivering the great Shakespearean speeches. That way of considering the matter has lost credit, and the clever people on the London stage today aim at a line of effect in which their being 'amateurs' is almost a positive advantage. Small, realistic comedy is their chosen field, and the art of acting as little as possible has—doubtless with good results in some ways—taken the place of the art of acting as much. Of course, the older actors, with all their superfluous science, as they deem it, left on their hands, have no patience with the infatuation of a public which passes from the drawing-room to the theatre only to look at an attempt, at best very imperfect, to reproduce the accidents and limitations of the drawing-room.

All this tends to prove, however, that the theatre is what is called an actuality, and that if it labours under appreciable disadvantages, these are not the result of a want of patronage. There is no want of patronage to complain of when many hundreds of people are found every night prepared to pay the sum of ten shillings for a stall. The privilege of spending the evening in a stall at any theatre in London is dearly purchased at that cost; the disparity between the price paid for your entertainment and the quality of the entertainment provided is often almost ludicrous. It is in the power of an enterprising play-goer to endeavour to extract a portion of that large amount of pleasure which is represented (to our possibly too frugal sense) by two dollars and a half, from a spectacle not unworthy of a booth at a fair. Pleasure, however, is usually expensive in England, and the theatre conforms simply to the common law. Books are dear, pictures are dear, music is dear, travelling is dear. Play-going, in other ways besides, comes under the usual London disadvantages—the great distance to be traversed before reaching the theatre, the repulsive character of many of the streets through which your aesthetic pilgrimage lies, the necessity of dining earlier than usual and of dressing as if for a private entertainment. These things testify to the theatre's being the fashion among a certain class, and the last luxury of a few, rather than taking its place in the common habits of the people, as it does in France. The difference in favour of the French is indicated by the very much more convenient form that play-going assumes in Paris, where the various temples of the drama are scattered along the clean, bright Boulevard and are guarded by no restriction, tacit or other, as to the costume of their frequenters. In New York as well, in these respects, we are better off than the good people who embark for an evening of the play in London. The New York theatres are all more or less adjacent to the great thoroughfare of the town, and the ceremony of 'dressing' does not, even feebly, impose itself. It must be admitted, however, that when once you are dressed and seated in London, your material comfort is greater than it is in Paris, greater, too, than it is in New York. The atmosphere, for inscrutable reasons, is a very much less poisonous compound than the suffocating medium through which the unexhausted Parisian is condemned to witness the masterpieces of Molière and Victor Hugo, of Sardou and the younger Dumas. You are much better seated, less crowded and jostled, than in Paris, and you are not bullied and irritated by the terrible tribe of *ouvreuses*. Your neighbours sit quietly and reasonably in their places, without trooping out between the acts, to the deep discomfort of your toes and knees. You have, in a word, the sense of passing your evening in better company than in Paris, and this, if it be not what you go to the theatre for, and if it be but a meagre compensation for a lame performance, may, nevertheless, be numbered among the encouragements to play-going. These encouragements, in all matters independent of the great matter—the acting itself—have multiplied greatly in London during the last few years, and have now reached a very high perfection. Everything has been done that can be done by beauty of scenery, completeness of furniture and costume, refinement of machinery, to put the auditor into good humour with what he is about to listen to. What will it matter what he listens to if he have real buhl cabinets, Persian carpets, and Venetian mirrors to look at? These tendencies have found a sumptuous home, within a small number of months, in three theatres which divide between them the honour of being the most important in London. To a stranger, inquiring which should be deemed the first of these houses, it would be difficult to give a very definite answer. 'Oh, the Lyceum,' it might be said, 'because at the Lyceum they play Shakespeare.' Yes; at the Lyceum they play Shakespeare; but the question is, *how* they play him. The greatest of poets is not, to our mind, interpreted at the Lyceum in a manner to assign a very high place to the scene of the attempt. At the St James's, they play translations of MM. Bayard and Scribe, and original productions of Mr Tom Taylor. At the Haymarket, they play Lord Lytton and M. Sardou. It is a nice question whether it is a nobler task to render Shakespeare inadequately, or to represent with sufficient skill rather pale adaptations of French *vaudevillistes*. It is a question, however, that we are not called upon to solve, and we will content ourselves with saying that at the three theatres just mentioned a great many things are very cleverly done.

Upward of two years ago the Lyceum passed into the hands of Mr Henry Irving, who is without doubt at present the most distinguished actor in England. He had been acting at the Lyceum for some years before, while the house was under the management of the late Mr Bateman, and then of his widow, who has within a few months, with a great deal of courage and zeal, attempted to awaken the long dormant echoes of Sadler's Wells—a theatre which had its season of prosperity (many years ago), but which finally, in its out-of-the-way position, was left stranded by ebbing tides. Mrs Bateman, to whom much of the credit of originally introducing Mr Irving to the public belongs, succeeded in some degree, we believe, in turning the tide back to the little theatre to which the late Mr Phelps's 'revivals' at one period attracted the town. Mr Irving for the last two years, then, has had his own way at the Lyceum, and a very successful way it has been. Hamlet and Shylock have constituted the stock of his enterprise, though he has also acted several of the parts in which he built up his reputation— Richelieu; Eugene Aram and Charles I, in Mr W. G. Wills's plays; Louis XI, in a translation of Casimir Delavigne's rather dull drama, and Matthias in *The Bells*. During the whole of last winter, however, *The Merchant of Venice* held the stage, and this performance disputes with that of *Hamlet* the chief place in his list of successes as an actor. Among his triumphs as a manager, the former play, we believe, quite heads the list; it has every appearance of being an immense financial success, and startling stories are told of the great sums of money it brings in to the happy lessee of the theatre. It is arranged upon the stage with a great deal of ingenuity and splendour, and has a strong element of popularity in the person of Miss Ellen Terry, who is the most conspicuous actress now before the London public, as the picturesque Shylock of her Portia is the most eminent actor. Mr Irving has been a topic in London any time these five years, and Miss Terry is at least as much of one. There is a difference, indeed, for about Mr Irving people are divided, and about Miss Terry they are pretty well agreed. The opinion flourishes on the one side that Mr Irving is a great and admirable artist, and on the other the impression prevails that his defects outnumber his qualities. He has at least the power of inspiring violent enthusiasms, and this faculty is almost always accompanied by a liability to excite protests. Those that it has been Mr Irving's destiny to call forth have been very downright, and many of them are sufficiently intelligible. He is what is called a picturesque actor; that is, he depends for his effects upon the art with which he presents a certain figure to the eye, rather than upon the manner in which he speaks his part. He is a thoroughly serious actor, and evidently bestows an immense deal of care and conscience upon his work; he meditates, elaborates, and, upon the line on which he moves, carries the part to a very high degree of finish. But it must be affirmed that this is a line with which the especial art of the actor, the art of utterance, of saying the thing, has almost nothing to do. Mr Irving's peculiarities and eccentricities of speech are so strange, so numerous, so personal to himself, his vices of pronunciation, of modulation, of elocution so highly developed, the tricks he plays with the divine mother-tongue so audacious and fantastic, that the spectator who desires to be in sympathy with him finds himself confronted with a bristling hedge of difficulties. He must scramble over the hedge, as best he can, in order to get at Mr Irving at all; to get at him, that is, as an exponent of great poetic meanings. Behind this hedge, as we may say, the actor disports himself with a great deal of ingenuity, and passes through a succession of picturesque attitudes and costumes; but we look at him only through its thorny interstices. In so doing, we get glimpses of a large and various ability. He is always full of intention, and when the intention is a matter of by-play, it is brilliantly carried out. He is, of course, much better in the modern drama than in the Shakespearian; because, if it is a question of sacrificing the text, the less we are obliged to sacrifice the better. It is better to lose the verses of Mr Wills than to fail to recognise those of the poet whom the French have sometimes spoken of as Mr Williams. Mr Irving's rendering of Shakespeare, however, is satisfactory in a varying degree. His Macbeth appeared to us wide of the mark, but his Hamlet is very much better. In *Macbeth*, as we remember his performance, he failed even to look the part satisfactorily—a rare mistake in an actor who has evidently a strong sense of what may be called the plastic side of the characters he represents. His Hamlet is a magnificent young prince: few actors can wear a cloak and a bunch of sable plumes with a greater grace than Mr Irving; few of them can rest a well-shaped hand on the hilt of a sword in a manner more suggestive of the models of Vandyke. The great trouble with the Hamlet was that it was inordinately slow—and this, indeed, is the fault throughout of Mr Irving, who places minutes between his words, and strange strides and balancings between his movements. Heat, rapidity, passion, magic—these qualities are the absent ones, and a good general description of him is to say that he is picturesque but diffuse. Of his Shylock during last winter, it was often said that it presents his faults in their mildest and his merits in their highest form. In this there is possibly a great deal of truth; his representation of the rapacious and rancorous Jew has many elements of interest. He looks the part to a charm, or rather we should say, to a repulsion, and he might be painted as he stands. His conception of it is a sentimental one, and he has endeavoured to give us a sympathetic, and, above all, a pathetic Shylock. How well he reconciles us to this aspect of the character we ourselves shall not undertake to say, for our attention was fixed primarily upon the superficial execution of the thing, and here, without going further, we found much to arrest and perplex it. The actor struck us as rigid and frigid, and above all as painfully behind the stroke of the clock. The deep-welling malignity, the grotesque horror, the red-hot excitement of the long-baffled, sore-hearted member of a despised trade, who has been all his life at a disadvantage, and who at last finds his hour and catches his opportunity—these elements had dropped out. Mr Irving's Shylock is neither excited nor exciting, and many of the admirable speeches, on his lips, lack much of their incision; notably the outbreak of passion and prospective revenge after he finds that Antonio has become forfeit, and that his daughter has fled from him, carrying off her dowry. The great speech, with its grim refrain: 'Let him look to his bond!' rising each time to an intenser pitch and culminating in a pregnant menace, this superb opportunity is missed; the actor, instead of being 'hissing hot', as we have heard Edmund Kean described at the same moment, draws the scene out and blunts all its points. The best thing that Mr Irving does is, to our taste, the Louis XI of Casimir Delavigne, a part in which his defects to a certain degree stand him in stead of qualities. His peculiarities of voice and enunciation are not in contradiction to those of the mumbling old monarch and dotard whom he represents with so much effective detail. Two years ago he played Claude Melnotte for several months, sacrificing himself with the most commendable generosity to the artistic needs of Miss Ellen Terry, who was the Pauline of the season. We say sacrificing himself, for his inaptitude for the part was so distinct that he must have been aware of it. We may mention two other characters in which Mr Irving composes a figure to the eye with brilliant taste and skill—the Charles I of Mr Wills, and the Vanderdecken, of (if we mistake not) the same author. His Charles I might have stepped down from the canvas of Vandyke, and his Vanderdecken is also superb. We say he looks these parts, but we do not add that he acts them, for, to the best of our recollection, there is nothing in them to act. The more there is to act, and the less there is simply to declaim, the better for Mr Irving, who owes his great success in *The Bells* to the fact that the part of the distracted burgomaster is so largly pantomimic.

Miss Terry is at present his constant coadjutor, and Miss Terry is supposed to represent the maximum of feminine effort on the English stage. The feminine side, in all the London theatres, is regrettably weak, and Miss Terry is easily distinguished. It is difficult to speak of her fairly, for if a large part of the public are wrong about her, they are altogether wrong, and one hesitates to bring such sweeping charges. By many intelligent persons she is regarded as an actress of exquisite genius, and is supposed to impart an extraordinary interest to everything that she touches. This is not, in our opinion, the truth, and yet to gainsay the assertion too broadly is to fall into an extreme of injustice. The difficulty is that Miss Terry has charm—remarkable charm; and this beguiles people into thinking her an accomplished actress. There is a natural quality about her that is extremely pleasing—something wholesome and English and womanly which often touches easily where art, to touch, has to be finer than we often see it. The writer of these lines once heard her highly commended by one of the most distinguished members of the Comédie Française, who had not understood a word she spoke.

> '*Ah, Miss Terry, for instance; I liked her extremely.*'
> '*And why did you like her?*'
> 'Mon Dieu, *I found her very natural.*'

This seemed to us an interesting impression, and a proof the more of the truism that we enjoy things in proportion to their rarity. To our own English vision Miss Terry has too much nature, and we should like a little more art. On the other side, when a French actress is eminent she is eminent by her finish, by what she has acquired, by the perfection of her art, and the critic I have just quoted, who had had this sort of merit before his eyes all his life, was refreshed by seeing what could be achieved in lieu of it by a sort of sympathetic spontaneity. Miss Terry has that excellent thing, a quality; she gives one the sense of something fine. Add to this that though she is not regularly beautiful, she has a face altogether in the taste of the period, a face that Burne-Jones might have drawn, and that she arranges herself (always in the taste of the period) wonderfully well for the stage. She makes an admirable picture, and it would be difficult to imagine a more striking embodiment of sumptuous sweetness than her Ophelia, her Portia, her Pauline, or her Olivia, in a version of Goldsmith's immortal novel prepared for the Court Theatre a couple of years ago by the indefatigable Mr Wills. Her Ophelia, in particular, was lovely, and of a type altogether different from the young lady in white muslin, bristling with strange grasses, whom we are accustomed to see in the part. In Miss Terry's hands the bewildered daughter of Polonius became a somewhat angular maiden of the Gothic ages, with her hair cropped short, like a boy's, and a straight and clinging robe, wrought over with contemporary needlework. As for her acting, she has happy impulses; but this seems to us to be the limit of it. She has nothing of the style, nothing of what the French call the authority, of the genuine *comédienne*. Her perception lacks acuteness, and her execution is often rough; the expression of her face itself is frequently amateurish, and her voice has a curious husky monotony, which, though it often strikes a touching note in pathetic passages, yet on the whole interferes seriously with finish of elocution. This latter weakness is especially noticeable when Miss Terry plays Shakespeare. Her manner of dealing with the delightful speeches of Portia, with all their play of irony, of wit and temper, savours, to put it harshly, of the school-girlish. We have ventured to say that her comprehension of a character is sometimes weak, and we may illustrate it by a reference to her whole handling of this same rich opportunity. Miss Terry's mistress of Belmont giggles too much, plays too much with her fingers, is too free and familiar, too osculatory, in her relations with Bassanio. The mistress of Belmont was a great lady, as well as a tender and a clever woman; but this side of the part quite eludes the actress, whose deportment is not such as we should expect in the splendid spinster who has princes for wooers. When Bassanio has chosen the casket which contains the key of her heart, she approaches him, and begins to pat and stroke him. This seems to us an appallingly false note. 'Good heavens, she's touching him!' a person sitting next to us exclaimed—a person whose judgement in such matters is always unerring. But in truth there would be a great deal to say upon this whole question of demonstration of tenderness on the English stage, and an adequate treatment of it would carry us far. The amount of kissing and hugging that goes on in London in the interest of the drama is quite incalculable, and to spectators who find their ideal of taste more nearly fulfilled in the French theatre, it has the drollest, and often the most displeasing effect. Of such demonstrations French comedians are singularly sparing; it is apparently understood that French modesty may be ruffled by them. The English would be greatly—and naturally—surprised if one should undertake to suggest to them that they have a shallower sense of decency than the French, and yet they view with complacency, in the high glare of the footlights, a redundancy of physical endearment which the taste of their neighbours across the channel would never accept. It is wholly a matter of taste, and taste is not the great English quality. English spectators delight in broad effects, and English actors and authors are often restricted to them. It is a broad effect, it tells, or 'fetches,' as the phrase is, to make a lover and his mistress, or a husband and his wife, cling about each other's necks and return again to the charge; and when other expedients are wanting, this one always succeeds. It is when the embrace is strictly conjugal that it is especially serviceable. The public relish of it is then extreme, and is to be condemned only on aesthetic grounds. It speaks of the soundness and sincerity of the people, but it speaks also of their want of a certain delicacy. The French contention is that such moments, such situations should be merely hinted at—that they are too sacred, too touching to linger upon, and that, moreover, at bottom they are not dramatic. Mr George Rignold, an actor who has had some success in America, has lately been playing in *Black-eyed Susan*, Douglas Jerrold's curiously antiquated drama, which tells so strange a tale of what the English stage had become fifty years ago; and this performance consists almost exclusively of the variety of situation in which the unfortunate William presses his devoted spouse to his bosom. It is admirable, but it is too admirable; and it is as great a mistake to give us so much of it as it would be to represent people saying their prayers. We have a vivid recollection of the tone in which a clever French lady narrated to us her impressions of a representation of Robertson's comedy of *Caste*, which she had seen at the Prince of Wales's Theatre. One of the principal incidents in this piece is the leave-taking of a young officer and his newly wedded wife, he being ordered away on foreign service. The pangs of parting, as the scene is played, are so protracted and insisted upon that our friend at last was scandalised; and when the young couple were indulging in their twentieth embrace—'*Mais, baissez donc le rideau!*' she found herself crying—'Put down the curtain! Such things are not done in public!'— while the company about her applauded so great a stroke of art, or rather, we ought to say, of nature—a distinction too often lost sight of in England.

In speaking of the performances of Shakespeare at the Lyceum just now as 'inadequate', we meant more particularly that no representation of Shakespeare can be regarded as at all adequate which is not excellent as a whole. Many of the poet's noblest and most exquisite speeches are given to secondary characters to utter, and we need hardly remind the reader how the actors who play secondary characters (putting, for the moment, those who play primary ones quite aside) are in the habit of speaking poetic lines. It is usually a misery to hear them, and there is something monstrous in seeing the most precious intellectual heritage of the human race so fearfully knocked about. Mr Irving has evidently done his best in distributing the parts in *The Merchant of Venice*, and with what sorry results this best is attended! What an Antonio! what a Bassanio! what a Nerissa! what a Jessica! The scene between Lorenzo and Jessica on the terrace at Belmont, in which the young lovers, sitting hand in hand, breathe out, in rhythmic alternation, their homage to the southern night—this enchanting scene, as it is given at the Lyceum, should be listened to for curiosity's sake. But who, indeed, it may be asked, can rise to the level of such poetry? who can speak such things as they should be spoken? Not, assuredly, the untrained and undedicated performers of whom the great stock of actors and actresses presenting themselves to the English and American public is composed. Shakespeare cannot be acted by way of a change from Messrs Byron and Burnand, Messrs Robertson and Wills. He is a school and a specialty in himself, and he is not to be taken up off-hand by players who have been interpreting vulgarity the day before, and who are to return to vulgarity on the morrow.

Miss Marie Litton, an enterprising actress, has lately been conducting the small theatre attached to the Westminster Aquarium, and wooing success by revivals of 'old comedies'. Success, we believe, was at first rather coy; for about the Westminster Aquarium there hovers a sensibly bad odour. The impurities of its atmosphere, however, are chiefly perceptible after nightfall, and Miss Litton has conjured away ill-fortune by giving her performances during the more innocent hours, and renaming the little play-house the 'Afternoon Theatre'. It is a dusky and incommodious establishment, with that accidental, provincial look which is so fatal to the spectator's confidence in a would-be 'home of the drama'. But, such as it is, it has lately witnessed an attempt to bring out *As You Like It* in style, as they say at the restaurants. The style consists chiefly in Miss Litton's doing Rosalind, in Mr Lionel Brough's doing Touchstone, and in Mr Hermann Vezin's doing Jacques. Mr Hermann Vezin, who is of American origin, is one of the best actors in London. He plays a remarkable variety of parts, and plays some of them extremely well. He is what is called in London an elocutionist—he speaks blank verse more artfully than most of his neighbours. His Jacques, however, appeared to us to lack colour and vivacity, humour and irony. The last occasion on which we had seen Mr Lionel Brough was that of his playing in a fierce burlesque, at the Folly Theatre, in conjunction with Miss Lydia Thompson. As for Miss Litton herself, she has this qualification for the part of Rosalind, that as Rosalind, during most of the play, endeavours to pass herself off as a young man, so the actress's natural organism is remarkably man-like. Miss Litton is too bulky for Rosalind's nimble wit. But what an artistic education it supposes, a proper rendering of the part! What grace, what finish, what taste, what sentiment, what archness! In London there is no House of Shakespeare, as there is in Paris a House of Molière, and in his undomiciled condition, between the Lyceum and the 'fishy' Aquarium, the poor great poet has strange bedfellows.

Among the three or four best theatres there has lately been a changing of hands. The company of the Prince of Wales's have lately established themselves at the Haymarket, which has been 'done up,' as they say in England, with great magnificence; and that of the Court has transferred itself to the St James's, where, for a long time, no such promise of prosperity had reigned. The two forsaken theatres have meanwhile re-opened their doors in creditable conditions. The Prince of Wales's, indeed, has been the scene of an interesting performance, of which we shall presently speak. The Haymarket has gained by being taken by Mr and Mrs Bancroft, but we are not sure that this humorous couple have bettered themselves with the public by leaving the diminutive play-house to which they taught the public the road. The Prince of Wales's is a little theatre, and the pieces produced there dealt mainly in little things—presupposing a great many chairs and tables, carpets, curtains, and knickknacks, and an audience placed close to the stage. They might, for the most part, have been written by a cleverish visitor at a country-house, and acted in the drawing-room by his fellow-inmates. The comedies of the late Mr Robertson were of this number, and these certainly are among the most diminutive experiments ever attempted in the drama. It is among the habits formed upon Mr Robertson's pieces that the company of the Prince of Wales's have grown up, and it is possible that they may not have all the success they desire in accommodating themselves to a larger theatre. Upon this point, however, it is quite too early to pronounce; and meanwhile Mr Bancroft has transformed the Haymarket—which was an antiquated and uncomfortable house with honourable traditions, which had latterly declined—into the perfection of a place of entertainment. Brilliant, luxuriant, softly cushioned and perfectly aired, it is almost entertainment enough to sit there and admire the excellent device by which the old-fashioned and awkward proscenium has been suppressed and the stage set all around in an immense gilded frame, like that of some magnificent picture. Within this frame the stage, with everything that is upon it, glows with a radiance that seems the very atmosphere of comedy.

So much for the house, but for the rest, there is less to say. As soon as we come to speak of a theatre of which the specialty is the comedy of contemporary manners, our appreciation stumbles into the bottomless gulf of the poverty of the repertory. There can be no better proof of such poverty than the fact that the *genius loci* at the Prince of Wales's was always the just-mentioned Mr Robertson. This gentleman's plays are infantile, and seem addressed to the comprehension of infants. Mr and Mrs Bancroft's actors and actresses could not go on playing them for year after year without falling into the small manner. It is not incumbent on us to say that this manner has been found wanting on being applied to larger things, for the simple reason that it has been rarely put to the test. To consecrate his new enterprise, Mr Bancroft has brought forward the late Lord Lytton's hackneyed comedy of *Money*, and the acting of this inanimate composition cannot be said to make formidable demands. That it should have been brought forward at all at a moment when a brilliant stroke was needed, speaks volumes as to the degree in which an English manager may be unacquainted with the *embarras de choix*. In opening anew the best of English theatres, Mr and Mrs Bancroft were probably conscious of high responsibility; they had apparently decided that they ought to be local and national, and that it would be a false note to usher in their season with a drama extorted, after the usual fashion, from the French. They looked about them for an 'original' English comedy, and it is certainly not their fault if they found nothing fresher nor weightier than this poor artificial *Money*, covered with the dust of a hundred prompters' boxes, and faded with the glare of a thousand footlights. An original English comedy is not to be had by whistling—no, nor apparently even by praying—for it. There are, however, members of the company at the new Haymarket who are fit for better things; fit, some of them, for the best things. The weak side, as on the London stage throughout, is that of the women. With the exception of Mrs Bancroft, there is not an actress who calls for mention. Miss Marion Terry, who does the young ladies, is a pale reflection of her sister, and, although a graceful and sympathetic figure, has, as an actress, no appreciable identity whatever. It will be interesting to see what they will do at the Haymarket when they have to mount a piece with an important part for a young woman. What they will do apparently will be—not to mount it. Mrs Kendal (Miss Madge Robertson), at the Prince of Wales's, used to play the important young women; but Mrs Kendal has now passed over to the new St James's, the management of which her husband divides with Mr Hare. Mrs Bancroft in the line of broad comedy is a delightful actress, with an admirable sense of the humorous, an abundance of animation and gaiety, and a great deal of art and finish. The only other actress in London who possesses these gifts (or some of them) in as high a degree is Mrs John Wood, who is even more broadly comic than Mrs Bancroft, and moves the springs of laughter with a powerful hand. She is brilliantly farcical, but she is also frankly and uncompromisingly vulgar, and Mrs Bancroft has more discretion and more taste. The part most typical of Mrs Bancroft's best ability is that of Polly Eccles, in *Caste*, of which she makes both a charming and an exhilarating creation. She also does her best with Lady Franklin, the widow with a turn for practical jokes, in *Money*, but the part has so little stuff that there is not much to be made of it. Mrs Bancroft is limited to the field we have indicated, which is a very ample one; she has made two or three excursions into the region of serious effect, which have not been felicitous. Her Countess Zicka, in a version of Sardou's *Dora*, is an example in point.

Since we have begun to speak of the ladies, we will remain a little longer in their company—apologising for our want of gallantry in again expressing our vivid sense of the fact that they do not shine on the London stage at the present hour. It takes more to make an accomplished actress than the usual Englishwoman who embraces the profession can easily lay her hands upon; a want of frankness, of brightness, of elegance, of art, is commonly, before the footlights, this lady's principal impediment. The situation may be measured by the fact that Miss Adelaide Neilson (whose principal laurels, we believe, were won in the United States) was one of its most brilliant ornaments. Miss Neilson was a remarkably pretty woman; but she added to this advantage, so far as we could perceive, none of the higher qualifications of an actress. We shall not soon forget a visit we paid over a year ago to the musty and fog-haunted Adelphi, where Miss Neilson was then representing the character of Julia in *The Hunchback*. The performance lingers in our mind as something ineffaceably lugubrious. Mr Hermann Vezin did Master Walter, and Mr Henry Neville, Sir Thomas Clifford. They are both clever actors; but either they were very much out of place, or they were playing without their usual spirit; for a sense of melancholy poverty lay heavily upon the auditor's mind, which was not enlivened by the manner in which Miss Lydia Foote, an actress enjoying great credit, expressed the characteristics of the merry-making Helen. We have passed some bad hours at the Adelphi—an establishment which we remember in the 'good old' days, as they are called, of Mr Benjamin Webster and Madame Celeste. Mr Benjamin Webster used to be very effective in *The Dead Heart*, a drama of the French Revolution, pervaded by the clanking of chains and the uproar of rescuing populace. As for Madame Celeste, who that ever saw her in the *Green Bushes* can forget the manner in which, as The Huntress of the Mississippi, she stalked about the stage with a musket on her shoulder, her fine eyes rolling, as the phrase is, all over the place, and her lower limbs, much exposed, encased in remarkably neat Indian leggings? It is not these memories that are painful, but several more recent ones. We spoke of the Adelphi just now as a 'fog-haunted' house, and literally, from some mysterious reason, of winter nights the murky atmosphere of the Strand is as thick within the theatre as outside of it. It is a very palpable presence at most of the London theatres; but at the Adelphi a perpetual yellow mist, half dust, half dampness, seems to hover above the stalls, and to stretch itself across the stage, like a screen of dirty gauze. Was it because we beheld it through this unflattering medium that a certain performance of *Nicholas Nickleby*, which Mr Andrew Halliday had done into a drama, recently appeared to us a terribly abortive entertainment? We are unable to say; but we remember receiving the impression that it was vain to attempt to galvanise the drama into life by expensive upholstery, for a public whose taste could resist the shock of such a performance. There was a vulgar ferocity, a shabby brutality about it which were quite indefinable; and we felt that the taste of the community that could tolerate it really offered no soil in which the theatre might revive. If that was possible, better things were impossible. Mr Hermann Vezin, Mr Henry Neville, Miss Lydia Foote, were again in the cast, together with Mrs Alfred Mellon, a praiseworthy actress, who many years ago was almost brilliant, and who now, in a costume worthy of a masquerade in Bedlam, gave visible form to the savage humours of Mrs Squeers. In spite of the valuable aid of these performers, however, there is nothing comfortable in our recollection of *Nicholas Nickleby*, unless it be the acquirement of a conviction. We mean the conviction that it is a great mistake to attempt to transform Dickens's works into dramas. The extreme oddity of his figures, which constantly endangers them for the reader, is doubled when they are presented to the eye. Dramatic effect is not missed, but overdone, and we receive an impression of something intolerably salient and violent. Add to which the simple cutting up of a novel into episodes, tacked together anyhow, is always an abomination.

Mrs Kendal (to return to the ladies whom we have left) is a thoroughly accomplished, business-like actress, with a great deal of intelligence, a great deal of practice, and a great deal of charm. She is not, we should say, highly imaginative, but she has always the manner of reality, and her reality is always graceful. At the St James's she carries the weight of the whole feminine side of the house—she reigns alone; and it is a proof of the great value which in London attaches to a competent actress, once she is secured, that Mrs Kendal does all sorts of business. Yesterday she was a young girl, of the period of white muslin and blushes; today she plays Mrs Sternhold, in a revival of Tom Taylor's *Still Waters*. The former Court and the former Prince of Wales's (that is, the St James's and the Haymarket) keep very well abreast of each other, and their rivalry is altogether friendly; but as we cited the recent revival of *Money* at the second-named of these houses as an evidence of scanty resources, so we may say that it was rather pitiful to see Mr Hare, when he came to open his new theatre, with nothing to set out as a birthday feast but an adaptation of a stale French vaudeville of twenty or thirty years ago, entitled *Le Fils de Famille*. This performance had not even the merit of novelty, for it had been played at the Court for many weeks before Mr Hare left this house. *The Queen's Shilling*, however, as the English version of the play is called, offered Mr Kendal some opportunities for very good acting. He and his wife, a few weeks after the opening of the St James's, undertook the grave responsibility of making a success of the little drama which Mr Tennyson has lately contributed to the stage. *The Falcon* is an attempt to convert into a poetic comedy one of the most familiar and most touching of the tales of Boccaccio, a tale which a dozen poets have

reproduced in narrative verse. Mr Tennyson's verse, in this last repro-
duction, aspires to be dramatic; but it works in awkward conditions. The
story of the poor gentleman who, to give a breakfast to the proud lady
whom he secretly adores, sends his falcon—a solitary treasure—to the
pot, and then learns that the purpose of the lady's visit (she is a noble
widow, of the neighbourhood) had been to ask for the gift of the bird for
her little boy, who is lying ill and has taken a fancy to it—this simple and
affecting tale is capital reading, but it is very indifferent acting. The
dénouement consists exclusively in the poor man's saying 'My falcon?
why, madam, you have had it for your breakfast!'—and before an
audience with an irreverent sense of the ridiculous such a *dénouement*, in
a pathetic piece, might have provoked a dangerous titter. The English
public, however, is not ironical, nor analytic; it takes things on the whole
very simply. *The Falcon* therefore was for a few weeks a moderate
success—the author having taken the precaution not to bid for loud
applause by any great splendour of verse. Mr and Mrs Kendal, on the
other hand, who recited the text with a great deal of care—the former
indeed with a degree of ready art remarkable in an actor who has formed
his manner upon current colloquialism, and has had the fear of the
artificial constantly in his eyes—Mr and Mrs Kendal, in their Italian
dresses of the fifteenth century, were splendidly picturesque figures.
The arrangement of the stage also remains in our mind as a supremely
successful thing of the kind—the cool, inclosed light of a thick-walled
cabin among Italian hills, with a glimpse of a glowing summer's day
outside. So you stand and look, from a window with a deep embrasure,
at the country about Siena.

We have spoken of Miss Ellen Terry, of Mrs Bancroft, of Mrs
Kendal; but we have not spoken of the most interesting actress in
London. It is agreeable to be able to say that she is an American; but
as she is doubtless as well known in New York as in London, we ought
perhaps to do no more than briefly allude to her. Miss Geneviève Ward's
appearances in London take place at considerable intervals, and she has
seemingly never made it her business to obtain a regular footing here.
Indeed, to the best of our knowledge, she has not, until the present
year, made what is called a hit. This fact is remarkable when Miss
Ward's exceptional ability is considered. She acts with a finish, an
intelligence, a style, an understanding of what she is about, which are as
agreeable as they are rare. We know not whether she was born under an
evil star, or whether there is an insufficient demand for her peculiar
qualities to produce a reputation; at any rate, the actress strikes us as
having hitherto been less appreciated than she deserves. It may be
hoped that now she has made a hit she will obtain her deserts; it is only
a pity that her success is not bound up with a more solid opportunity.

Forget-Me-Not, the piece in which Miss Ward has lately appeared at the Prince of Wales's under the new management (she had already brought it out, shortly before the close of the summer season at the Lyceum), is the joint production of Messrs Herman Merivale and Crawford Grove. The play is of very slender pattern, being almost totally destitute of action, and much overburdened with talk. The worst of it is that the talk is about nothing worth while—hovering perpetually round the question of whether a low French adventuress, whom the authors have not attempted to make anything but sordid, shall or shall not quarter herself upon certain young English ladies in Rome, with whom she is connected by mysterious ties. An English gentleman, befriending his young countrywomen, undertakes to dislodge the intruder, who resists with great energy, but is finally eliminated. Of these materials Miss Ward has made herself a part. It is a very bad one, but such as it is, she plays it with uncommon brilliancy. Her natural advantages are great, and, to our perception, she comes nearer than any other actress upon the London stage to being a mistress of her art.

At the Haymarket, among the men, Mr Arthur Cecil is easily first—first, we mean, in the sense of being most of an artist. His art is the art of pure comedy, but it never loses sight of nature; it is always delicate and fine. Few English actors, we suspect, have ever achieved such a command of laughter with an equal lightness of touch. It is true that we remember Charles Mathews. There was more of Charles Mathews than of Arthur Cecil—he was much greater in quantity; but we doubt whether he was more exquisite in quality. Mr Arthur Cecil is young; but it is his fate to represent elderly men—though when he occasionally does one of his own contemporaries (Sam Gerridge, for instance, in *Caste*) he loses nothing of his cunning. An actor whose situation is the same, who in the vitality of youth is often condemned to depict senility, is Mr Hare, of the St James's. He does many things admirably, his line, however, being less humorous than Arthur Cecil's. He is less genial and less comical, but his old men, whether natural or grotesque, are always minutely studied, and brought before us with elaborate art. He should be seen in a little piece called *A Quiet Rubber* (an adaptation of *Une Partie de Piquet*), in which his Lord Kildare, an impoverished and irascible Irish nobleman, whose high temper and good-breeding are constantly at odds, is a remarkable creation. Among the actors of the younger school, the votaries of that quiet realism which brings down on the heads of those who practice it the denomination of 'amateurs', John Hare certainly divides with Arthur Cecil the first place. Among the latter's companions, at the Haymarket, Mr Bancroft and Mr Conway must be mentioned. Mr Bancroft has always had a speciality—that of the well-dressed, drawling, empty-headed but presumably soft-hearted heavy dragoon, or man about town, of whom a specimen is usually found in the comedies of Mr Robertson. Mr Bancroft represents him with a humour that is not too broad, and in which the characteristics of the gentleman are not lost sight of. But he recently gave proof that he was capable of more serious work; and his Count Orloff, in the version of Victorien Sardou's *Dora*, played at the Prince of Wales's two years ago, was a vigorous and manly piece of acting. In *Diplomacy*, indeed, several of the performers we have mentioned, with two or three others, showed to exceptional advantage. Mrs Kendal was not so good as the heroine as we have sometimes seen her; she was too mature for the part. We have also said that Mrs Bancroft, as the Countess Zicka, showed a good deal of misdirected energy. But Arthur Cecil, Mr Kendal, and Mr Clayton were all excellent, and the critical scene of the play, the scene of the three men, which on the first production of the piece in Paris did so much to secure its success, was rendered by the two latter gentlemen and by Mr Bancroft in a manner which left little to be desired. We may say here, in parenthesis, that the part of the mother, in *Diplomacy*, the grotesque old widow of a South American general, was weakly filled. We mention the fact as a sign that on the London stage there is a plentiful lack of accomplished old women. There is no one that seems to us half so good as that wonderful Mrs Vernon, who for so many years was the delightful old lady of comedy at Wallack's. Mr Clayton, of whom we just spoke, deserves a paragraph to himself—though he has lately, if we are not mistaken, been playing in New York, and taking care himself of his credit. He is one of the best representatives of what may be called the man of the world in the contemporary drama. He has an agreeable combination of polish and robustness, and he cultivates ease without that tendency to underact which is the pitfall of the new generation. He made a great hit some five or six years ago in the *All for Her*, of Messrs Herman Merivale and Palgrave Simpson, a drama suggested by Charles Dickens's *Tale of Two Cities*. We remember thinking his acting picturesque, but the piece infelicitous. At the time we write, he is playing Sir Horace Welby, the gentleman who fights a duel with Miss Geneviève Ward in *Forget-Me-Not*. The part is a painfully weak one, but Mr Clayton acts it in a manner which shows that he is capable of much more brilliant things. Mr Conway, whose name we set down above, is at present an ornament of the Haymarket, where he plays the young lovers. We say an ornament advisedly; for Mr Conway's first claim to distinction is his remarkably good looks, which may be admired, along with those of the other professional beauties, at half the photograph shops in London. Mr Conway follows the same line as that elegant young actor, the late Mr Montague, who was for several years, at Wallack's, the admiration of New York. He acts with care and intention; but the spectator can hardly rid himself of the feeling that the cut of his garments bears an unduly large part in his success. He has been playing Alfred Evelyn in the revival of *Money*, of which we have already spoken, and he throws a great deal of effort and animation into the part. But he is overweighted by it, flimsy as it is, and he labours under the disadvantage of a harsh and inflexible voice. We remember seeing Mr Charles Coghlan play Alfred Evelyn, upward of five years since, when the play was brought out at the Prince of Wales's. He did it better, for Mr Coghlan is a serious and interesting actor. Mr Coghlan is *par excellence* a votary of quiet realism; the only criticism we shall make of him is that he sometimes confounds the real with the quiet. He has lately been playing in an English arrangement of an American piece—*The Banker's Daughter. The Old Love and the New*, as it is renamed, was brought out by the new management of the Court, with every appearance of success. There is something so truthful, touching and manly in Mr Coghlan's acting that it is a satisfaction to see him; but he should remember that good acting consists in doing, not the real thing, but the thing which from the scenic point of view *appears* the real thing—a very different affair. This would be a guarantee against his turning his back too much to the audience and delivering too many of his speeches into corners and cupboards. We cannot speak of *The Old Love and the New* without a word of applause for a very clever actor, Mr Anson, who plays the part of a New York commercial traveller with remarkable comic force. The wonder of it is that the actor is not, as we at first supposed, an American. His rendering of the part is a real study in linguistics. The intonation, the accent of his model, are reproduced with a verity and a sobriety together which do great honour to Mr Anson's powers of observation. He has caught the vulgar side of his dealer in 'samples' so well that for the actor's sake we could not wish the former less vulgar. We have reached our limits, and we have left a great many things unsaid and a great many names unnoted. We have pretended only to mention the actors of the moment; we have no space even for immediate retrospect. We have omitted, for instance, to say anything of Mr Toole, who has at present a small theatre of his own, an establishment of frivolous traditions, known as the 'Folly'. Mr Toole is a rich and elaborate comedian, whom we remember seeing and enjoying in all his parts when he visited the United States some years ago; but in London, we must confess, he does not interest us so much as he did in America. This is partly, we suspect, because much of the quality that we enjoyed in him, the savour of the soil, the cockney humour, was generic, as we may say, and not individual. In London this quality is in the air; every one, in certain classes, has a little of it; so that it becomes commonplace and ceases to be picturesque. Moreover Mr Toole sometimes nods, and when he does, it is portentous. No less an adjective than this will express the lugubrious quality of his unsuccessful attempt to produce a great comic effect in Mr Byron's dreary little drama entitled *A Fool and His Money*. The source of laughter, for the spectator of this misguided effort of actor and author alike, converts itself into a fountain of tears— tears of humility for our common liability to err. Though we have not said it hitherto, we must here say a good word for Mr Charles Warner, who for unnumbered months distinguished himself as the Anglicised hero of the dramatisation of Emile Zola's *Assommoir*, which Mr Charles Reade did into English (under the name of *Drink*) for the Princess's. Mr Warner's Coupeau is one of the best pieces of acting seen in London for many a day; it revealed, as the French say, the actor, who, though he had played much, had never played half so well. His Coupeau was an inspiration. We know not whether Mr Edward Terry, who is the comic gentleman at the Gaiety, ever has inspirations, but it would be a happy one for him that should lead him to escape from the baleful circle of the punning farces and burlesques of Messrs Byron and Burnand. He is one of the most amusing actors in London, and strikes us as having a comic vein that might be worked much more profitably than we see it worked in *Little Doctor Faust* and *Robbing Roy*. The same may be said of his comrade, Miss Nelly Farren, whom we ought to have included in our group of noticeable actresses. Many knowing critics in London will tell you that Miss Farren is a great actress, and that if she only had a chance her genius would kindle a blaze. This may be; but meanwhile the chance is wanting. We have seen Miss Farren in two or three parts in which she gave a glimpse of original comic power; but these bright moments were swallowed up in the inanities and vulgarities of the comic drama, as practised by the indefatigable punsters we have mentioned. Both she and Mr Terry appear to be sacrificed to that infantile con- ception of dramatic entertainment which is the only contribution of the English imagination of the day to the literature of the theatre.

POSTSCRIPT. LONDON, NOVEMBER, 1880

Since the foregoing pages were written, nothing has occurred to falsify the various judgements they contain. Very little, indeed, has occurred in any way—the months of August, September, and October being usually a period of theatrical repose and sterility. At the present writing, however, most of the play-houses are open, and the winter season may be said to have begun. The writer may add that if he was warranted a few months since in deploring the destitution of the English stage—its want of plays, of authors, of resources—he is today even more justified by the facts. Mr Irving, desiring to open his winter brilliantly at the

Lyceum, can invent nothing better than a revival of that hackneyed and preposterous drama, *The Corsican Brothers*—a piece of which the principal feature is a gentleman of supernatural antecedents, in a blood-stained shirt, moving obliquely along a groove in the stage, under a shower of electric light. *The Corsican Brothers* is brilliantly mounted, with that perfection of detail, that science of the picturesque, which, in default of more pertinent triumphs, is the great achievement of the contemporary stage. It contains a little of everything except acting. Mr Irving's proceedings in the first act of this drama, and especially the manner in which he delivers himself of the long explanatory narrative put into the mouth of the hero, are of a nature to cause a fiendish satisfaction on the part of such critics as may hitherto have ventured to judge him severely. An incident which points in exactly the same direction as this extremely successful, but none the less significant, enterprise at the Lyceum is the production (unattended in this case with great success) of *William and Susan* at the St James's. *William and Susan* is an arrangement of *Black-eyed Susan*. Dougals Jerrold's first two acts have been rewritten and provided with scenery as trim and tidy as a Dutch picture —Mr Wills being the author charged with the delicate task of pouring the old wine into new bottles. Mr Wills has made a flat and monotonous little play, into which even the singularly charming and touching acting of Mrs Kendal has failed to infuse the vital spark. Mrs Kendal is natural and delightful; she has the art of representing goodness and yet redeeming it from insipidity. Mr Kendal, who plays the high-toned and unfortunate tar, is a graceful and gentlemanly actor, but he is not another T. P. Cooke. He has not the breadth and body the part requires. The play, as it now stands, is of about the intellectual substance of a nursery-rhyme. The *mise en scène* is as usual delightful.

By far the most agreeable theatrical event that has lately taken place in London is the highly successful appearance of Madame Modjeska, who is so well known and generally appreciated in America. This charming and touching actress has hitherto appeared but in two parts; but in these parts she has given evidence of a remarkably delicate and cultivated talent. There are actresses in London whose proceedings upon the stage are absolute horse-play by the side of the quiet felicities of Madame Modjeska. A dismal translation of *La Dame aux Camélias* (in which the situation of the heroine is enveloped in the most bewildering and mystifying pruderies of allusion) permitted Madame Modjeska to achieve a success which was not assisted by any element of the real or the reasonable in the character represented. But she has lately been playing a business-like version of Schiller's *Mary Stuart*, and in this case has shown herself able to handle with brilliancy a part of greater solidity. She is a very exquisite and pathetic Queen of Scots. Madame Modjeska is the attraction of the hour; but it only points the moral of these desultory remarks that the principal ornament of the English stage just now should be a Polish actress performing in a German play.

From *Scribner's Monthly*, January 1881.

Laurence Irving (b. 1897) is the son of H. B. and therefore grandson to the legendary Sir Henry whose biography he published in 1951. Alongside Daphne du Maurier's Gerald, *which we'll come to later and is anyway written in an altogether different key, it stands on the theatre bookshelf as one of the rarest examples of a truly great biography written from within the family. In a chapter entitled 'Curtain: Westminster Abbey', Irving (himself a distinguished artist and designer) takes up his grandfather's story in October 1905 by which time the first actor ever to have been granted a knighthood, and the one who was by general reckoning the father-figure of the modern British theatre, was within a fortnight of his death. He was then in his 68th year.*

I

WHEN THE company assembled at Sheffield on Monday, October 2nd, they were alarmed by his evident frailty which courageous pretence could not conceal. His answer to enquiries after his health was invariably the same—'Quite well—thank you!' spoken with a quiet insistence. The Lord Mayor of Sheffield gave a luncheon in his honour. In his speech of thanks, Irving spoke of himself as of a man 'the sands of whose life are running fast'. That night, waiting for his cues, he sat in the wings, worn out and fighting for breath; but when they came he answered them like a battle-weary and disciplined soldier automatically obeying orders. Once upon the stage he wrought the old miracle. At Bradford, the following Monday night he played Shylock. When Gerald Lawrence came off the stage he found the Chief sitting in the wings waiting for his first entrance. Instead of his usual enquiry, 'Well—me boy, what are they like—cast iron?' Irving said meditatively: 'It's a pity—just as one is beginning to know a little about this work of ours—it's time to leave it.'

On Tuesday he played Becket. In the morning he had written a letter to Harry who had asked his advice about a contract he had been offered by Frohman. However feeble his body, his mind was as alert as ever to the business of the theatre:

'My dear Harry,

The contract or agreement would be *no* agreement after the first month or two. It is full of pitfalls and I should not bind myself to anybody for five years. If you don't both agree, better to part and if you do—well—all right and have fresh contract every year. Anyhow you are not entering into anything of the sort. As you say, they are all so mixed up and play into one another's hands that you cannot be too careful. Between ourselves—it has come to my knowledge that it needed the most influential interest to get Mrs Pat's contract carried out after her accident in spite of clauses in black and white providing for such a contingency as hers.

I return the document, which is really impudent in its one-sidedness. There are really only seven good months in America and these people would send you almost at any time, North, South, E. and West—up and down and across the continent—one night stands and all such horrors and I see nothing at all about Sundays being excepted. Whichever way you went to America it would be well to have a representative of your own to look after your interest and save you worry and vexation.

By the way, I don't believe in your lawyer being Frohman's. I never found a man serve two masters properly and even such a friend as George Lewis fails at it.

God bless you,
With all love,

H.I.'

On Wednesday, when Stoker came to fetch him for a luncheon at which the Mayor of Bradford was to present him with an address, he seemed very feeble. As he climbed the steps in front of the Town Hall, he played the old comedy which hitherto had so successfully disguised his infirmity. He halted a moment, pointed to a local feature and made some enquiry about it. While he listened to the answer, he managed to regain his breath. At the lunch, though he looked desperately ill, he spoke well; his theme was the need for municipal theatres. 'It may be,' he concluded, 'that in years to come our countrymen will scarcely understand how in our times so potent an instrument for good or ill as the stage was left entirely outside the sphere of public administration.'

That night he played *The Bells*—a performance which the company had come to dread. They found it an agony to watch him. When the curtain fell, he collapsed and sat in the prompt entrance, fighting for breath for ten minutes before Loveday and Walter could help him to his dressing-room. At last he recognised partial defeat. He gave orders for *The Bells* to be sent back to London—it had made him and now it threatened to destroy him. Stoker had anticipated his order.

The following morning, Friday, October 13th, Irving seemed a little better, though Loveday and Stoker were alarmed by his too easy acquiescence to the abandonment of the projected American tour. 'A kindly continent to me,' he said, 'but I will not leave my bones there if I can help it.' In the evening he seemed stronger and was very serene. The curtain rose upon a performance of *Becket*, which left a deep impression on all those who saw it; those who played that night with Irving hovered on the borderland of supernature. It had seemed to them, during the past ten days, as though he was consciously dying—they had spoken openly of this to one another. The first inkling of approaching crisis was felt by Gerald Lawrence when Irving, stooping over his hand as Becket made obeisance to the king, brushed it with his lips. He had never done so before—normally his gestures never varied by a hair's breadth. At the end of the third act, after Becket had parted from Rosamund, his words were 'Poor soul! Poor soul!' Edith Wynne Matthison heard Irving repeat the words after she had left the stage. When the curtain rose and fell to thunders of applause, he kept repeating to himself 'Poor soul' as he was led away to his dressing-room—as though, she felt, he meant the human soul in general, as though it was a prayer for his own.

In the third and last act Rosamund leaves Becket with these words:

BECKET: '. . . Think not of the King: Farewell!'
ROSAMUND: 'My Lord, the city is full of armèd men.'
BECKET: 'Ev'n so: Farewell!'
ROSAMUND: 'I will but pass to Vespers
                   And breathe one word for my liege-lord the King,
                   His child and mine own soul, and so return.'
BECKET: 'Pray for me too; much need of prayer have I.'
                   (Rosamund kneels for his benediction and goes.)

On the second line, Edith Wynne Matthison made a rhythmic slip—pronouncing armed as a monosyllable. Her mistake did not pass unnoticed by Irving. With the ghost of a twinkle in his eye, he murmured: '. . . Armèd, my dear, armèd.' Disconcerted, she stumbled again, substituting his own words: 'And so farewell' for 'And so return'. The repetition of his earlier line seemed to strike a chord in his spirit. 'Pray for me too—much need of prayer have I,' he said, and then added, 'Farewell—farewell', as she left the stage, with such profundity of meaning that it seemed as though he was on the brink of eternity and was striving to tell her so.

During Becket's last scene with John Salisbury came these lines:

BECKET: 'My counsel is already taken, John.
        I am prepared to die.'
JOHN: 'We are sinners all,
        The best of all not all prepared to die.'
BECKET: 'God's will be done.'

Those standing in the wings and hanging breathlessly on his every word, heard him, in place of the last line say: 'God is my judge'.

When Fitzurse struck him, he did not grasp his adversary as was his habit, but gently laid his hand upon his arm. Those anxiously waiting in the wings heard him recite clearly and resonantly Becket's last words: 'Into thy Hands, O Lord, into thy Hands!' Then he fell, not as he usually did with his head downstage, but upstage towards the steps which led to the choir—another alarming departure from his meticulous practice.

The curtain fell. Loveday and Belmore, his assistant, helped Irving to his feet. He seemed dazed and bewildered. 'What now . . .?' he muttered, as though he hoped that the devoutly desired end had come and was ready to obey the supreme mandate. His people led him downstage to take the calls for which the audience was clamouring. The curtain rose and fell many times before he began a halting speech—losing himself a little and paying tribute to Shakespeare instead of to Tennyson. He rested for a minute or so in the wings before Loveday helped him to his dressing-room. While he was changing his clothes he seemed to rally. He chatted a little with Loveday and Stoker about the future of the tour and showed concern lest his advance agent, who had been kept needlessly at the theatre waiting to see him, might miss his supper if he was to catch the last train to Birmingham where they were due to play the following week. As Stoker was leaving to dismiss the man, Irving stretched out his hand to say good night. Stoker grasped it. They were too intimately associated normally to exchange such courtesies. This gesture and the pressure of Irving's hand were disturbing variations in the routine of their nightly parting.

'Muffle up your throat, old chap!' advised Irving, '—it is a bitterly cold night—you have a cold—take care of yourself. Good night. God bless you.'

After Stoker had gone, Irving was brought a charcoal study of himself drawn by a local boy; the young artist was waiting outside to have his work hallowed by his signature. He signed it and turned to wash his hands—very carefully and methodically as was his custom. Walter helped him into his heavy overcoat and, with Loveday, escorted him to his waiting cab. Shepherd, his assistant and messenger, was standing near and, as sometimes happened, Irving told him to get in with Walter.

'You ought to have a cab,' he said to Loveday. 'It's very cold. See you tomorrow—Good night.'

He himself got in and sat with his back to the driver to avoid the draught. He did not speak during the short journey. As he entered the hotel he stumbled, but Shepherd caught him and helped him to the inner hall. 'That chair . . . !' he gasped, pointing to the nearest one. He sat down to rest for a moment. His tired heart no longer sustained the fight for breath. Losing consciousness, he slipped from the chair to the ground.

A country doctor, who had been at the play and had missed his train, was having a drink in the manager's private room. Hearing someone call for a doctor, he went at once into the hall. An old gentleman, whom he did not recognise, lay unconscious on the floor; his head was supported by a frail little fellow who was quietly weeping. Somebody nearby told him that the prostrate man was Sir Henry Irving. He was too late. Irving and Brodribb had once again linked hands and were on their way.

2

The news of Irving's death was carried swiftly to his company in their scattered lodgings; shocked as they were, it seemed to be the climax to a tragedy long rehearsed. A porter brought the news to Tree as he sat with his friends at supper in the Garrick Club; in silence the message was passed round the table and in silence the members rose, and left the Club. His sons journeyed to Bradford through the night. The next day Toole, dazed and broken-hearted by the news of his friend's death, bade his servants recover from the waste-paper basket the last words which Irving had written to him—his address on a wrapper round a newspaper containing an account of the civic reception at Bradford. In Manchester, on the following night, Ellen Terry strove to keep faith with her public. She was playing *Alice Sit-By-the-Fire*. When she came to the lines: 'It's summer done, autumn begun . . . I had a beautiful husband once . . . black as raven was his hair . . .', she broke down. The curtain was lowered and in respectful silence the audience left the theatre. Mrs Aria, hearing that the end had come as he desired, was content; she expended her grief in fashioning a pall of fresh laurel leaves such as she knew would have pleased him.

When the people heard of his death, the expression of their sorrow was akin to that inspired by Nelson, for, like the great sailor, Irving was honoured and respected for his actions and for his nature loved.

The flags throughout the kingdom were flown at half mast. The pillars of the desecrated Lyceum were hung with crêpe and every London cab-driver tied a black bow upon his whip. The newspapers of the world published columns of eulogy and appreciation; the humble and the great subscribed their tributes. A few dissentient voices recapitulated the old contentions, but they were scarcely heard. Yet, while Irving's body lay in state in the house of the Baroness Burdett-Coutts, the controversy which had been the background of his life survived his death.

Ellen Terry once had asked him, half in jest, if he thought it possible that he might be buried in Westminster Abbey. 'I should like them to do their duty by me and they will—they will,' was his reply. His confidence in the people was not misplaced. Alexander and a few of Irving's close friends so gauged public feeling that they asked the Dean of St Paul's if they might bury their dead leader in his cathedral. Their request was refused. They waited upon Dr Armytage Robinson, the Dean of Westminster, with a memorial signed by the leaders of their profession and by the great men of literature, art and science and of a society whose intellectual recreation Irving had enriched. The Dean had been threatened with blindness and lay in a darkened upper room attended by his sister, in whom the old prejudices against players and playhouses lingered. When she heard the purpose of the petition she protested vehemently against the burial of any more actors in the Poet's Corner. The members of the deputation were still waiting for an answer when Sir Anderson Critchett, who had become the leading oculist in the country, passed through the room in which they sat, on his way to see his patient. Recognising several of his friends, he asked what they were waiting for. When he heard the purpose of their mission, he promised that he would do all he could to help them. He reminded the Dean that, when he had saved his sight, he had asked what return he could make as a token of his gratitude. Now, said Critchett, was the time and opportunity to make that return by granting the request of the gentlemen waiting below. The Dean's sister repeated her protest—'No actors—no actors!' but in vain. The Dean honoured his debt.

On the eve of the funeral, Irving's cremated remains were carried through the streets lined with silent crowds. The people had finished their day's work and were grateful for this opportunity to pay their last tribute to the dead actor—for on the morrow there would be no room for them in the Abbey.

The actors and actresses whose working lives he had dignified, the craftsmen and handymen in the well-found theatres for which the Lyceum had been the model, the generations of patrons, humble and great, in whom he had created a hunger for the higher drama, the troops of friends he had known and those who had been but a blur of faces beyond the footlights—these Alexander and his helpers laboured to accommodate in the nave and transepts of the Abbey where in homage they would accord the great actor an ovation, silent but more eloquent than the applause that had so often thundered in his ears.

During the night, the coffin which contained the ashes of Irving lay in St Faith's Chapel. On October 20th, shrouded with its laurel pall, it was borne upon the shoulders of his friends into the Abbey, where, in the presence of a vast congregation, it was laid at the feet of the statue of his beloved Shakespeare and at the side of his fellow-player, David Garrick.

Irving died penniless. On this account, there was no cause for tears, for pity or for disparagement. As he said, he had not been sent into the world to collect money. He may or may not have known that Toole and Mrs James had, in their separate wills, left him ample provision for his old age had he survived them. The sale of his pictures, theatrical relics and the clothes and properties he had used in his most notable parts, which were contested for keenly by his friends and admirers, afforded enough to provide for his only dependant—his widow.

The Knight from Nowhere left no successor. The continuity of the Shakespearian succession was broken. The sceptre of the Globe Theatre had passed through only four hands before it reached his own. The brightest jewel in that sceptre was Hamlet, created first by Burbage. The second Hamlet, Joseph Taylor, an actor in the King's company at the Globe and Blackfriars theatres, was rehearsed by Burbage and succeeded him in the part. Betterton studied Hamlet with Sir William D'Avenant, who had seen Taylor. Garrick learnt his business from the veteran companions of Betterton. The survivors of Garrick's company communicated his method to Edmund Kean on whose interpretation—rehearsed by Kean's Polonius, Chippendale—Irving fashioned his own. The generation of actors who saw Irving in *Hamlet* passed away; in that and in the next generation no supreme actor took the stage capable of transmitting the fiery message, through his genius—no actor of whom it might be said, as Théophile Silvestre wrote of Delacroix:

'There was a sun in his head and storms in his heart who for forty years had played upon the keyboard of human passions and whose brush grandiose, terrible and suave, passed from saints to warriors, from warriors to lovers, from lovers to tigers and from tigers to flowers.'

Such a man was Henry Irving.

From *Henry Irving: The Actor and his World*, 1955.

Another of my godfathers (see also Peter Bull and Alexander Woollcott,
for I was singularly or rather triply blessed), Sewell Stokes (b. 1902) first
made his name as an arts journalist, then as a playwright and novelist.
With his brother Leslie he wrote the first English-language play about
Oscar Wilde, and in a long and varied career he has also been a film critic,
a probation officer and a theatrical biographer. The first of his biographies,
Isadora Duncan, was published in 1928 and lived on to become forty years
later the basis of a Ken Russell documentary about the dancer whose close
friend Sewell Stokes had been at the end of her life and the beginning of
his.

ARRIVED AT the studio we sat and drank beer, because, as Isadora
remarked, there was no champagne. And, she added, one *must* drink
something. Then, remembering how little I drank myself, she said:
'Though of course you and Mr Selfridge never touch wine. I can't
understand it. Life only gives one glimpses of ephemeral joy, and these
through love, or art, or wine.'
Isadora talked always of Mr Selfridge as she talked of Mussolini. She
had met him on several occasions. Personally she liked him. But in
the abstract he was her enemy. He was included in her attack on
millionaires.
'Millionaires don't do anything for beauty,' she would cry. 'I ask
them for a few paltry thousands for my school, and they say they have
nothing to give.'
Once she told me that she would be able to run Mr Selfridge's store
for him, on her own lines. I laughed. But she was serious. Recently I sat
opposite Mr Selfridge in his palatial office at the very top of the still more
palatial building his genius has brought into being.
'Could Isadora have helped you to run your business?' I asked
him.
Mr Selfridge removed his pince-nez, shook his head.
'I admired Miss Duncan,' he said. 'I admired her great intellect. I
found her conversation most interesting. But she was an artist, with all
the eccentricities of an artist. I could have found no place for her in my
store.'
Leaving Mr Selfridge after this interview I had the impression that he
was a very tired man. Beneath the spotless perfection of his city clothes

he appeared weary. As weary as Isadora herself had been. Neither of them had seemed to me to be happy. Probably Mr Selfridge is less happy than the hundreds of clerks in his store. Certainly Isadora, except when she was dancing or heard music, was more miserable than any little dancer in the back row of the ballet.

Putting down the glass out of which she had been slowly sipping her beer, Isadora suddenly decided to entertain me with an impromptu burlesque. In precisely the deferential tone of a 'society' entertainer, she said, as she walked to the middle of the room:

'Just a few impersonations. With your kind permission I will first endeavour . . .'

Then, to my utter surprise, she began to impersonate the Theory of Isadora Duncan. Several times before I had seen people, without sufficient knowledge to appreciate Isadora's art, caricature it; but never had I watched such a brilliant travesty of it as now. Nobody, except possibly Ruth Draper, could have been so completely a *diseuse* as Isadora was then, and the satire of herself might have been written by Noël Coward, so devastatingly true was every word of it.

Without warning Isadora turned herself into a conscientious mistress in one of the many schools of dancing, which, since her own first school began, have sprung up all over the world. Before her one imagined a class of ambitious, if unsuitable girls, whose fond parents were all anxious for them to learn the beauty of movement.

'Girls,' cried this teacher archly, 'I want you all to remember the words of the great Isadora. Remember, Isadora says: "Dance the sky, dance the air, dance the sea." Now, girls, I want you all, with me, to dance the sky, and the air, and the sea. Ready girls . . . ?'

Isadora then quickly became one of the 'girls' in question. How she accomplished this illusion, I do not know. Simply, I suppose, she had the art of the *diseuse* at her finger-tips. For immediately there stood in the teacher's place a plump and sullen schoolgirl of eighteen. Actually a heavy-footed schoolgirl, on whose pink suety face one could count the pimples of adolescence.

This girl, with comic results, did her best to follow the teacher's instructions. While endeavouring to 'dance the air' she succeeded only in convincing the spectator that her poor feet were eternally clamped to the ground.

'*Poise*, Isadora says *poise*,'—the teacher's voice, returning for a moment, cried—and watching the poise of the unfortunate girl, who reminded one of the children trying to fly in *Peter Pan*, my eyes filled with the tears of laughter. While her arms made fruitless efforts to raise her large body towards the ceiling, her feet buried themselves in the ground; and her determined expression suggested, especially about the lines of her mouth, that of a harassed goldfish. It was convulsively amusing.

'Antics like those I've just performed,' said Isadora, returning, and drinking the beer left in her glass, 'are being made by schoolgirls all over the world, every day. And *I'm* blamed for it. No wonder my methods are laughed at, caricatured. But schools like these are just burlesques of my ideas. That's what I want to put right. The women who run these institutions on the shadows of my inspiration are artistic frauds. I'm told that in America there is now a woman calling herself the Crimson Mother, who supervises one of these schools. She appears each morning, just for a few moments, from behind curtains, and addresses her disciples, using a distortion of my own ideas. For that she receives an enormous income. I'm penniless. Nobody will listen to me. I started the revival of classical dancing, but now the whole thing has grown beyond me, in a hopelessly wrong direction. I feel sometimes that my art has been wasted . . .'

To avoid those tears which so easily came to the surface with Isadora when she allowed her mind to dwell on the futility of life—as it always did when she could not find some kind of soporific—I changed the subject by handing her a letter I had that morning received from Bernard Shaw. It was an amusing reply to a letter of mine, in which I had asked Mr Shaw to confirm a point in the discussion (which I think has not been made public) between himself and Mr Frank Harris, concerning his play *Saint Joan*.

'I could have played the part of Saint Joan,' Isadora declared. 'I *ought* to have played it. I have the ample figure, the hardy physique of a farm-servant. Joan was a buxom creature. Yet she is always played by thin little actresses like Gramatica and Pitoeff.'

I believe she would have played the heroine of Shaw's drama magnificently. I have seen *Saint Joan* acted in Italy, in France, and in England; well acted on each occasion, but I cannot help feeling that Isadora would have triumphed over the other actresses. She had about her as she moved and spoke that fiery inspiration, which, for all the brilliance of their technique, I have never noticed in the work of Gramatica, Pitoeff, or Sybil Thorndike. Had she wished it, Isadora could have become as great an actress as she was a dancer. And what a dramatic critic she would have made, too. Of her great friend she wrote:

'In 1899 I first saw Eleonora Duse in London, playing in a third-rate play called *The Second Mrs Tanqueray*. The play goes through two acts of utter vulgarity and banality and I was shocked to see the divine Duse lending herself to such commonplace characterisation. At the end of the third act, where Mrs Tanqueray is driven to the wall by her enemies, and, overcome with ennui, resolves to commit suicide, there was a moment when the Duse stood quite still, alone on the stage. Suddenly, without any special outward movement, she seemed to grow and grow until her head appeared to touch the roof of the theatre, like the moment when Demeter appeared before the house of Metaneira and disclosed herself a Goddess. In that supreme gesture Duse was no longer the second Mrs Tanqueray, but some wonderful Goddess of all ages, and her growth before the eyes of the audience into that divine presence was one of the greatest artistic achievements I have ever witnessed. I remember that I went home dazed with the wonder of it. I said to myself, when I can come on the stage and stand as still as Eleonora Duse did tonight, and, at the same time, create the tremendous force of dynamic movement, then I will be the greatest dancer in the world. At that point in *The Second Mrs Tanqueray*, Duse's spirit rose to such exalted heights that she became a part of the movement of the spheres.'

My thoughts of how great Isadora would have been in the rôle of *Saint Joan* were interrupted by her doing a sudden and very convincing character sketch.

She stood, one elbow resting on the piano, and her legs crossed, and there seemed to sprout from her the skirt of a frock-coat: her neck engulfed itself in a high stiff collar, and a moustache, one end of which she stroked affectionately between the lines of her deep-voiced recitation, appeared actually to be there. As she brought forth, with studied solemnity, some lines from Tennyson, the whole atmosphere of the studio became changed. Where a few minutes before Jean Cocteau might have felt at home, was now scarcely room, between the plush and antimacassars, for the ghosts of Aubrey Beardsley and Queen Victoria to squeeze past.

Her brilliant performance came to an end. And, as there was no more beer left in the bottles, Isadora returned to the only topic left which was at all likely to distract her mind from the depression which filled it. She talked again of love. She read through the love-story she had written for the films, and asked me what I thought of it. Quite candidly I was able to tell her that I thought, as a film story, it was a very excellent piece of work. It was, too. Somehow Isadora had managed, after her infrequent visits to the cinema, to derive a perfect conception of what the mass of the public will always like; and had at the same time preserved her own intelligence.

'Take it,' she said, handing me the script. 'Try to persuade some producer to accept it. As an added inducement to whoever becomes interested in it, tell them that if they like I'll play the part of the Marchesa Romananini, the vampire. Can you think of anybody to play the hero?'

Several handsome young men, whose names are household-words, whose faces are household-dreams among the film 'fans' of the world, suggested themselves to my mind, when Isadora said:

'I know Ivor Novello. He could play the hero. If I played in the film, too, I'd probably fall in love with him. That wouldn't matter, would it?'

'Of course not!'

'Only I'm not pretty.'

'You're more than pretty, Isadora. You're almost beautiful.'

'*Almost?*'

Isadora was silent for a moment.

'You young men,' she sighed; 'your generation is so *frank*.'

'And not too *gallant*? I'm sorry, Isadora, I didn't mean . . .'

'Now Sir Herbert Tree,' Isadora waved aside my weak apology, 'said to me in Berlin—I think it was in Berlin—that I was the most beautiful creature he'd ever set eyes on.'

'Did his words flatter you?'

'At the time—not a bit. They bored me. While the sight of the dinner he'd ordered, especially for me, tempted my appetite—for I was exceedingly hungry—he just looked at me longingly and kept repeating to himself:

'So beautiful. So *very* beautiful. But not for me. Not for me.'

'He would keep on'—Isadora imitated Tree's voice perfectly—'saying the same thing over and over again. "So very beautiful. But not for me".'

'Why not for him?'

'That,' responded Isadora, 'is what I've often asked myself since. Why not for him? Unless of course,' she naïvely added, 'he was thinking of Lady Tree. Some people dare so little—even for beauty.'

'And you've dared everything,' I said; 'like George Sand. I expect you're rather like George Sand.'

'Perhaps.'

'She had a great many lovers, but she was man enough to get rid of people when they ceased to please her.'

'We're different there. It's always the other people who get rid of me.'

The words with which W. L. George defended George Sand against the attack made on her manner of living by Franz Liszt, might equally well serve Isadora. He said:

'. . . though she was not a technically chaste woman, she always looked upon an alliance as a marriage: thus she was absolutely faithful. In her long life there was not one story of intrigue; she keeps herself entirely unto the man whom she has chosen. She gives herself freely, entrusts herself wholly and withdraws herself honestly. She behaved like an honourable man, and this should entitle her to some respect.'

From *Isadora, an intimate portrait*, 1928.

Of all the plays I have seen and/or reviewed over the past twenty years,
and there have, at a rough calculation by courtesy of my Hanimex pocket
calculator with which I do not always agree, been an average of two a week
(more like four now, but only one or two twenty years ago) that's to say
two times fifty-two, well, say fifty allowing for a fortnight off in the summer,
that's a hundred plays a year across twenty years, that's two thousand
plays which is more or less what I've done with my life so far; anyway, of
all those plays I cannot think of a single new one which had a greater
immediate impact on me than The Entertainer *by John Osborne (b. 1929).*
That's not to say it's the greatest modern play I've seen, since it clearly
isn't; but in its overwhelmingly seedy theatricality, in the chances it gave
Olivier as Archie Rice, and in the parallels it drew between the crumbling
of a pier show and the crumbling of a nation, I cannot think of a more
stunning evening. Admittedly I first saw it exactly twenty years ago and I
was therefore fifteen, an impressionable age, particularly as Olivier's epic
Titus Andronicus *had only been a year or so lodged in the memory and*
here was the selfsame actor improving on what I'd decided was already an
unbeatably high-definition performance, while I'd also only just seen Look
Back in Anger *and here was the selfsame playwright making a comparable*
artistic polevault. Seen again now, so much longer after Suez, and without
Sir Laurence, I'm inclined to think that The Entertainer's *power is*
historic rather than for all time; seen then, it was electric and tragic and
magnificent and everything the theatre ought to be and almost never is.

ROCK-N-ROLL. Nude tableau, behind first act gauze. Britannia. Then;
the Archie Rice music, the one and only, interrupting the programme.
The stage blacks out. A lime picks out the prompt corner, and ARCHIE
makes his entrance. He sings a few bars of 'We're all out for good old
Number One'.

> ARCHIE: We're all out for good old Number One
> Number One's the only one for me.
> Good old England, you're my cup of tea,
> But I don't want no drab equality.
> Don't let your feelings roam,
> But remember that charity begins at home.
> What we've got left back

We'll keep—and blow you, Jack.
Number One's the only one for me.
—God bless you,
Number One's the only one for me.

I've just come to tell you about the wife. She's gone back to her husband. She has, straight. Don't clap too hard, we're all in a very old building. Yes, very old. Old. What about *that*? What about *her*, eh—Madam with the helmet on? I reckon she's sagging a bit, if you ask me. She needs some beef putting into her—the roast beef of old England. No, nobody's asking me, never mind. Nice couple of fried eggs, anyway. She's a nice girl, though—a nice girl. Going steady with Charlie here—isn't she, Charlie? (*To the conductor.*) She met him in a revolving door, and they've been going around together ever since. I'm doing me nut, you know that, don't you? I'm doing me nut up here. Nudes, that's what they call them, lady, nudes. Blimey, she's got more clothes on than I have. It's a lot of madam, that's all it is. A lot of madam. Oh, I put a line in there. Never mind, it doesn't matter. I've made a few tumbles in my time. I have, honest. You wouldn't think I was sexy to look at me, would you? No, honestly, you wouldn't, would you, lady. I always reckon you feel stronger after it? (*Sings.*) 'Say, your jelly-roll is fine, but it don't compare with mine!' There's a bloke at the side here with a hook, you know that, don't you? He is, he's standing there. I can see him. Must be the income-tax man. Life's funny though, isn't it? It is —life's funny. It's like sucking a sweet with the wrapper on. Oh, well, we're all in the fertiliser business now, I suppose. Well, I'd rather have a glass of beer any day—I would. You don't believe me, but I would. You think I'm gone, don't you? Go on, say it, you think I'm gone. You think I'm gone, don't you? Well, I am. What's the matter, you feeling cold up there? Before I do go, ladies and gentlemen, I should just like to tell you a little story, a little story. This story is about a man, just a little, ordinary man, like you and me, and one day he woke up and found himself in paradise. Well, he looks up, you see, and he sees a feller standing next to him. It turns out that this feller is a saint or something. Anyway, he's on the welcoming committee. And the feller says to him —the Saint—says to him: 'Well,' he says, 'you're now in paradise.' 'Am I?' he says. 'You are,' says the Saint. 'What's more, you have earned yourself eternal happiness.' 'Have I?' he says. 'You most certainly have,' says the Saint. 'Oh, you're well away,' he says. 'Can't you hear the multitudes? Why, everyone is singing, everyone is joyful. What do you say, my son?' So the little man took a look around him at all the multitudes of the earth, spread out against the universe. So he says to the Saint: 'Well, can I get up where you're standing, and take a proper

136

look?' So the Saint says: 'Of course you can, my son' and makes way for him. And the little man stood up where the Saint was and gazed up at the sight around him. At all the Hosts of Heaven, and all the rest of it. 'All the wonder and the joy of eternity is round about you,' said the Saint. 'You mean, this is all eternity and I'm in Paradise?' 'That is so, my son. Well, what have you to say?' So the little man looks around again for a bit, and the Saint says: 'Well, my son?' 'Well,' he says, 'I've often wondered what I'd say if this ever happened to me. I couldn't think somehow.' And the Saint smiled at him kindly and says again: 'And what *do* you say, my son?' 'Only one thing I can say,' says the little man. And he said it! Well, the Saint looked as if he had been struck across the face by some great hand. The Hosts stopped singing and all the Angels hid their faces, and for a tiny splash in eternity there was no sound at all in Paradise. The Saint couldn't speak for a while, and then he threw his arms round the little man, and kissed him. And he said: 'I love you, my son. With all my soul, I shall love you always. I have been waiting to hear that word ever since I came here.' He's there with his little hook, I can see him. Oh, well, I have a go, don't I? I 'ave a go.

The cloth goes up, revealing a dark bare stage. The music starts up softly, and ARCHIE RICE stands on the stage in a little round world of light, and swaggers gently into his song:

> Why should I care
> Why should I let it touch me,
> Why shouldn't I sit down and cry
> To let it pass over me?

He begins to falter a little.

> Why should——
> Why should I let it get me——
> What's the use of despair?

He stops and stares ahead of him. The music goes on, then he picks up.

> If they see that you're blue
> They'll look down on you.

He stares up, then goes on.

> So why oh why should I bother to care?

PHOEBE appears L. holding a raincoat and hat.

ARCHIE: Why should I care,
　　　　Why should I let it touch me,
　　　　Why shouldn't I?——

He stops, the music goes on, as he walks over to PHOEBE, who helps him on with his coat, and gives him his hat. He hesitates, comes back down to the floats.

You've been a good audience. Very good. A very *good* audience. Let me know where you're working tomorrow night—and I'll come and see *YOU*.

He walks upstage with PHOEBE. The spotlight is hitting the apron, where ARCHIE has been standing. The orchestra goes on playing: 'Why should I care'; suddenly, the little world of light snaps out, the stage is bare and dark. ARCHIE RICE has gone. There is only the music.

From *The Entertainer*, 1957.

About Mrs Patrick Campbell there is considerable detail to be found in an earlier essay by John Gielgud; about what many would consider her finest hour, the first night of Pygmalion *at His Majesty's on 11 April 1914, the greatest expert I know is the actor and author Richard Huggett (b. 1929) who describes here precisely what happened.*

THE DAY, when it finally came, was warm and sunny, a fact gratefully noted by those who queued all day for the unreserved seats in the gallery and the pit. First in the queue was Harald Melville, the scenic designer, then a fourteen-year-old Highgate schoolboy. It was not the accepted theatrical custom to have premières at the end of the week but Tree, who cared little for established customs and liked to organise matters his own way, preferred to open his new plays on a Saturday for a number of sensible reasons. It gave him all Sunday to relax quietly after the ordeal; it gave his glorious, hard-working company two whole days to recover from the tensions and agonies of the first performance and to prepare for the anti-climactical misery of the second; and, finally, it allowed the critics a long leisurely week-end to write those long, leisurely notices, instead of the usual quick scramble at the end to meet their deadline.

The curtain was due to go up at eight o'clock. By seven-thirty the Haymarket, Pall Mall, Lower Regent Street and Piccadilly Circus were choked with the biggest traffic block since the Coronation, three years earlier. Carriages, motor-cars and taxi-cabs disgorged their splendidly dressed occupants who streamed into the marble-paved foyer, discarded their top-hats and fur coats under Charles Buchell's portrait of Tree as King John, and progressed slowly up and down the staircase into their stall and circle seats. It was a star-studded occasion: English and Continental royalty; society and the theatrical aristocracy, the Alexanders, the Forbes-Robertsons, the Wyndhams, the H. B. Irvings; everybody was there, it was an audience which gossip-columnists dream about. Shaw made a spectacular late entrance wearing a badly fitting dress-suit, a flapping Inverness cape and a bulgy blue peaked cap which made him look rather like a disgruntled French schoolboy. Disdaining the cloakroom, he thrust his rolled-up cape and cap under his seat and glowered furiously at the people round him.

Then, as now, programmes were given away free of charge on first nights, but even the closest scrutiny of its contents did not take long.

The days of the glossy, splendidly illustrated souvenir programme had not yet arrived. It is a sad and mystifying fact that although Tree was accustomed to presenting his plays with a truly lavish hand and an Olympian disregard of money, although this was a unique theatrical and social occasion, the programme which he was content to give to his privileged audience was a drab, bleak document, little more than a cast list, printed on the plainest paper and containing nothing but the essential items of information . . . the list of scenes ('what *is* a phonetic laboratory?' they could be heard saying), the programme of music to be played in what was then always described as the *entr'acte*, in which Percy Grainger rubbed shoulders with Sibelius and Wagner; an item about matinée teas which cost sixpence per person, and a reassuring announcement that the theatre was ventilated by Ozonair, supplied by a firm of that name on Victoria Street. There were no advertisements except for one, which was printed in a prominent place on page three; 'Special Theatre Edition of *Thoughts and Afterthoughts* by Herbert Beerbohm Tree, can be obtained at the Box Office or from the Attendants. Price 1/-.'

There was an even greater tension than usual because this was no ordinary première. When did the theatre last offer such an exciting combination of talents? The older playgoers might mumble nostalgically about the great days at the Lyceum with Irving, Ellen Terry, Forbes Robertson, Martin Harvey and Alexander, but this evening it was to be a Tree first night with its spectacle and grandeur; a Mrs Pat first night with all the scandal which that might entail—older playgoers might eagerly speculate as to which item of her clothing she would contrive to lose *this* time; and a Shaw first night with the ever-present possibility of riots and demonstrations—with Shaw you never knew *what* was going to happen.

All this speculation and uncertainty was the result of a sensational article which had appeared only that morning in the *Daily Sketch*. Tree's publicity campaign had been gathering momentum during the last two weeks with an unexpected bonus in Mrs Pat's remarriage; this had been given an excellent press coverage with the most gratifying results. By themselves, Tree, Mrs Pat and Shaw were newsworthy but together they took priority over everything else. With superb timing and a shrewd realisation of its effect, Tree saved his final bombshell for that Saturday morning, and allowed it to explode in the early editions of the morning papers. The news value of *Pygmalion* can be judged from the fact that the *Daily Sketch* devoted its entire front page to pictures of Mrs Pat in her best known parts—when in modern times did a play get this sort of publicity?—together with an announcement which made the public rub their eyes with amazement and alarm over their breakfast tables.

One word in Shaw's new play will cause sensation.
Mr Shaw introduces a certain forbidden word.
WILL MRS PATRICK CAMPBELL SPEAK IT?
Has the censor stepped in or will the word spread?
If he does not forbid it, then anything might happen!
It is a word, although held by many to be merely a meaningless vulgarism, is certainly not used in decent society.
It is a word which the *Daily Sketch* cannot possibly print, and tonight it is to be uttered on the stage.
There can be little doubt of the word actually being used in the play. And this evening the most respectable audience in London is to hear that appalling word fall with bombshell suddenness from Mrs Pat's lips. This audience has been brought up on Shakespeare, but they are not yet accustomed to Shaw.
In the German version of the play which has just been published, a literal translation of the relevant dialogue is as follows:

FREDDIE: Are you going to walk across the park?
ELIZA: Walk across the park? . . . *Muck*!
(Sensation.)

Literary men and women will be there from Chelsea and Hampstead and the Garden Suburb, leaders of London society, middle-class matrons and maidens, all accustomed to hearing only what is pure and clean and wholesome—and Shakespearean. It will come as a shock to the Upper Circle if they hear Mrs Pat uttering a word never before heard except from Covent Garden porters, and never before read except in the poetry of Mr John Masefield.

But if the censor does pass the word, and if the audience at His Majesty's does approve it, then it will become the catchword of the season. And girls from Golders Green, maidens from Maidstone, young ladies from Lewisham will all pick up this revolting epithet like the suburban girl does in the play. She shocks and distresses her mother. So will they!

In view of this announcement, it is hardly surprising that the normal tension of a first-night audience should have been increased on this occasion to a fever-pitch of nervous anticipation. As they settled down

141

into their plush-lined stall and circle seats, their diamond tiaras, evening-gowns and stiff shirt-fronts a dazzling display, eagerly scanning their programmes for any further tit-bits of information, all topics of conversation were overridden by one which made these hardened first-nighters quiver with unsuppressed excitement—just what was The Word which Mrs Pat was going to say, and whatever It was, *would she dare to say it*?

This was a question which was giving Tree a considerable amount of anxiety. In the spacious suite on the first floor which was the Number One dressing-room, the wretched man was in a pitiful state of nerves. The careless optimism of those early rehearsal days had faded; he had now convinced himself that the play would be a dreadful failure and that Shaw's handling of the production was going to result in total disaster. But in addition to the first night terrors to which he was more than usually prone, he was now having alarming doubts about The Word. When he had embarked on the venture, it had all seemed a tremendous joke to shock the public. But that convention-defying courage had quickly dwindled when he saw the papers that morning at breakfast. For once his talent for publicity seemed to have over-reached itself—he had never expected quite such an ominously strong reaction, and his friends at the Club had shaken their heads and had prophesied disaster. 'You've gone too far this time, you'll never get away with it,' was the theme of the lunchtime conversation. The more he thought about it, the more worried he became: even though the Censor had passed it without comment, public opinion was the final censor, and it might take a very different view. There might be hostile demonstrations; they might boo; if they were *really* shocked they might even walk out or throw things. All these things had happened before and might happen again. Royalty was to be present and after all, he was a Knight Bachelor; he really should not, *could* not, take the risk of creating a nasty public scandal. The prospects were really frightening; he paced up and down his dressing-room in an agony of indecision, and it was the callboy tapping on his door and shouting 'Overture and Beginners, please. Your call, Sir Herbert,' which brought him with a sharp jerk back to the present moment. Even now it was not too late to save the situation. He left his dressing-room and went down on to the stage where the excited murmuring of the audience could be clearly heard above the tuning of the orchestra. The time was now five minutes to eight.

Mrs Pat's dressing-room had been specially erected on the stage-level to spare her the tedious necessity of going up and down the stairs for her many costume changes, and was considerably larger than the Number Two dressing-room which she would otherwise have had. For the last ten minutes she had been struggling to take off her wedding-rings which she obviously couldn't wear during the play. Neither hot water nor soap would move them an inch so she covered them with a skin-coloured tape. This produced strange ridges and lumps on her fingers provoking one critic into ecstasies over what he described as her skill in making her normally beautiful hands look bony and worn with arthritis. As Tree approached the dressing-room, she was sitting at her table in her muddy skirt and shawl and, with the aid of her dresser and a special make-up devised by Leichner, was skilfully transforming her beautifully sculptured features into those of an unwashed, grimy flower-girl.

The little incident which followed was really rather extraordinary, almost incredible, but since it was mentioned in the gossip columns of the popular press during the following week and later found its way into a number of theatrical autobiographies, and since it was also vouched for by Mrs Pat herself in her memoirs, *My Life and Some Letters*, published eight years later, it is probably true. The story has passed from mouth to mouth, is heard from old actors at parties and has thus become part of the verbal tradition of the theatre. When all the colourful details have been stripped away, the plain fact emerges. Mrs Pat's account is brief and is banished to a footnote in her memoirs. 'Sir Herbert Tree implored me to cut the word, but, if I must say it, to say it "beautifully".' An old actor, Sydney Blow, whose memoirs were published in 1958 confirms it. 'It is difficult to imagine in those days that Tree was against her saying "bloody". He wanted her to cut it. Even on the first night he went to her dressing-room and begged her not to say it. She absolutely refused.'

By now the stage was rapidly filling up with the flower-girls and costermongers, and the gorgeously dressed opera-goers who appear at the beginning of the play. Tree's dresser, Alfred Trebell, handed him the raincoat, umbrella, notebook and pencil he required in the first scene. Tree walked on to the stage and took up his position behind one of the pillars of St Paul's Church; this moment just before the opening was always the most agonising for him, and not all the whispers of, 'Good Luck, Chief,' from the company and stage-staff could bring a particle of comfort. The orchestra played the National Anthem, the house-lights went down, the huge, gold-fringed red velvet curtain swept up with a heavy muffled swish and at eleven minutes past eight precisely, the English première of *Pygmalion* started.

Tree's fears turned out to be entirely groundless. The play went smoothly, without a single hitch: it was one of those golden evenings in the theatre when the gods were smiling happily down from their theatrical heaven and nothing could go wrong.

Alfred Craven's colourful and authentic reconstruction of Covent Garden market, with a crowd of over fifty scrambling through real rain to the shelter of the church, was given a rapturous ovation when the curtain rose on the first act. The appearance of the solitary and much publicised taxi-cab and its departure with Mrs Pat and her flower-basket was the signal for a tornado of cheers from all parts of the house. There was a buzz of keen curiosity at the contents of the Wimpole Street laboratory, and Mrs Higgins's charmingly Pre-Raphaelite sitting-room with its beautiful view of the river was loudly applauded.

As for the performances, they were, for the most part, superb. The qualification is necessary because Tree introduced, as he invariably did on first nights, an element of carefree improvisation, artfully contriving to suggest that he had actually made up some of his own lines, which in some cases he certainly had. This did not bother anybody except Shaw and the other actors—acting with Tree was well known in the Profession to be an exceptionally hazardous ordeal—for the regular patrons of His Majesty's, connoisseurs of Treedom, were quite accustomed to the spectacle of the First Gentleman of the Theatre having a little trouble with his memory. Tree had taken his usual precaution of writing out the difficult sections of his part on little pieces of paper and hiding them all round the stage: they were pinned to the backs of the columns, on to chairs and tables, on the desk, the piano and the mantelpiece. To make assurance doubly sure, he took the extra precaution of installing a team of prompters at strategic points all round the back of the stage, behind doors and windows, behind the fireplace, behind the balcony, behind the sofa, underneath the tea-table and desk, so that wherever he found himself in trouble, help would be near at hand. Not that it made the slightest difference: his stumbling and floundering was distressingly evident. However, it was generally agreed that he had caught Higgins's obstinacy, aggressiveness, brutality and childish enthusiasm with splendid conviction. He certainly had the *feel* of the part—the *words* would doubtless come later. He bumbled and dithered and roared with enormous satisfaction. He flourished his black and cerise smoking jacket with soft collar, he peeled and munched bananas, juggled with apples, vaulted on and off the piano and tried hard, oh, *so* hard, to be breezy. And if the result was not entirely convincing, one could applaud the effort if not the achievement.

When Mrs Pat made her first entrance in Act One, it was immediately clear to the company that in spite of her absence from the rehearsals and her apparent inattention during them, she really knew her part inside out. Every direction Shaw had given her was faithfully obeyed, she didn't miss a single trick; and if there were any lingering doubts as to the advisability of a middle-aged woman impersonating a young flower-girl, these were quickly swept aside when confronted by her superb comic timing and that sheer radiance of personality which only the greatest stars possess. In the rejuvenating ecstasy of her week-old second marriage, with George Cornwallis-West sitting proudly in the front row of the stalls, she achieved a dazzling youthfulness which amazed everybody: it is significant that none of the critics who saw her, and there were over sixty, were sufficiently ungallant to mention her age or to give the least hint that she was thirty years too old for the part. Although it was to deteriorate badly during the subsequent season, on that first night her performance was hailed as a truly splendid and astonishing achievement.

But much as the critics admired her, they reserved their choicest superlatives for Edmund Gurney to whom the acting honours were unanimously awarded. All his life he had waited for a part like Alfred Doolittle, the philosophical, unprincipled dustman, and when it fell into his lap, he played it with all the stops pulled out, with a splendid, heart-warming comic vitality. He delivered those long speeches which are almost operatic arias without music, with a melancholy passion and a sly cynical relish which was enormously funny, and his gloomy repetition of the catchphrases, 'middle-class morality' and 'undeserving poor' was irresistible: 'it's the jolliest stuff,' said the *Daily Telegraph*.

The great sensation of the evening was, rightly and predictably, the public utterance by Mrs Pat of the now legendary words '*not bloody likely*'. The effect of this on an audience, which had been waiting tense and expectant for half the evening, was a sharp intake of breath which might have been mistaken for a protracted hiss, a few seconds of stunned disbelieving silence—and then, laughter, which screamed and echoed and multiplied round the theatre. It went on and on and on, it seemed as if it was never going to stop. When it threatened to die away, a fresh wave would burst out, louder and more frenzied than before. People rocked and shook and cried with hysteria. According to Stanley Bell's stop watch, it lasted a minute and a quarter, which may not seem much, but when it is considered that a big laugh in the theatre lasts on an average between ten and fifteen seconds, the *Pygmalion* laugh was unparalleled in theatrical history. 'People laughed so much,' said Mrs Pat afterwards, 'it nearly ruined the play'. After that, nothing could go wrong and nothing did. The audience which was clearly doting on every single minute of the play, screamed its approval so uninhibitedly, that Shaw rose in disgust after the tea-party scene and stormed angrily out of the theatre. The news of Shaw's departure was quickly passed on to Tree while he was changing into his dress-suit for Act Four. 'Aaaaah, so the cat's away,' he said with a relieved smile, and then, knowing he was quite safe, proceeded to do everything Shaw had forbidden. At the end, the audience went mad with delight; Tree was quite openly crying and cut his usual curtain speech to the minimum, though he could not forbear to mention Shaw's early departure. Then there were bouquets, flowers, endless curtain-calls, more speeches, tears and cheers and a cascade of roses thrown from the gallery. There were a few chords of dissent from the suffragettes in the gallery but these merely added spice to the occasion: no triumph is ever quite complete without a few boos. It was well past midnight before the happy but exhausted company were allowed to leave the stage and go up to the Dome where a first night party, complete with champagne, chicken and caviare, was held for them and a hundred of Tree's most intimate personal friends.

The following day there was a brisk exchange of telegrams between Shaw and Mrs Pat. 'MAGNIFICENT. SUPERB. NEVER BETTER' cabled Shaw. These were the first kind words she'd had from him for a long time and she was, understandably, very touched. 'YOUR GENEROUS PRAISE QUITE UNDESERVED' she replied. Even in his most tender moments, Shaw had no time for false modesty. He replied: 'DEAR STELLA. I WAS TALKING ABOUT THE PLAY.' But Mrs Pat was equal to this and her riposte was swift. 'DEAR JOEY. SO WAS I!'

From *The truth about 'Pygmalion'*, 1969.

In August 1904, on the verge of her 22nd birthday, plump, innocent and already desperately over-enthusiastic, Sybil Thorndike (1882-1976) set sail from Greenock to tour America in the company of Ben Greet and his sometime Pastoral Players. That first tour was to last more than a year, and on almost every day of it Sybil would write home to the family in Kent—long, gossipy, evocative letters dealing with company news and American geography in roughly equal proportions. Sybil travelled, she wrote later, 'thousands and thousands of miles, to big towns and one-eyed towns all over the country from coast to coast . . . and all the while I was trying to describe to myself and the family at home the wonders of this land seen through my very young, Walt Whitman-dazzled eyes and brains and feeling.'

By the time they reached California, Sybil was getting twenty-five dollars a week and living frugally enough (often sharing a bed with Greet's niece Daisy, her best friend on the tour) to save most of it. She had, however, developed an unfortunate tendency to giggle on stage, especially during Greet's Hamlet, for which she was fined two dollars. Her parts at this stage of the tour were small and generally unrewarding; but then, in Stockton, came the big chance—one she described next day in a letter to her family.

'DARLING ANGELS, Father, Mother and Russ and everyone at home. I've had my "great chance"—I played Viola last night. Hold on to your chairs and I'll tell you from the start. We arrived at a place called Stockton yesterday morning—such a sweet place, with a square. I'm looking out on the Square now—and palm-trees and geraniums growing on the pavements and barrows of apricots and peaches and all sorts of heavenly fruit. Mrs Crawley didn't feel at all well on the train and Mr Crawley came to me (Oh! he's a perfect lamb with the nicest face rather like Cassius), and he said, "Do you know Viola?" I said, "Rather, I should say I did. Not only have I played her in the barn but at the Ben Greet Academy of Acting—better than any part I know her." "Well," he said, "I've not told B. G., yet, but I think Minnie"—that's Mrs Crawley; she calls him Rawdon like *Vanity Fair*—"won't be fit to go on to-night, and if you can play it she will be greatly relieved." So I relieved his mind of all doubts as to my ability, and then I prayed hard—and oh!

Father, what I wanted to pray was this, "Oh! Lord God, please smite her with a fell disease so that she can't play for weeks, and let me play the parts, oh! Lord!" But no, not your good Christian kind little daughter. I said meekly, "Oh! Lord God, please make her better, but let it be necessary for her to have one night off at least." And the Lord hearkened unto my prayer, for as soon as I'd unpacked my bag at Stockton (praying all the while, you may be quite sure), a message was sent me from B. G. to say would I run thro' the words with some of the company in the afternoon. Horrors! at lunch-time someone again came and said she was getting better, and might be able to play, and the rehearsal wasn't necessary! Did I give up hope? No, I went thro' the part myself, and then Eric Blind would go thro' Orsino's scenes with me, which was extremely kind considering how weary and ill he has been. Then, my angel dears, at 6 o'c. Dai rushes to me. "I've seen Uncle, and you've got to play." So off I go to the theatre to see about clothes, and Dai brings me a sandwich and a cup of coffee. I felt too terribly thrilled to eat much, and she was too sweet the way she helped me to dress and kept on saying things like, "For goodness' sake, Syb, keep your knees straight, or you'll look like a girl"—and "don't waggle your head at every word when you get emotional, and you'll be all right." Then "it came—the hour of starting came—and in a carriage grand, the vain Matilda lightly sprung" (see "Matilda Bligh", recited with such gusto by our mother when young), and I went on.—Well, I've never enjoyed myself so much in all my life. In fact, I felt I was Viola, she didn't seem different to anything I felt deep down—the scenes with Orsino were lovely—oh! and so was the scene with Olivia—"honourable lady of the house" one, and when Sebastian comes in the end and I saw him I felt exactly like seeing you, Russ, after years and ages of separation, and I cried like anything, but it didn't matter really, did it? The audience were lovely and laughed at everything I wanted them to laugh at, which was most kind. Ben Greet said, "Good girl, you never missed a word," and Dai said, "It was lovely, Syb, and you only waggled your head once badly, and I never even looked at your knees because I was enjoying it all so," and all the company were so nice, especially Mr Crawley, who felt relieved, I expect, that the show hadn't been a failure because of Mrs Crawley being ill. The paper (they have a special one even in a tiny place like this—the Americans *do* seem to care so much about papers) said, "Mrs Crawley" (they didn't know it wasn't her, you see) "gave a most charming performance, naïve and touching." Ha! ha! now my foot is on the ladder truly and really and I mean to swot terribly hard to know every single part, in case any kind person gets stricken with the plague and can't appear. Good-bye now—I'm writing this in bed— fancy me—I couldn't wait to dress before I told you. I had break-

fast in bed—Dai made me, and she brought me a paper with my
notice in. I feel more pleased than ever to have such a good friend
as her.'

From *Sybil Thorndike*, 1929.

Daphne du Maurier wrote Gerald, *a biography of her actor-manager father, in 1934 when she was 27 and he had just died at the age of 61. It was I think the first theatre book, and also the first biography, I ever read and it lives in my memory as a more expertly touching and brilliantly convincing summary of a life than almost any I have ever encountered since. Du Maurier, son of the artist-novelist George, creator of Raffles and namer of the cigarettes, was not by all accounts an easy man and it cannot have been an altogether easy book to write; when it first appeared, there was even some amazement that a daughter had dared to refer to a father throughout the text by his christian name.* Gerald *(now happily available in paperback) will not tell you the precise dates of every one of his first nights, nor yet the names of all the people he worked with; it will tell you what it was like to be the last of the actor-managers and the last of the great matinée charmers at a time when charm and actor-management were both going rapidly out of public favour. I would like at this point simply to reprint the whole book; space forbidding, we pick it up in the summer of 1931.*

THE SUMMER and autumn loomed ahead, and the outlook was not a particularly cheerful one. Gerald could not afford to be idle, but he had no play in mind. Something had got to be done. The old successful days at Wyndham's seemed very long ago, with Tom Vaughan sitting in a corner of the dressing-room sipping his whiskey and soda, and announcing in his solid, confident voice that there wasn't a seat book-able in the house for six months, and that the new play was in for a year's run. It was no use sighing and regretting the days that had gone for ever; the present clamoured for security, and the future was a menace. Advice, of course, was cheap. Go to America. Go to New York. Go to Australia and South Africa. There was heaps of money to be made. You only had to get on the boat. It was so easy to talk, so easy to conjure up ideas of the income tax paid off at last, of a bank balance that could be looked at without shuddering, of a triumphant return to England with pockets full of bank-notes and hysterical Press-cuttings. But, when he really got down to it, the picture was not quite so brilliant. Like all the big under-takings in life, it required confidence and energy, and he wasn't sure if he had either any more. The very thought of setting out on a long journey, from which one might not return for two years; of travelling, of continually meeting new people, of being entertained by governors and viceroys, of staying in hotels, railway carriages, ships . . . no, he was too old, too tired; he simply could not cope. England one might manage; after all, one had toured the provinces with Tree and Forbes-Robertson so often in the past, they would be familiar ground. So there was an idea. And Gladys had done it a few years ago and made a packet of money. It was true that Gladys had a courage and a determination that was hard to equal and impossible to defeat, whereas he was never certain, never sure; but, even so, he might get away with it with a slice of luck.

If only Frank Curzon had been behind him, and Tommy Vaughan at his side! The trouble was to find a play, and a new one, to give the provincial audiences. Films had rather spoilt the market, for one thing; there were big cinemas in every town, and almost every old play had been adapted and turned into a film story which was old history by now. There were no new plays—nothing, at least, that was worth producing, and certainly nothing that was worth risking for the first time. It looked as though he would have to take an old play that was a proved success. *Bull-Dog* had been done to death in the provinces; besides, it had been made into a film. *Dear Brutus*—no, not again so soon; and anyway it was not suitable. *Diplomacy* might suit, and he owned the rights, but apparently a tour of it had been done not long ago. Wherever he looked it seemed as though the plays had been done before. What about *The Ware Case*? It was a rattling good play, had not dated, and would always bear revival. Nor had it been on tour—or, at least, not for many years. The more he thought about it the more he liked the idea of *The Ware Case* and finally it was decided upon.

A four-months tour of the provinces was arranged, the cast was engaged, and, in August, Gerald, accompanied by Mo, drove off to Southsea to appear before a provincial audience for the first time for thirty years.

There was something rather strange about arriving in his own car and staying at the best hotel, with reporters waiting for him at the theatre door and his name in huge letters above the entrance, when once he had herded with six or seven others in a third-class carriage, and shared dingy lodgings in a back street, had bacon and eggs for supper and sung 'Frosty Weather' amid shrieks of delight. It had been very pleasant living without responsibilities. Whether this tour was a success or not, at least he had made up his mind to one thing, and that was that he would make some money for charity. Besides being President of the Actors' Orphanage and of Denville Hall, a home for aged actors and actresses, he had this year been elected President of the Actors'

Benevolent Fund, and he was determined to work hard for it in his first year. Shy and diffident about his own financial affairs, and utterly incapable of striking a bargain for himself, Gerald would go to any lengths to raise money for his charities, and during the tour of *The Ware Case* he set himself the huge task of raising a thousand pounds for the Actors' Benevolent Fund. Originally starting as a bet, and by saying half jokingly, 'I know it can be done,' this task developed into the most serious and vital object of the tour, and the success of *The Ware Case* became a minor affair. It was characteristic of his whole life that the tour, as a tour, was not the brilliant triumph that everybody but Gerald himself had anticipated. The play had dated slightly, and it had been seen before; and the box-office returns were disappointing even if the reception was enthusiastic. But the Actors' Benevolent Fund overtopped its thousand pounds by a large margin.

Gerald deliberately made his task more difficult, and more exciting, by wagering that he would raise over a hundred pounds in each individual town, and he did not fail. It spoke well for the generous sporting spirit of the provincial audiences, whom he took into his confidence, that they never let him down; and it became a matter of honour for Nottingham to beat Birmingham, and Leicester to beat Leeds. After the curtain had fallen on each performance, Gerald would come in front and make a personal appeal, which would be received with good-natured cheers and promises to respond. He asked those who had not, until the last act, discovered the murderer in *The Ware Case*, to put a sum of money in the box towards his thousand pounds, or, better still, to send him a cheque. Although tired after playing the exhausting part of Hubert Ware all the evening, he gave his audience another little performance on his own, and made up as Henry Irving, the founder of the Actors' Benevolent Fund, speaking to them with his voice and his mannerisms as he remembered them over forty years ago. As a guest to various Rotary Club luncheons he made speeches on behalf of his charity, and, mixing up his appeal very cleverly with some reminiscences and anecdotes, he would relieve the members of their pocket-money in the space of a few minutes.

Nobody escaped his eagle eye, from the Mayor of the city to the smallest schoolboy in the pit on matinée days, and in all the fourteen weeks of the tour he met with no refusal from any member of the community.

It was a triumph for the Actors' Benevolent Fund and a really wonderful piece of work by its President. Gerald felt that for the first time for years he had accomplished something that was worth while, something which more than made up for the little disappointments and depressions of middle age.

After all, it showed a small mind and an ungrateful memory to grumble. He had enjoyed over thirty years in the profession which had brought him so much success and happiness, and the least he could do was to make some small gesture in return. What did it matter if *The Ware Case* had not turned out to be a big financial proposition? At least the company had enjoyed themselves, they had all had plenty to laugh about, there had been many excellent opportunities for practical joking, and Mo had looked after him in her own inimitable way.

They returned to London in time for Christmas and celebrated, as usual, with holly and mistletoe, turkey and plum pudding, crackers and a conjurer. And Gerald, with a paper cap on his head and a whistle in his hand, talked at the top of his voice, hid half-sovereigns in his neighbours' mince pies, and looked as though he had never heard the word depression.

Edgar Wallace was writing a play for him. It was to be produced at Wyndham's. He was entering upon his sixtieth year, and damnation to all who stood in his way, and particularly the Inland Revenue!

The responsibility of *The Green Pack* lay upon his shoulders entirely, as Edgar was out in Hollywood, and the only means of communication was by cables or by long-distance telephone calls at a prohibitive cost.

Scenes had to be altered, and characters changed, and a new ending to the play worked out. Edgar had written it in his usual tearing hurry—twenty-four hours or something phenomenal—and, though it looked good on paper, it did not look quite so good at rehearsal. The play could not be produced as it stood; that was obvious. It would have to be turned upside down and pulled about like a jig-saw puzzle, which, with Edgar's cabled permission, Gerald proceeded to do. Actually it came to every member of the company walking about with pencils and pieces of paper, lips moving silently, foreheads creased in a frown, and every now and then one of them breaking into a cry: 'Look, what about this for an idea?' It was not the way the greatest plays of all time have been written, but, then, nobody was suggesting for a moment that *The Green Pack* was a great play. It was doubtful if it was even a moderately good play. The only thing Gerald and the company hoped to do was to make it into a good enough play to warrant full houses at Wyndham's Theatre for three or four months.

'Do what you like with the play,' Edgar had wired from Hollywood, 'and God love you, Gerald.' The message of faith and affection made Gerald more determined than ever to produce a success and to be able to repay Edgar for his trust and generosity. By a tremendous effort the play was pulled into shape and presented to the public on the 9th of February, but it was overshadowed on the opening night with the grave news that the author was dangerously ill in Hollywood with a sudden attack of double pneumonia. The following day the message came that Edgar Wallace was dead.

It was a terrible blow to all his friends and the world in general. It seemed unbelievable that the flame of his personality should be quenched at last, his great, generous heart be still, and his dynamic force and brilliant brain be silenced for evermore. That Edgar should die—Edgar, with his super-human energy, his strength, his grip upon life; Edgar, who, sinister and serene, with his Napoleonic head, should have straddled the world when the rest of us lay dead. It was a shock to faith and an attack upon courage. It was one more argument in favour of futility. Not until Time had brought a light of reason and understanding to bear upon it did the mind accept with thankfulness that Providence or God Almighty had chosen both wisely and well. It is known now that Edgar would have been an invalid had he lived longer, without hope of recovery, and probably in pain. With the supreme good fortune that had favoured his meteoric path through life, he went out of his little world at the right moment, with a smile on his lips and without a gesture of farewell.

With heavy hearts and saddened spirit the company at Wyndham's continued the performance of *The Green Pack*. But, with Edgar dead, it was a joyless undertaking, almost in the nature of a requiem, and neither actors nor audience could forget the tragedy of the author and lose themselves whole-heartedly in the story of the play. It did not possess the excitement of *The Ringer*, nor the grim realism of *On the Spot*, nor, yet again, the quick pace and vivid story that made *The Calendar* memorable. It was, and always had been, an indifferent play that all the artifices of production could not turn into a winner. It ran for nearly five months, however, which was not so poor in these days of short runs, and Gerald considered that, taking into account the tragic circumstances that had overshadowed it from the beginning, the play had done very well. It was like old times, too, being back at Wyndham's, with the original staff and his original dressing-room. It only needed Tommy Vaughan to wander in with his inevitable handshake and his genial, 'Well, Gerald, old man,' to bring back the old days of ease, and enthusiasm, and security.

With the final night of *The Green Pack* it was a plunge once more into the unknown, a last farewell to Wyndham's, and another lone and weary search for the right play to produce at the right time.

For the first time, Gerald began to look a little older, a little weary, a little worn. He complained of not sleeping, of feeling eternally tired, of having 'Mummie's pain' under his heart. He was always going into chemists' shops and buying quack medicines with mysterious names.

He wandered about with great medical volumes under his arm, profusely illustrated, which told him in a wealth of detail all the diseases from A to Z. He was losing his eagerness, his curiosity about people and their ways of living; it was an effort to think clearly about things, to give an opinion, to make plans.

He spent much of his time pottering in the drawing-room and looking through old letters of Guy's, old sketches of Papa's. It was as though he wanted to soak himself in the past and shut away the present and the future.

Fewer people came to Sunday lunches. He began to appreciate quiet days, sitting about, playing bridge with Angela and Jeanne. Daphne suddenly wrote from Fowey and said she was going to be married, and Gerald burst into tears, just as Kicky had done over Trixie, and said, 'It isn't fair,' like a little boy. At any rate, the fellow was a soldier, and Guy had been a soldier, so perhaps it was all for the best, he sighed, and she would settle down like the du Maurier girls in pictures that Papa had drawn—like Trixie, and Sylvia, and May; but oh! damn and blast! Why did one's daughters fall in love?

Getting married, bearing children, growing old . . . things happened so swiftly in life, and the moments passed. He pondered on the why and wherefore of little things, and he never came to a definite understanding. He never learnt wisdom finally and for ever.

And here he was, the head of his profession, nearly sixty, and sick to death of acting; frittering away the days in doing nothing, in lunching with a pal, in having a yarn, in hanging about; wondering at the back of his mind why he was alive at all, and if there was any riddle to the universe after the long day was over. And, in spite of everything, he had to go on acting, because he could not afford to retire.

'Which do you prefer, Sir Gerald?' asked an anxious and hopeful reporter, his stub of pencil in his hand. 'Acting for the films or acting on the stage?' 'I prefer strolling down the street,' said Gerald, smothering a yawn. It was a typical reply, and must have astonished the young journalist, used to interviewing actors and actresses who declaimed about their Work with a capital letter. 'And your plans for the future?' continued the newspaper man in some trepidation, while Gerald solemnly wound up a clockwork animal and placed it on the floor. 'I'm going to read the most amazing play in the world which has not yet been written, by a man I don't know, and who doesn't exist,' Gerald answered. 'And,' he went on, 'if I accept it, I shall produce it in a theatre which has not yet been built.' The reporter thanked him for his information and went away wondering why Sir Gerald had ever been knighted —which sentiment serves as a reminder of one of Mo's classic remarks. When asked by one of the children suddenly out of the blue, 'Mummy, why was Daddy knighted?' she looked up from her knitting, pushed back her spectacles, thought solemnly for a few minutes, and then replied, 'I don't think we've ever quite known.'

Gerald was certainly not a satisfactory person to interview from a journalistic point of view. He never answered questions in the right way, and always wandered from the point; and, as he had never in his whole life 'truckled to the Press', as he called it, newspaper proprietors could hardly be blamed for disliking him. One or two unfortunate experiences had led Gerald into declaring a vendetta against the Press in general, and he was often deliberately rude. This was not a helpful factor in his public life, and he was obliged, especially in the last years, to fight a lone battle, without allies, against Time and depression in the theatre, a battle which a little tact and good will on either side might have made entirely unnecessary.

They thought Gerald snobbish and conceited when he was merely bored or not particularly interested, and he thought them rude and offensive when they were merely earning their daily bread. They could not believe that his dislike of publicity was genuine and not a pose, and he could not believe that their general attitude was critically honest and not deliberately malicious. Circumstances had combined to make the Press unpopular with Gerald and Gerald equally unpopular with the Press, and so the vendetta continued to the end. Meanwhile, in '32, Gerald was still looking for a play. Recent evidence had shown him that the public no longer came to see a play for the sake of one big name alone; they liked a combination and a variety of talent. *Cynara* had been a success because both he and Gladys had played in it together. Therefore as well as a play he must find a leading lady whom stalls and gallery and pit would pay to see. His choice fell upon a play by John van Druten called *Behold, We Live*, and he presented it in August at the St James's, with Gertrude Lawrence playing the part of the woman. It was a gloomy story, surely written under the stress of some emotion, and did not have much popular appeal, but it managed to survive through the autumn. At the same time Gerald and Gertrude Lawrence took part in a film, *Lord Camber's Ladies*, that was being directed at Elstree. His dislike of film-acting increased tenfold during this period, though no one would have believed it to look at him, with his pockets full of tricks and practical jokes that he let fly amongst the feet of cameramen, electricians, and directors in a sort of desperate effort to relieve the tedium. Practical joking during these months developed to a pitch of positive frenzy, until both theatre and studio resembled another Bedlam. The nervy, highly strung Gertie was a boon companion in mischief, and the round-faced Hitchcock a surprising ally down at Elstree. It was a wonder that the picture was ever completed at all, for hardly a moment would pass without some faked telegram arriving, some bogus message being delivered, some supposed telephone bell ringing, until the practical jokers were haggard and worn with their tremendous efforts, and had lived so long in an atmosphere of pretence that they had forgotten what it was like to be natural.

It was a game that could be carried too far, and, settling as it did into a daily routine, ceased before long to be genuinely amusing, and almost developed into a vice. It served, however, as a form of safety-valve, and prevented Gerald from dwelling too deeply on his future, which to his discerning eye appeared to be forbidding. Half-heartedly he would read plays, none of which seemed to him worth while producing, and he would turn them down with a shrug of his shoulder and 'I don't know; perhaps I've lost my sense of judgement, but it seems unholy muck to me.' And then, a few weeks later, he would hear that the play he had refused had been read and accepted by someone else; and it would be produced, and become a moderate or even a definite success.

This would not annoy him in the least. He would not grudge the success that might have been his. Instead, he would shrug his shoulders again and say, 'All right; I suppose I was wrong. Thank God I'm not acting in it all the same.'

In the spring he revived that hardy veteran, *Diplomacy*, and produced it at the Prince's Theatre. The public had not seen it since '24, when Gladys gave it ten months' run at the Adelphi, and now Gerald took some little trouble with the wording of the play itself, substituting certain modern expressions for some of the decidedly Victorian phrases. It was always an actor-proof play, and could be relied upon, like a dependable car, to run smoothly, despite its age, and tide over a difficult period. Gerald played his original part of Henry Beauclere, which had always suited him admirably, and made no great demand upon his strength or his powers of concentration, especially now that he had brought this particular type of acting to perfection; and, with his years of experience behind him, he could not fail to give an accomplished, polished, absolutely first-class performance.

It survived through the early summer, and, in August, Gerald and Mo went off to Wales for a holiday, finishing up at Fowey in September.

For the first time for many years Gerald appeared to enjoy his holiday, both at Port Merion and in Cornwall. He did not complain of boredom, he was not restless, and he did not hanker after London. He seemed happy pottering about, and reading, and laughing at everything and everybody; the weather was generally fine and he had none of his fits of depression. It seemed premature to talk, but was it possible that he was going to enjoy resting at last, and would be content to pass quiet holidays, lying about, playing bridge with the girls, sleeping in the sun?

There had been a great agitation earlier in the summer to sell the house at Fowey and thereby cut down one of the expenses. Gerald's dislike of the place had been the chief argument in favour of the plan. And then, with the motion practically carried through and the paper signed, Gerald made one of his sudden decisions. 'Don't do it,' he said. 'I can't explain why, but I feel it would be a terrible mistake. It's a thing that might be regretted for a lifetime. Never do anything like that in a hurry.' And so the house was not sold, and in that month of September at any rate Gerald appeared to be content. Films claimed him once again in the autumn, much as he detested them, and the weary grind of early rising and being ready made up at the studio at an impossible hour in the morning, only to find he was not wanted for some hours, became once more the order of the day.

By this time he was resigned, more or less, to the confusion and the delay that is apparently a necessary feature to the making of pictures. He did not expect anything else. It was all part of the show. Even if he loathed every poisonous moment, it was something that had to be endured; it was not his concern; he was only a unit out of a thousand other units; he was not even playing a leading part. He did it because he could not at the moment bring himself to consider any other means of making money; it was one stop-gap after another, one more straw floating on the surface of the water.

He persisted in being vague about his plans. When urged to consider the future, he began to talk about birds, or a new trick from Hamley's, or somebody he had been lunching with the day before. 'I can't be bothered with the income tax, Billy dear,' he said when a distraught Sybil presented him with buff-coloured forms; 'they're probably quite decent fellows. Write and tell them I haven't any money. Look, there's a starling outside my window, behaving in the most curious way.' And he would put on one of his enormous pairs of glasses and lean out of his window to make an inspection.

At one moment there would be suggestions of a big tour in the Dominions; at another, tentative plans would be discussed as to the production of a new film, engagements in London, engagements in South Africa, contracts to appear in a stated number of pictures; but none of these ideas came to maturity.

Gerald would not make up his mind, he would not come to an agreement; it was as though something whispered in his heart and behind his brain that these things were to no purpose. He was like one who, glancing at his watch and smoking a last cigarette, stands on the brink of an adventure, marking time. . . .

From *Gerald: A Portrait*, 1934.

Tyrone Guthrie (1900-71) was a giant and a rebel and arguably the most influential albeit also the most erratic theatre director of his time. A prophet without much honour in either of his own countries, he had an overwhelming belief in the open stage at a time when London and Belfast were still locked inside the proscenium arch, and his dissension led him to found not just new theatres but whole new theatrical communities in Canada and the United States. That there is no Guthrie theatre in the United Kingdom is both sad and ludicrous; there is however still the memory of the man and his massive eccentricity. When he died, a worker on the Irish estate from where Guthrie ran (among other things) a jam factory told his widow that a great oak had fallen. So it had. This brief Guthrie guide to acting comes from a manual he wrote shortly before his death.

BY DEFINITION Acting is no more than Doing, Taking Action. But in a specialised sense, the term Acting is used for the Art or Craft of Acting. This implies pretending to be someone or something other than yourself; or even, while retaining your own identity, expressing thoughts or feelings which do not in fact correspond with your own thoughts and feelings at a particular moment. Indeed in this sense of the word we all spend a great deal of our lives in acting, a greater part, I suspect, than most of us realise. Most of it is done in a good-natured endeavour to lubricate the creaking mechanism of social intercourse. This is particularly the case in business or professional dealings. Employees have to make a show to employers of being industrious and respectful, while employers have to make a show of being kind and just and taking an interest. 'How's *Mrs* Wetherbee? . . . Oh, not *again* (in a tone of extreme concern) . . . that's her second this winter.' (With even deeper concern) '*Has* she tried those sort of inhaler things?' Fortunately at this moment the telephone rings and the actor can switch from the rôle of Considerate Employer to that of Jolly Fellow-Rotarian and by the time the 'kidding' and the roars of assumed laughter have run their dreadful course, old Wetherbee, thank God, has slipped out of your office and Miss Scales is ready to take dictation. Whereupon yet another Act begins: the iron-clad, ice-cold Man of Affairs creating order and profit out of chaos; and, at the self-same time, yet another impersonation: the dominant Male allowing a Female to help him, so far as such a flighty, fluffy little thing can be a help in business.

Is this kind of hypocrisy really acting? I think so, because, though you are not pretending to an identity or appearance other than your own, and though you are inventing your own dialogue and choreography, you are, nevertheless, expressing many different facets of yourself, and this, I believe, means that from time to time you are forced, if the facets are to be convincingly displayed, to think of yourself as many different kinds of people, similar only because they all look like you, wear your clothes, speak in your voice and are limited by your, admittedly considerable, limitations.

Yet isn't it possible that most of us are not quite so severely limited as we suppose, and that this sort of acting, which can also be called social adaptability, is a considerable help in expanding our limitations? Incidentally, most of us perform these tricks of adaptability so habitually that we are hardly conscious of them as not being our absolutely 'natural' behaviour.

Of course, practically no social behaviour is 'natural'. It is natural to rush and grab what we want like a baby or an untrained animal; it is natural to growl and scream when our desire is thwarted, be it for a bone, a rattle or a bishopric. Socially acceptable behaviour is a highly unnatural performance, only attainable after considerable training. I sometimes think that if professional actors reflected a little more on how we all learn acceptable social manners, it would be a valuable guide to many of the techniques of their craft.

To return to the definition of acting: in general we use the word to signify pretending to be somebody else in the particular context of drama, a character in a play, of which the theme, the sequence of events (or plot), the nature of the persons and the very words which they speak have all been previously conceived by an author, then written down, then rehearsed (or repeated over and over) by actors. And even this more artificial kind of acting bears a resemblance to the less conscious pretences of social life: the success of the performance depends upon being 'convincing'. In the one case your cheery 'Good morning' must convince Mrs Arbuthnot that you sincerely wish her well. In the other case you must convince an audience, even many successive audiences, that your Hamlet is sufficiently interesting to justify the considerable effort which is demanded of them at this particular play. You must also convince an audience that your assumption is plausible in the given circumstances; that a person, who looks and sounds as you do in the part, might have said the words, felt the sentiments, done the deeds which the author has indicated.

Emphatically this is not the same thing as convincing an audience that you actually are Hamlet. Quite obviously you are not. The intention of the actor should never be to try to deceive the audience into confusing fiction with fact. He should, rather, go through the *ritual* of performance in such a manner as to make the fiction acceptable—not as fact, but as an interesting and pleasurable experience.

How to make acting plausible

How does an actor set out to make his performance plausible?

First, by imagination. To impersonate a character successfully you must imagine what it would feel like to *be* that character, how he would move, what his voice would be like, why he says and does whatever he says and does in the play. Of course he says and does these things because he is a person of a certain character, and characters are conditioned partly by their heredity, partly by their environment. Therefore acquaintance with the character whom you are to play involves having a point of view about that character's heredity and environment. Put another way, the actor's study of his rôle must be based first on the factual evidence of the text: what the character reveals about himself and what other people in the play reveal about him. Sometimes there may be good reason to suspect the truthfulness of other people. (In *Hamlet*, for instance, in the soliloquies Hamlet is giving the audience his own perfectly frank point of view and Horatio's evidence about Hamlet is apt to be very reliable. The evidence, however, of Claudius or Polonius is more suspect, for both are repeatedly exposed to the audience as untrustworthy. Consequently, when, for instance, they assert that Hamlet is mad, we do not necessarily believe that Hamlet is in fact mad, especially since Claudius and Polonius both have interested motives in saying so.)

Next the actor must draw deductions from the *actions* of the character he is to impersonate. The statement that Hamlet is mad must be weighed against whether Hamlet does indeed behave like a madman or merely as a man pretending to be mad. His actions now and then are wild enough, but is it a pretended wildness? The extreme lucidity of his reasoning throughout the play does not suggest mental disorder. Again, the widely-held critical theory that he is irresolute does not easily square with the events of the play—the murder of Polonius, for example, the execution of Rosencrantz and Guildenstern, his own dealings with the pirates, to say nothing of his break with Ophelia, which may suggest madness or extreme nervous pressure, but is absolutely not irresolute.

Therefore, in determining how he will play his part, the serious actor must do a great deal of preliminary work, putting himself into this or that imaginary situation, not only those expressed in the text, but others deducible from the text. For instance, how did Hamlet's father feel about his son's career at Wittenberg? Was Uncle Claudius the first to express disapproval? On the evidence of the text, was Hamlet really fond of his father or only afraid of him? How account for his mature, sophisticated advice to the players, spoken 'off the cuff' to people much older than himself? Is it not more than the gracious condescension of a well-informed princely amateur? One cannot quite imagine the Prince of Wales in the green-room before a Command Performance at Windsor Castle thus addressing Mr and Mrs Lunt and Bob Hope.

All this preliminary and largely psychoanalytic work must, in the case of so famous and complex a rôle as Hamlet, be based on extensive reading, comparison of the writings of critics and scholars, discussion with colleagues, director, older actors who have played the rôle, and so on. If, however, you are called upon to play only a small part, Francisco, for example, or the second Gravedigger, the preparatory imagining will be easier and take less time.

But, whether the part be long or short, complex or simple, the actor will, sooner or later, have to translate imagination into practice, theory into action, and to this end it will not come amiss if he has paid some attention not only to *what* is to be expressed and *why* but also *how*. Here he will, inevitably, have to pay some attention to what is called theatrical technique.

Imagination and technique

It should be remembered that the division of an actor's work into two compartments, Imagination and Technique, is merely a matter of logical convenience. In fact the two compartments should not, indeed cannot, be kept entirely separate. They overlap and interlock at every stage and in every aspect of the preparation of a play. In the previous paragraph I may have given the impression that thinking and imagination come first, preceding in time the technical matters of giving breath and body to previously conceived ideas. If so, this was simply for the sake of convenience, of trying to be clear and at the same time brief.

With beginners the imaginative process probably does come first, because beginners are as capable of imaginative effort as are veterans and because beginners do not have the veteran's technical accomplishment. They have to learn, almost entirely by experience and at the expense of themselves and the public, how to use their physical equipment: when to move, when to keep still, when to speak slowly and emphatically, when fast and lightly—and not only when but also, harder to learn, how.

Ideally an imaginative intuition should be inseparable from the physical means of its expression. With the most gifted players this is almost always so. But now and again it happens that even the greatest actor will imagine an idea but be unable immediately to find a physical means to express it. He may have to experiment with different emphases, different vocal colours, different inflexions or different movements before he finds the right one. Or, vice versa, he may feel impelled to turn his head, to move his eyes, to breathe more quickly or deeply without immediately knowing why. In general, however, the more gifted the actor, the more completely will his ideas be co-ordinated with the physical means of their expression, and this without the slightest consciousness of such co-ordination. It is the ham who thinks: 'At this point I show anger. Therefore I shout, I stamp, I dilate the nostrils, I clench and unclench the fist.' The truly gifted actor will just feel angry and the technical expressions will occur automatically and in a far less stereotyped manner than those of the ham.

While from time to time imagination may seem to be in one compartment and technique in another, this is an almost entirely artificial distinction. It must be made by teachers and critics and theorists, and by actors, when they are considering the craft which underlies their art. But in the practice of their art they should seek the most complete and unconscious synthesis of theory with practice, imagination with technique.

A logical distinction between imagination and technique and a hoped-for synthesis between the two, exists in all the arts, indeed in all human activity. For instance, the pianist or violinist does not 'put in the expression' by means of solely technical effects. His performance is a mixture of planned form and prearranged effect (analogous to the actor's intellectual and imaginative preparation) with emotional and instinctive reaction to this or that particular occasion. The writer can theoretically distinguish between form and matter, and in the practice of a good writer they are completely interlocked; the one neither precedes nor dominates the other. Indeed one of the measures of the quality of a writer is the degree to which he has achieved the synthesis of form and matter. A great military leader or business administrator or lawyer, doctor or priest is so, in so far as he can unconsciously synthesise theory and practice, form and matter, imagination and technique.

Good and bad

Good acting demands that you are 'convincing' in your part. The audience must be willing to take part in a *ritual*, in which you represent, say, Hamlet. You must be able to sustain this representation 'convincingly': that is to say, you must consistently satisfy the audience's imagination and never outrage its acceptance of the fact that yours is a 'convincing', or consistently credible, Hamlet, Mrs Tanqueray or whatever character you are impersonating.

Now, if you want to make someone believe something, there must be at least some correspondence between the impression which you make and the preconception of your auditor. At a very elementary level, if you say, even to so co-operative an audience as a small child, who is not merely willing but eager to suspend disbelief . . . if you say to him: 'I am a bear and I am going to eat you for my supper', the performance will fall pretty flat if your tone and demeanour are implausible. This does not mean that you must literally imitate a bear's growl and put on a bearskin. That would probably scare your audience into a fit. Your voice and demeanour, however, must, to some limited degree, suggest qualities which your audience will recognise as appropriate to the idea of a bear.

At a less elementary level, if the part of Hamlet is to be convincingly played, the actor must make his auditors believe that his Hamlet has at least some clear connection with their preconception. If they have listened carefully to the first scene of the play, they will have heard that Hamlet is a prince, is young and the heir to a troubled kingdom. So an elderly and vulgar actor will have difficulty in being accepted. But literate people come to *Hamlet* with many, many preconceptions, derived from all sorts of sources. Many of these it is almost the actor's duty NOT to embody; but many of them he cannot avoid. To play Hamlet you must be not only adequately youthful and princely, you must deliver the rhetoric with musicianly appreciation and skill, the passion must be credibly passionate, the wit witty, the grief grievous. The audience must be able to accept that, at every single moment of that gigantically demanding impersonation, your words, gestures, what you seem to be thinking and feeling sufficiently correspond with what the text is telli ng them about Hamlet and with the preconceptions which they have formed. Performance and preconceptions must correspond sufficiently but not necessarily fully: first, no two people's preconceptions are identical and no one's preconception is very detailed or complete. Second, most audiences are willing to take part in the theatre's make-believe (in Coleridge's 'willing suspension of dis-belief') to the extent that they will go half-way to meet the actor, will accept him as a prince unless his lack of princely qualities is acute. The point is that the actor need not completely fulfil the demands of his part; he simply must not fall too short.

Clearly it is harder to meet the demands of parts like Hamlet or King Oedipus, which cover immense ranges of feeling and thought, than those of little parts where you are not called upon to do more than come on and say, 'Tennis, anyone?' But even here you must be able to swing your racket convincingly and when, a little later, your rôle expands to 'I say, Monica, you look divine in blue,' you must eye Monica as though, she really were divine. More than that, you must suggest that you too are divine, since in this, and ten thousand similar light comedies, you and

Monica supply what is called the Love Interest. You must maintain the audience's belief not only in your own impersonation but in the whole goings-on of which you are but one part. To be 'convincing' you must create for yourself and the other actors a convincing environment. This means that the way you use furniture, props, doors, even mere space, the way you look at imaginary objects—all these must be appropriate to the context.

You must learn when to move and when to keep still. Broadly speaking, you must not move when movement would seem unnatural or when a move on your part would draw attention away from something more relevant. For instance, if you are suddenly told a piece of horrifying news you do not, in real life, gesticulate. You may sit, even fall, but more probably for several seconds your whole energy will be concentrated on the message and its implications. Thereafter all sorts of movements and sounds may follow; but at first absolute stillness. There are times when it may be natural for the character whom you are playing to move, but when such movement would distract the focus of attention from something else on stage. You have to learn where, at any given moment, this focus should be, and why; and then learn appropriate ways, and appropriate moments, to shift it.

It is not always realised how easily an audience can be distracted. In ordinary life we accept a great deal of distraction both in sight and sound. Out of a complex of noise, out of many diverse, conspicuous objects, we select what is relevant and reject the rest. But this is not so in the theatre. The audience expects the selective process to have been achieved by the author and director; it expects to have the focus of its attention *directed* to what is relevant, and is easily distracted and irritated if irrelevant impressions are offered. Part of the audience's pleasure in the theatrical experience is that, at any given moment, something significant is happening. This may be no more than an intake of breath, the lifting of an eyebrow. It is intended to be significant. The audience knows this and resents the least distraction.

Of course there are moments when the focus is not so concentrated on a single effect: crowd-scenes, for instance, or group-scenes, like the murder of Julius Caesar, or the sort of ensemble which Chekhov presents, where some people are playing cards, others drinking tea, but where, at any moment, the focus must shift from the ensemble to one individual. Clearly at that moment it is highly inappropriate if one of those who is 'out of focus' pretends to play a trump or spills his tea. One keeps out of focus by avoiding any rapid or jerky movement or change of rhythm. Complete but unnatural stillness is almost more distracting than violent movement.

You must learn how to do only one important thing at a time.

Beginners are for ever trying to run to the door, open it and react to what they see, with gesture, facial expression and audible sounds, all at the same time. You must plan a *sequence* of impressions for the audience. For instance, first indicate that something is happening outside the door. Second, go to the door and open it—the rhythm of these movements will be determined by the nature and urgency of the feeling. Third, look out. Be sure at this point to give the audience time to see you see whatever it is. Finally—react. This may take several seconds. But, if your ideas are intelligibly and feelingly expressed, they will be several interesting seconds for the audience and the tension, amusement or curiosity can be progressively played upon, that is to say the little sequence of impressions must be worked up to a peak. The beginner, frightened of a pause which he does not know how to fill, rushes through the business so fast that nothing is clear and the whole moment is a meaningless blur.

Therefore, to be 'convincing' in even a small part, you need to have not only some aptitude but to know quite a few tricks of the trade. And being 'convincing' is only the beginning of being a good actor. More important than merely to convince is to enlighten. The good actor reveals feelings and ideas and 'nuances' which are only implicit in the text. This means that he must be sufficiently imaginative to discover such implications and sufficiently skilful to express them.

Finally, a good actor must have a quality in his personality which commands the eyes and ears of an audience. The eye of an audience is not held solely by physical beauty—and, anyway, beauty lies in the eye of the beholder and can be considerably enhanced by artifice. Audiences look at actors who have some kind of magnetism. This is largely a matter of self-confidence on the actor's part, the belief that he is, in fact, worth looking at. Similarly, the ear of an audience inclines towards voices which are varied and expressive, rather than merely 'beautiful'. The Voice Beautiful is generally, alas, the Voice Dull. The people to whom one's ear is literally compelled to listen have not necessarily the sweetest, gentlest or even the loudest voices. Probably the most compelling appearances and voices are the most sexually potent; but here again nature can be powerfully reinforced by art.

Good acting, is, first, convincing; then, enlightening; finally compelling. Likewise, bad acting is unconvincing, unenlightening and boring. I have known bad actors with compelling attributes: stunning physique, a magnificent voice. For this reason opera-singers and ballet-dancers can have highly successful careers and be simply terrible actors. I have known bad actors to succeed brilliantly in parts which permitted their very badness to be an advantage. I have known good actors, who through lack of taste or education, can only succeed when well-directed;

and even more good actors who are prevented from being better by egotism, by being unable to realise that the whole of a work of art, in this case the performance of a play, must be greater than even the most brilliant of its parts.

Finally, let us remind ourselves that 'good' and 'bad' are exceedingly subjective terms. Nothing and no one is good all the time and in all circumstances. But a really good actor will never be utterly terrible in anything; and a really bad one, though he may do well in certain parts, will never cause an experienced observer to mistake success for talent.

From *Tyrone Guthrie on Acting*, 1971.

Addicts of the Broadway musical will not need to be told who wrote the words for Wintergreen's campaign song ('He's the man the people choose/ Loves the Irish and the Jews') in Of Thee I Sing, *nor yet that it was the same man who rhymed 'free 'n' easy' with 'Viennesey' for a song unsurprisingly having to do with Strauss. The aforementioned addicts might not even be surprised to discover that this was also the man who came up with 'He will be six foot two/My son-in-law/His haircut will be crew/My son-in-law' nor yet that having penned that he went on to write an entire romantic duet in Spoonerisms.*

But in the end nothing matters about Ira Gershwin (b. 1896) as much as the fact that he wrote the lyrics for Porgy and Bess, *thereby achieving— with his brother George who of course wrote the music—the finest triumph of the American musical theatre. But apart from Cole Porter and now perhaps also Stephen Sondheim, Ira Gershwin was the closest America ever came to Wodehouse and Coward: the same delight in wordplay, the same high-society satire, the same juggler's knack with one-syllable sounds. Ira's lyrics may not always read like the height of literary or poetic achievement, yet in them lies the twentieth-century history of America and no one with access to a gramophone or memories of Astaire and Gertrude Lawrence (two of his most consistent interpreters) need be told any more about that particular magic. Here's how he came to write just one of the standards.*

The Saga of Jenny

LADY IN THE DARK (1941). Music, Kurt Weill. '*Allegretto quasi andantino*'—actually, a sort of blues bordello. In the Third Dream Sequence, Gertrude Lawrence as Liza Elliot is being Tried for Breach of Promise. Having led Kendall Nesbitt to believe she will marry him, she now Cannot Make Up Her Mind. Her Defense is that Dire Complications Frequently Result from Being Too Positive—as follows:

Liza
There once was a girl named Jenny
Whose virtues were varied and many—
Excepting that she was inclined
Always to make up her mind;

168

And Jenny points a moral
With which you cannot quarrel—
As you will find.

Refrain

Jenny made her mind up when she was three
She, herself, was going to trim the Christmas tree.
Christmas Eve she lit the candles—tossed the taper away.
Little Jenny was an orphan on Christmas Day.

Poor Jenny! Bright as a penny!
Her equal would be hard to find.
She lost one dad and mother,
A sister and a brother—
But she would make up her mind.

Jenny made her mind up when she was twelve
That into foreign languages she would delve;
But at seventeen to Vassar it was quite a blow
That in twenty-seven languages she couldn't say no.

Jenny made her mind up at twenty-two
To get herself a husband was the thing to do.
She got herself all dolled up in her satins and furs
And got herself a husband—but he wasn't hers.

Jenny made her mind up at thirty-nine
She would take a trip to the Argentine.
She was only on vacation but the Latins agree
Jenny was the one who started the Good Neighbor Policy.

Jury

Poor Jenny! Bright as a penny!
Her equal would be hard to find.
Oh, passion doesn't vanish
In Portuguese or Spanish—
But she would make up her mind.

Liza

Jenny made her mind up at fifty-one
She would write her memoirs before she was done.
The very day her book was published, hist'ry relates
There were wives who shot their husbands in some
thirty-three states.

Jury

Poor Jenny! Bright as a penny!
Her equal would be hard to find.
　　She could give cards and spade-ies
　　To many other ladies—
But she would make up her mind.

Liza

Jenny made her mind up at seventy-six
She would live to be the oldest woman alive.
But gin and rum and destiny play funny tricks,
And poor Jenny kicked the bucket at seventy-six.

Jury

Jenny points a moral
With which we cannot quarrel.
Makes a lot of common sense!

Liza

Jenny and her saga
Prove that you are gaga
If you don't keep sitting on the fence.

Jury

Jenny and her story
Point the way to glory
To all man and womankind.

All

Anyone with vision
Comes to this decision:
Don't make up—You shouldn't make up—
You mustn't make up—Oh, never make up—
Anyone with vision
Comes to this decision:
DON'T MAKE UP YOUR MIND!

The third musical dream sequence in *Lady in the Dark*, a mixture of Court Trial and Minstrel Show, was practically completed when it was decided that minstrel costume and background weren't novel enough. Agreeing that a circus setting seemed preferable—there could be more riotous colour and regalia—we changed the opening, the jury patters, and most of the recitatives, from an environment of burnt cork and sanded floor to putty nose and tanbark.

One section of this sequence, however, remained unchanged: Liza Elliott's defense of her actions. It was a six- or seven-minute pseudo-metaphysical dissertation based on the signs of the Zodiac and their influences, all pretty fatalistic; in short, she'd done what she did because she couldn't help doing whatever she did do. We were quite proud of this bizarre and *Three Penny Opera*-like effort and felt it could be the play's musical highlight. (We wrote a fourth dream sequence, but this one was not for her analyst. It was a rather extravagant daydream—following a marriage proposal by the Western movie star—in which Liza envisions her possible Hollywood life: an enormous ranch in the San Fernando Valley with a palatial home furnished from the Hearst Collection, butlers galore, private golf course, Chinese cooks, fifty-thousand-barrel gushers on the property, &c. But this twenty-minute daydream—not to be heard by the analyst—was also unheard and unseen by the audience, as the show was already about fifteen or more minutes too long.) Anyway, after some four months of hard work—twelve to sixteen hours a day, and through one of the hottest summers New York had ever known—our contributions to *Lady in the Dark* were completed; and Kurt could now remain in New City across the Hudson to orchestrate, and I return home until the start of rehearsals.

I had been back in California only about a week when producer Sam Harris telephoned me. After long and careful consideration he and Moss Hart felt that the Zodiac number, impressive as it was, might prove too dour and oppressive; something lighter and perhaps gayer was required. I telephoned Kurt. His feeling was, right or wrong, we owed them a go at it, since, generally, everything else we'd done had been found so acceptable. So, a few days later I was again in New York. At one conference Moss had a suggestion that we do a number about a woman who couldn't make up her mind. That sounded possible; and after a week or so of experimenting with style, format, and complete change of melodic mood from the Zodiac song, we started 'Jenny', and finished Liza's new defense about ten days later.

All through rehearsals Miss Lawrence did 'Jenny' most acceptably. But I kept wondering whether it would be as effective as the Zodiac song. This is what happened opening night in Boston: We were playing to a packed house, and the show was holding the audience tensely. It was working out. I was among the standees at the back of the house; next to me was one of the Sam Harris staff. In the circus scene when Danny Kaye completed the last note of 'Tschaikowsky', thunderous applause rocked the theatre for at least a solid minute. The staff member clutched my arm, muttered: 'Christ, we've lost our star!', couldn't take it, and rushed for the lobby. Obviously he felt that nothing could top Danny's rendition, that 'Jenny' couldn't compete with it, and that either Miss Lawrence would leave the show or that Danny Kaye would have to be cut down to size.

But he should have waited. The next few lines of dialogue weren't heard because of the continuing applause. Then, as Danny deferred to Miss Lawrence, it ended; and 'Jenny' began. She hadn't been singing more than a few lines when I realised an interpretation we'd never seen at rehearsal was materialising. Not only were there new nuances and approaches, but on top of this she 'bumped' it and 'ground' it, to the complete devastation of the audience. At the conclusion, there was an ovation which lasted twice as long as that for 'Tschaikowsky.' 'Tschaikowsky' had shown us the emergence of a new star in Danny Kaye. But 'Jenny' revealed to us that we didn't have to worry about losing our brighter-than-ever star.

It is easier to predict correctly what will happen to the stock market than what show numbers will do. One hopes for the best, but one best remain non-committal. Not everyone does, though. Three or four nights after the Boston opening, with *Lady* looking like a big hit, Kurt told me he hadn't wanted to worry me but this is what occurred after the dress rehearsal. Hassard Short, a top revue man of excellent taste, in charge of the show's physical production and lighting, took Kurt aside and said: 'If you take my advice, you boys had better get two new numbers ready in a hurry. You'll find that "Jenny" and the Russian number won't make it.'

From *Lyrics on Several Occasions*, 1959.

Sir Max Beerbohm (1872-1956) succeeded Bernard Shaw (who first named him 'the incomparable Max') as drama critic of the Saturday Review *in 1898, and wrote this study of GBS in December 1905 at the time of the Vedrenne-Barker seasons at the Court. It is followed by* The Art of Rehearsal, *a letter written by Shaw (1856-1950) in 1921 to an Irish theatre colleague who'd asked him for advice and information.*

Mr Shaw's Position

IT MUST amuse him, whenever he surveys it; and I hope he will some day write a comedy around it. It bristles with side-lights on so many things—on human character in general, and on the English character in particular, and on the particular difficulties that genius encounters in England, and on the right manner of surmounting them.

For years Mr Shaw was writing plays, some of which, by hook or crook, in holes and corners, were produced. They were witnessed, and loudly applauded, by such ladies and gentlemen as were in or around the Fabian Society. Not that these people took their socialist seriously as a playwright. They applauded his work in just the spirit in which, had he started a racing-stable, they would have backed his horses. He was taken with some measure of seriousness by such of the professional critics as were his personal friends, and were not hide-bound by theatrical tradition. Here, they perceived, was something new in the theatre; and, liking to be in advance of the time, they blew their trumpets in their friend's honour. The rest of the professional critics merely sniffed or cursed, according to their manners. The public took no notice at all. Time passed. In Berlin, Munich, Vienna, and elsewhere, Mr Shaw was now a popular success. Perhaps in the hope that England had caught an echo of this exotic enthusiasm, Messrs Vedrenne and Barker ventured to produce *John Bull's Other Island.* England had not caught that echo. There was only the usual little succès d'estime. But, not long after its production, the play was witnessed by a great lady, who advised an august person to witness it; and this august person persuaded a person yet more august to witness it. It had been withdrawn, meanwhile; so there was 'a command performance'. All the great ladies, and all the great gentlemen, were present; also, several paragraphists. That evening

Mr Shaw became a fashionable craze; and within a few days all London knew it. The Savoy restaurant is much frequented by fashion, and by paragraphy; and its revenues are drawn mainly from the many un-fashionable people who go to feast their eyes on the people who are fashionable beyond dispute. No large restaurant can live by the aristo-cracy alone. Nor can even a small theatre. Mr Shaw 'pays' now because now the English middle class pays to see that which is seen and approved by the English upper class, and (more especially) to see the English upper class. Whether either of these classes really rejoices in Mr Shaw, as yet, is a point on which I am doubtful. I went to see *Man and Super-man* a few nights ago. The whole audience was frequently rocking with laughter, but mostly at the wrong moments. (I admit that Mr Shaw's thoughts are often so profound, and his wit is always so swift, that to appreciate his plays rightly and fully at a first hearing is rather an achievement.) But it was obvious that the whole audience was very happy indeed. It was obvious that Mr Shaw is an enormous success. And in the round-about way by which success has come to him is cast a delicious light on that quality for which England is specially notable among the nations.

His success is not gratifying to the critics. To those critics who are incapable of exercising their brains, and who have always resented Mr Shaw vehemently, it is of course, galling to find themselves suddenly at odds with public opinion—the opinion which they are accustomed to 'voice'. Having slated *John Bull*, and slated *Man and Superman*, they must have been in a fearful dilemma about the play produced at the Court Theatre last week, *Major Barbara*. Perhaps this, too, was going to 'catch on'. Would it not be safer to climb down, and write moderate eulogies? I suspect it was stupidity as much as pride that diverted them from this ignominious course. They really could not make head or tail of the play. They were sure that this time Shaw really had come a cropper—had really delivered himself into their hands. 'A success, are you? Pet of the public, are you? We'll see about that. *We*'ll pet-of-the-public you. *We*'ll' etc., etc. The old cries—'no drama-tist,' 'laughing at his audience,' and the like—were not sufficient, this time. 'Brute' and 'blasphemer' were added. In the second act of the play, Mr Shaw has tried to show some of the difficulties with which the Salvation Army has to cope. A ruffian comes to one of the shelters in quest of a woman who has been rescued from living with him. A Salvation 'lass' bars his way, and refuses to yield. He strikes her in the face. The incident is not dragged in. It is necessary to the purpose of the whole scene. Nor has any one ventured to suggest that it is an exaggeration of real life. Nor is the incident enacted realistically on the stage of the Court Theatre. At the first performance, anyhow, the actor impersonating the ruffian aimed a noticeably gentle blow in the air, at a noticeably great distance from the face of the actress impersonating the lass. I happen to be particularly squeamish in the matter of physical violence on the stage. I have winced at the smothering of Desdemona, for example, when it has been done with anything like realism. The mere symbolism at the Court Theatre gave me not the faintest qualm— not, I mean, the faintest physical qualm: æsthetically, of course, I was touched, as Mr Shaw had a right to touch me. And it seems to me that the critics who profess to have been disgusted and outraged must have been very hard up for a fair means of attack. Equally unfair, for that it may carry conviction to the minds of people who have not seen the play, is the imputation of blasphemy. Mr Shaw is held up to execration because he has put into the mouth of Major Barbara certain poignant words of Our Lord. To many people, doubtless, it is a screamingly funny joke that a female should have a military prefix. Also, there is no doubt that Mr Shaw's play abounds in verbal wit, and in humorous situations. But the purport of the play is serious; and the character of Major Barbara is one of the two great factors in it. With keenest insight and sense of spiritual beauty, Mr Shaw reveals to us in her the typical religious fanatic of her kind. Sense of spiritual beauty is not one of the qualities hitherto suspected in Mr Shaw; but here it certainly is; and I defy even the coarsest mind not to perceive it. (To respect it is another matter.) When Major Barbara comes to the great spiritual crisis of her life, and when she believes that all the things she had trusted in have fallen away from her, what were more natural than that she should utter the words of agony that are most familiar to her? That any sane creature in the audience could have been offended by the utterance, I refuse to believe. It was as inoffensive as it was dramatically right. And the critics who have turned up the whites of their eyes, and have doubtless prejudiced against the play many worthy people who have not, like them, had the opportunity of seeing it, must submit to one of two verdicts—insanity or hypocrisy. I have no doubt that of these two qualities they will prefer to confess the latter. It is the more typically British.

In that delicate comedy, *Mr Shaw's Position*, the parts played by these critics seem rather crude. There is a subtler fun in the parts played by some of the superior critics—the critics who were eager to lend helping hands to Mr Shaw in the time of his obscurity. So long as he was 'only *so* high,' and could be comfortably patted on the head, they made a pet of him. Now that he strides gigantic, they are less friendly. They seem even anxious to trip him up. Perhaps they do not believe in the genuineness of his growth, and suspect some trick of stilts. That would be a quite natural scepticism. A great man cannot be appreciated fully by his intimate contemporaries. Nor can his great success be ever quite palatable to them, however actively they may have striven to win it for him. To fight for a prince who has to be hiding in an oak-tree is a gallant and pleasant adventure; but when one sees the poor creature enthroned, with a crown on his head and a sceptre in his hand, one's sentiments are apt to cool. And thus the whilom champions of Mr Shaw's virtues are now preoccupied mainly with Mr Shaw's defects. The old torches are still waved, but perfunctorily; and the main energy is devoted to throwing cold water. Whereas the virtues of Mr Shaw used to be extolled with reservations for the defects, now the defects are condemned with reservations for the virtues. Mr Shaw, it is insisted, cannot draw life: he can only distort it. He has no knowledge of human nature: he is but a theorist. All his characters are but so many incarnations of himself. Above all, he cannot write plays. He has no dramatic instinct, no theatrical technique. And these objections are emphatically reiterated (often with much brilliancy and ingenuity) by the superior critics, while all the time the fact is staring them in the face that Mr Shaw has created in *Major Barbara* two characters—Barbara and her father—who live with an intense vitality; a crowd of minor characters that are accurately observed (though some are purposely exaggerated) from life; and one act—the second—which is as cunning and closely-knit a piece of craftsmanship as any conventional playwright could achieve, and a cumulative appeal to emotions which no other living playwright has touched. With all these facts staring them in the face, they still maintain that Mr Shaw is not a playwright.

That theory might have held water in the days before Mr Shaw's plays were acted. Indeed, I was in the habit of propounding it myself. I well remember that when the two volumes of *Plays, Pleasant and Unpleasant* were published, and the ordinary dramatic criticisms in this Review were still signed G.B.S., I wrote here a special article in which I pointed out that the plays, delightful to the reader, would be quite impossible on the stage. This simply proved that I had not enough theatrical imagination to see the potentialities of a play through reading it in print. When, later, I saw performances of *Mrs Warren's Profession*, *The Devil's Disciple*, and *You Never Can Tell*, I found, to my great surprise, that they gained much more than they lost by being seen and not read. Still, the old superstition lingered in my brain. I had not learnt my lesson. When *Man and Superman* was published, I called it 'Mr Shaw's Dialogues,' and said that (even without the philosophic scene in hell) it would be quite unsuited to any stage. When I saw it performed, I determined that I would not be caught tripping again. I found that as a piece of theatrical construction it was perfect. As in *John Bull's Other Island*, so in *Major Barbara* (excepting the aforesaid second act), there is none of that tight construction which was in the previous plays. There is little story, little action. Everything depends on the interplay of various types of character and of thought. But to order this process in such a way that it shall not be tedious requires a very great amount of technical skill. During the third act of *Major Barbara*, I admit, I found my attention wandering. But this aberration was not due to any loosening of Mr Shaw's grip on his material. It was due simply to the fact that my emotions had been stirred so much in the previous act that my cerebral machine was not in proper working order. Mr Shaw ought to have foreseen that effect. In not having done so, he is guilty of a technical error. But to deny that he is a dramatist merely because he chooses, for the most part, to get drama out of contrasted types of character and thought, without action, and without appeal to the emotions, seems to me both unjust and absurd. His technique is peculiar because his purpose is peculiar. But it is not the less technique.

There! I have climbed down. Gracefully enough to escape being ridiculous? I should like mine to be a 'sympathetic' part in *Mr Shaw's Position*.

From the *Saturday Review*, 9 December 1905.

The Art of Rehearsal

My Dear McNulty:

As to stage technique, there are several stage techniques; and people may be very clever in one or more of them without being good at them all, and may even—especially in acting—know bits of them and not the the rest. The beginning and end of the business from the author's point of view is the art of making the audience believe that real things are happening to real people. But the actor, male or female, may want the audience to believe that it is witnessing a magnificent display of acting by a great artist; and when the attempt to do this fails, the effect is disastrous, because then there is neither play nor great acting: the play is not credible nor the acting fascinating. To your star actor the play does not exist except as a mounting block. That is why comparatively humble actors, who do not dare to think they can succeed apart from the play, often give much better representations than star casts.

Many star actors have surprisingly little of what I call positive skill, and an amazing power of suggestion. You can safely write a play in which the audience is assured that the heroine is the most wonderful creature on earth, full of exquisite thoughts, and noble in character to the utmost degree, though, when it comes to the point, you find yourself unable to invent a single speech or action that would surprise you from your aunt. No matter: a star actress at $1,000 a week will do all that for you. She will utter your twaddle with such an air, and look such unutterable things between the lines, and dress so beautifully and move so enigmatically and enchantingly, that the imagination of the audience will supply more than Shakespeare could have written.

This art of suggestion has been developed to an abnormal degree by the emptiness of the mechanical 'well-made play' of the French school. And you may be tempted to say: 'If this woman is so wonderful when she is making bricks without straw, what heights would she not reach if I were to give her straw in abundance?' But if you did, you would be rudely disillusioned. You would have to say to the actress: 'Mere suggestion is no use here. I don't ask you to suggest anything: I give you the actual things to do and say. I don't want you to look as if you could say wonderful things if you uttered your thoughts: I give you both the thoughts and the words; and you must get them across the footlights.' On these conditions your star might be dreadfully at a loss. She might complain of having too many words. She would certainly try hard to get in her old suggestive business between the lines; to escape from the play; to substitute a personal performance of her own for the character you wanted to make the audience believe her to be; and thus your trouble with her would be in direct proportion to her charm as a fashionable leading lady.

The success of the Dublin Abbey Street Theatre was due to the fact that, when it began, none of the company was worth twopence a week for ordinary fashionable purposes, though some of them can now hold a London audience in the hollow of their hands. They were held down by Yeats and Lady Gregory ruthlessly to my formula of making the audience believe that real things were happening to real people. They were taught no tricks, because Yeats and Lady Gregory didn't know any, having found out experimentally only what any two people of high intelligence and fine taste could find out by sticking to the point of securing a good representation.

Now as to your daily business in the theatre. It will be more laborious than you expect. If before you begin rehearsing you sit down to the manuscript of your play and work out all the stage business; so that you know where every speech is to be spoken as well as what it is to convey, and where the chairs are to be and where they are to be taken to, and where the actors are to put their hats or anything else they have to take in their hands in the course of the play, and when they are to rise and when they are to sit, and if you arrange all this so as to get the maximum of effect out of every word, and thus make the actors feel that they are speaking at the utmost possible advantage—or at worst that they cannot improve on your business however little they may like it—and if you take care that they never distract attention from one another; that when they call to one another they are at a due distance; and that, when the audience is looking at one side of the stage and somebody cuts in on the other, some trick (which you must contrive) calls the attention of the audience to the new point of view or hearing, etc., then you will at the first rehearsal get a command of the production that nothing will shake afterward. There will be no time wasted in fumbling for positions, and trying back and disputing.

When you have put your actors through an act for the first time in this way, go through it again to settle the business firmly in their memory. Be on the stage, handling your people and prompting them with the appropriate tones, as they will, of course, be rather in the dark as to what it is all about, except what they may have gathered from your reading the play to them before rehearsal. Don't let them learn their parts until the end of the first week of rehearsal: nothing is a greater nuisance than an actor who is trying to remember his lines when he should be settling his position and getting the hang of the play with his book in his hand.

One or two acts twice over is enough for each preliminary rehearsal. When you have reached the end of this first stage, then call 'perfect' rehearsals (that is, without books). At these you must leave the stage and sit in the auditorium with a big notebook, *and from that time forth never interrupt a scene, nor allow anyone else to interrupt it or try back.* When anything goes wrong, or any improvement occurs to you, make a note; and at the end of the act go on the stage and explain your notes to the actors. Don't criticise. If a thing is wrong and you don't know exactly how to set it right say nothing. Wait until you find out the right thing to do, or until the actor does. It discourages and maddens an actor to be told merely that you are dissatisfied. If you cannot help him, let him alone. Tell him what to do if you know: if not, hold your tongue until it comes to you or to him, as it probably will if you wait.

Remember that when the 'perfect' rehearsals begin, the whole affair will collapse in apparent and most disappointing backsliding for at least a week as far as the long parts are concerned, because in the first agony of trying to remember the words everything else will be lost. You must remember that at this stage the actor, being under a heavy strain, is fearfully irritable. But after another week the words will come automatically; and the play will get under way again.

Remember (particularly during the irritable stage) that you must not tell an actor too much all at once. Not more than two or three important things can be borne at one rehearsal; and *don't* mention trifles, such as slips in business or in words, in a heartbroken desperate way, as if the world were crumbling in ruins. Don't mention anything that doesn't really matter. Be prepared for the same mistake being repeated time after time, and your directions being forgotten until you have given them three or four days running.

If you get angry, and complain that you have repeatedly called attention, etc, like a schoolmaster, you will destroy the whole atmosphere in which art breathes, and make a scene which is not in the play, and a very disagreeable and invariably unsuccessful scene at that. Your chief artistic activity will be to prevent the actors taking their tone and speed from one another, instead of from their own parts, and thus destroying the continual variety and contrast which are the soul of liveliness in comedy and truth in tragedy. An actor's cue is not a signal to take up the running thoughtlessly, but a provocation to retort or respond in some clearly differentiated way. He must, even on the thousandth night, make the audience believe that he has never heard his cue before.

180

In the final stage, when everybody is word perfect, and can give his or her whole mind to the play, you must watch, watch, watch, like a cat at a mouse hole, and make very well-considered notes. To some of them you will append a 'Rehearse this'; and at the end of the act you will ask them to go through the bit to get it right. But *don't* say when it doesn't come right: 'We must go on at this until we get it, if we have to stay here all night': the schoolmaster again. If it goes wrong, it will go wronger with every repetition on the same day. Leave it until next time.

At the last two rehearsals you ought to have very few notes: all the difficulties should have been cleared away. The first time I ever counted my notes was when I had to produce *Arms and the Man* in ten rehearsals. The total was 600. That is a minimum: I have run into thousands since. Do not forget that though at the first rehearsal you will know more about the parts than the actors, at the last rehearsal they ought to know more about them (through their undivided attention) than you, and therefore have something to teach you about them.

Be prepared for a spell of hard work. The incessant strain on one's attention (the actors have their exits and rests; but the producer is hard at it all the time), the social effort of keeping up everyone's spirits in view of a great event, the dryness of the previous study of the mechanical details, daunt most authors. But if you have not energy to face all that, you had better keep out of the theatre and trust to a professional producer. In fact, it sometimes happens that the author has to be put out. Unless he goes through the grind I have described, and which I face with greater reluctance as I grow older, he simply bothers and complains and obstructs, either saying that he does not like what the actors are doing without knowing what he wants instead, or at the first rehearsal expecting a perfect performance, or wanting things that can't be done, or making his suggestions ridiculous by unskilful demonstrations, or quarrelling, or devil knows what not.

Only geniuses can tell you exactly what is wrong with a scene, though plenty of people can tell that there is something wrong with it. So make a note of their dissatisfaction; but be very careful how you adopt their cure if they prescribe one. For instance, if they say a scene is too slow (meaning that it bores them), the remedy in nine cases out of ten is for the actors to go slower and bring out the meaning better by contrasts of tone and speed.

Never have a moment of silence on the stage except as an intentional stage effect. The play must not stop while an actor is sitting down or getting up or walking off the stage. The last word of an exit speech must get the actor off the stage. He must sit on a word and rise on a word; if he has to make a movement, he must move as he speaks and not before or after;

and the cues must be picked up as smartly as a ball is fielded in cricket. This is the secret of pace, and of holding an audience. It is a rule which you may set aside again and again to make a special effect; for a technical rule may always be broken on purpose. I once saw a fine play of Masefield's prolonged by half an hour and almost ruined because the actors made their movements in silence between the speeches. That does not happen when his plays are produced by Granville-Barker or by himself.

Remember that no strangers should be present at a rehearsal. It is sometimes expedient that strangers, and even journalists, be invited to witness a so-called rehearsal: and on such occasions a prearranged interruption by the producer may take place to affirm the fact that the occasion is only a rehearsal. But the interruption must be addressed to the mechanical staff about some mechanical detail. No direction should ever be given to an actor in the presence of a stranger; and the consent of every actor should be obtained before a stranger is admitted. The actor, of course, is bound to the same reticence. A stranger is a non-professional who is not in the theatre on business. Rehearsals are absolutely and sacredly confidential. The publication of gossip about rehearsals, or the disclosure of the plot of a play, is the blackest breach of stage etiquette.

I have tumbled all this out at express speed, as the best I can do for you out of my own experience, in reply to your innocent question about technique. I hope it is intelligible and may be helpful.

From *Arts League of Service Annual*, 1921–22.

The third and last of my godparents to appear in this archive, Alexander Woollcott (1887–1943) was the only one I never met. In 1941 my father had created for London the role of Sheridan Whiteside (widely believed to have been based on Woollcott) in the Kaufman and Hart comedy The Man Who Came To Dinner; because I was born on the first night, I acquired the christian name of the title character, and Woollcott agreed he'd be my godfather and wrote that one day when the war was over he'd come across the Atlantic to have a look at me.

One day in January 1943, by which time I was all of thirteen months, Woollcott went into a grocery store in New York, ordered a large tin of biscuits to be posted to us in Berkshire, went on to the CBS radio studios to do one of his coast-to-coast broadcasts, collapsed on the air and died a few hours later. I would like to have known him: an irascible but, by all accounts, enthralling figure, he was a playwright, biographer, essayist, journalist, gossip and critic who at the time of his death was probably the most powerful literary huckster in America and within only three decades of it had become largely unknown outside a small New York circle of friends and enemies. A kind of American amalgam of Cyril Connolly and Kenneth Tynan, Woollcott was a lifelong friend of (among many others) Harpo Marx and Dorothy Parker and Noël Coward, a member of the Algonquin Round Table, an inveterate editor of anthologies, a publicist for a wide range of appallingly sentimental novels, and a compulsive letter-writer to the famous.

He left almost nothing behind him except various collections, often of the same material : Ross of the New Yorker, who shared a long and acrimonious friendship with Woollcott, once said he had the 'damndest ability' of making double, triple and even quadruple use of everything he wrote. He was in short a hack of the very best kind, but Kaufman (who co-wrote the play about him), Rebecca West, the Marx Brothers and the Lunts all acknowledged a debt of some kind to him and that alone must suggest a certain catholicity of interest. An early defender of Faulkner and Hemingway and Steinbeck, he was also capable of broadcasting in fervent favour of a book called Beside the Bonnie Briar Bush and of another called The Chicken Wagon Family.

Still, Chaplin dedicated The Gold Rush to Woollcott and his opinion was always among the first sought by London actors about to tackle Broadway. He was in fact a man for all seasons and for most people some of the time. Here, in 1934, he is writing about Katharine Cornell, then 36 and already beginning to make her name as one of the first ladies of Broadway.

Miss Kitty Takes to the Road

THE LAST time I saw the Divine Sarah, she was a ravaged and desiccated old woman with one leg. And the foot of that one was already in the grave. Indeed, she had only two months left for living. But the prospect of such an untimely taking off was never in her jaunty scheme of things, and when I went around to call upon her in that fusty and frightening museum on the Boulevard Pereire, which was her home when she was in Paris, she made it clear that her thoughts were even then at play with the witching possibility of just one more farewell tour of America—that charming America where she had always been so uncritically applauded and so handsomely paid. My French was equal to the modest task of assuring her how ravished my country would be by these glad tidings. This time, she said, she would not attempt a long tour. In the voice of one who rather hopes to be shouted down, she explained that she was now much too old for such cross-country junketing. Too old? At this suggestion I was gallantly incredulous. 'Yes, young man, much too old,' she continued sadly. 'Of course, I shall play Boston and New York and Philadelphia and Baltimore and Washington. And perhaps Buffalo and Cleveland and Detroit and Kansas City and St Louis and Denver and San Francisco. But at my age I cannot attempt one of those really long tours.'

Thus, in all seriousness, the great Bernhardt when approaching her eighties. Hers was a viewpoint which seemed both alien and anachronistic in an era when there had come into possession of the New York stage a generation of players who regarded any departure from Broadway as penitential, who thought of Manhattan Transfer as a wild frontier town, and who, when induced to play three or four seacoast cities in the trial flight of a new play, would return to New York from the strain of such an exhausting expedition quite too prostrated to speak above a whisper. But Bernhardt, like all the great men and women of the theatre of her time, was a trouper. Of the younger stars now shining brightest in the theatrical firmament only one is entitled to be called by that name. That one is Katharine Cornell.

When, at the end of June, she sailed to take her well-earned ease beside the Mediterranean and brood over the prompt book of *Rosmersholm*, with which darkling tragedy she will make her first excursion into the leafy and beckoning depths of Henrik Ibsen, she had just completed an extraordinary season. With her repertory of three fine plays, her company of sixty persons—to say nothing of Flush—and her special car presided over by the only bearded porter in the entire personnel of the Pullman Company, that season had taken her on a journey of more than sixteen thousand miles and had involved her appearance in more than seventy-four cities. From Waco, Texas, to Portland, Maine, from Tacoma, Washington, to Montgomery, Alabama, she had taken to the road with such plays as the *Romeo and Juliet*, of Shakespeare, the *Candida*, of Mr Bernard Shaw and—most popular item in her bag of tricks—*The Barretts of Wimpole Street*, by Mr Rudolf Besier. She had taken along as fine a troupe as she could assemble, offering the country at large considerably better entertainment than had been offered it in twenty years. She had moved through sandstorms and blizzards and cloudbursts, and never failed to keep an engagement. She had come to towns where a large percentage of her eager audience had never seen a play before and were entirely unfamiliar with the idiom of the theatre. She had opened up mildewed and cobwebby opera houses which had stood dark so long that the guy ropes broke as they swung the scenery into place, the only surviving stage hands were so ancient that their palsied hands faltered at their tasks, and outraged rats ran startled along the footlight troughs during the performance. She had, incidentally, played to such huge and enthusiastic audiences that, by her unprecedented venture, she came home with a very considerable fortune.

It was a venture so personal and so isolated in the springs of its motive that it would be easy to exaggerate its importance as the harbinger of a new day. But with all due allowance for that reservation, it would still be true to say that Katharine Cornell had reminded the people of her day that there once had been and still was a vast and inviting province called 'the road'. The effect on her own career is a story only time can tell, but, as a direct result of the Cornell tour and triumph, Helen Hayes in *Mary of Scotland* and George M. Cohan in the delightful Eugene O'Neill play called *Ah, Wilderness* will embark in September on tours as heroic and as prolonged as hers. If Miss Hayes is even now booked for Wichita in Kansas and Shreveport in Louisiana, if the incomparable Cohan is planning now to play, if only for one night, in Erie, Pennsylvania, and Little Rock, Arkansas, it is only because in the season just past Katharine Cornell rediscovered America.

Perhaps, in what I have thus far said and in what I may hereinafter say, there is conveyed the suggestion that until Miss Cornell took to the road, the towns which lie off the small beaten track of the theatre had in recent years known no theatrical entertainment whatever. That is almost true, but not quite. There had been some. For example, many of these more remote ports of call did experience the visits of *The Green Pastures* and Walter Hampden. Some had bowed low when, three years ago,

Maude Adams and Otis Skinner took to the one-night stands. And only last season the dauntless Eva Le Gallienne tried her luck at a swing around the circle.

But at the risk of seeming invidious, I must make it clear that the arrival of one of these in any town could not possibly have seemed so glamorous and eventful as did the triumphant visit of Miss Cornell. No, if I lived in Sioux City, Iowa, or in Dallas, Texas, I would know that none of these proffered entertainments was faintly comparable with the advent of a gleaming and immensely successful young star at the crest of her career, bringing a fine troupe, either in a Shakespearean production which New York would not be privileged to see for another year or the watchfully refreshed masterpiece which had been one of the shining successes of the theatre. Such a boon—rain in abundance after a long drought—would be comparable only to the coming of Helen Hayes in *Mary of Scotland* or to the arrival, let us say, of the Lunts in *Reunion in Vienna*.

In these analogies it is implicit that such a tour can be successfully made only by one of such reputation that his or her name, written in lamps above a theatre door, is both a summons and a guaranty. The Lunts in *Reunion in Vienna*? Has Sioux City a chance of seeing them in that diverting climax of their partnership? I doubt it. Indeed, for their own sakes, I hope not. You see, they have already played it for a season in New York and in some fourteen of the larger American cities. They have also played it for a triumphant season in London. It is quite true that after a somnolent summer on their farm at Genesee Depot in Wisconsin, they could take it forth on a tour such as Miss Cornell so successfully completed. There would be at least another season of tremendous audiences and overflowing coffers. It would be pleasant for Austin, Texas, and for Mr Sherwood, who wrote the play. But it would mean another year's confinement to roles of which the Lunts have already exhausted the most important satisfactions. Their own pleasure in their profession and their growth in their art alike demand that they turn to the refreshment of new tasks.

It is stultifying for an actor to follow the vicious old American habit of continuing to play a part indefinitely just because there is a line at the box office waiting to see it. What of it? After five years of imprisonment in the success of *Rain*, the madness of the caged came upon poor Jeanne Eagels, and in a sense she died of that madness. Hers was the desperation and the death of the trapped. In protest against such bondage, John Barrymore was ever rebellious and it was largely on this account that he at last deserted the house of his fathers. In London, the matchless Elizabeth Bergner, an exile from Nazi Germany, who is probably the ablest actress in the world today, has found herself caught in a like success, and escaped from it for a time last spring only by a singularly persuasive fit of hysterics.

It was Miss Cornell herself who startled the money changers in the temple by striking out at the deeply planted but essentially absurd tradition that, like *Abie's Irish Rose* and *Chu-Chin-Chow*, a play must, for the sake of the management and the author's bank account, go on running as long as it is profitable. When *The Barretts* had completed its first year at the Empire Theatre in New York and was giving every sign of going on playing for at least another year, Miss Cornell, although more than twenty thousand dollars was pouring into the box office every week, calmly packed up her costumes and started off on tour. She did not want to get locked in the same play indefinitely and she was already deeply imbued with the wisdom of playing as many cities as possible. New York? As the late Minnie Maddern Fiske used to say, New York's just a stand.

By that notion of hers you must account for Miss Cornell's arriving, bag and baggage, in seventy-four towns last season. Her deepest motive may be no more complicated than the fact that she likes to travel. Like Mrs Fiske, she is instinctively vagrant. As the man in *The First Year* said of his wife when she wanted to go to Joplin, 'That woman's just train-crazy.'

But it is the guess of at least one onlooking neighbour that another force has contributed a good deal to Miss Cornell's decision to use for her career a pattern which everyone else had thought forever gone out of fashion. I mean the influence of her director and adviser, Guthrie McClintic, who is also, incidentally, her husband. In my diagnosis, considerable importance must be attached to the fact that he was once a stage-struck youngster in Seattle, his insatiable passion for the theatre nourished, or at least tantalised, by the visits of such stars as Olga Nethersole, Mrs Fiske and Maude Adams, by stray numbers of the old *Theatre Magazine*, from which he would clip half-tones for his scrapbook, and by the engagements of the Charles A. Taylor Rep Company, which used to take over the tottering old Third Avenue Theatre every summer. Taylor was the author of such hardy perennials as *From Rags to Riches* and *The Queen of the White Slaves*, and the McClintic boy became so interested that, when he wasn't sitting goggle-eyed in his balcony seat, he used to loiter around the stage door for forbidden glimpses of the shabby world behind the scenes. He thinks now that even then he discerned a real talent in old Taylor's young wife, who was introduced to Seattle in the ingénue roles and later became leading woman of the stock company. Her name was Laurette.

McClintic went from Seattle to New York to study at a dramatic school, but by the time Katharine Cornell made her first appearance on the stage, acting a tiny part with the Washington Square Players, he had become discouraged by the general apathy over his own prospects of ever becoming a Mansfield and had decided, instead, to be the David Belasco of the next generation. As a first step, he succeeded, by really alarming insistence, in getting the job of assistant to Winthrop Ames, an elegant, fastidious and overly meticulous producer from Boston in whose faintly Georgian Little Theatre startled and gratified guests used to be served after-dinner coffee between the acts. Sometimes some of the shows were good too. One of his new assistant's functions was that of scout. It was among his duties to attend all the plays and make programme notations after each new name for the voluminous files at the Ames office. Thus it befell that there is an actual record there of that otherwise undistinguished occasion when Mr McClintic first clapped eyes upon the young actress with whose destinies his own were later to be linked. Opposite her name when he filed the programme for reference next day was the notation: 'Monotonous. Interesting. Watch.'

Well, that was many years ago. Miss Kitty, as he calls her, is nominally under her own management, but, none the less, he is her chief counselor, and if it is now her policy to stir the dust in forgotten circuits, it is chiefly, I suspect, because she is living up to the notion of what a star should be which was formed in Seattle long ago. McClintic still thinks of a great star, not as one who rules a playhouse on Broadway or in London, but rather as an annual event, as one who is forever arriving by train, scenery and costumes and all, from some haze-hung and mysterious distance.

Let us admit that even in the palmiest days there were never enough of these to go around, that for the most part they were third and fourth rate actors who used to hit Seattle with a tremendous and unpersuasive pretence of being Marlowes and Mansfields. It is these which have vanished from the scene, unable to compete with the movies. Wherefore, for a time only a few plays came each year and then only one or none at all.

Stand with me in the lobby of a West Coast theatre watching the line at the box office. One woman, puzzled by the price of the ticket, discovers only from the ticket seller himself that this is a cast of real flesh-and-blood actors who have come by train instead of by parcel post. At such a dazzling prospect, she is beside herself with excitement. She has never seen a real play before. Behind her in line is a small boy who wants to know how many bread coupons you must collect before you can get a ticket. I know not in what heathenish school of entertainment he has been brought up. Behind him a woman is hesitant because the seats offered her are so far forward. She is afraid the flicker will disturb her.

And so on and so on. When I think of what, in my salad days, the theatre meant to me, as I came to know it at the old Coates Opera House in Kansas City or later at the Broad Street Theatre in Philadelphia, where I kept the red plush of the gallery moist with my tears over the nightly death of Nat Goodwin as Nathan Hale, I feel a pang in my heart at the sight of these dark deserted theatres throughout the country and even find myself thinking of a tour like Miss Cornell's as akin to the adventure which long ago in Polynesia befell one black sheep whose folks I knew. Lost or strayed from some pearl-diving expedition, he stumbled upon a long-forgotten colony of Puritans who still guarded the Bible their forefathers had brought with them out of England three centuries before. But now none of them knew how to penetrate to the gospel imprisoned in the black characters on every page and, because they had nursed my friend back to health, he stayed with them long enough to teach their youngsters the lost art of reading.

If you crave testimony to the deep hunger for the theatre which the turn of the wheel and the play of economic forces have left unsatisfied in our time throughout the greater part of America, you should have seen the vast audiences which, in the decaying death of the depression, were mobilised in Iowa and Kansas and Tennessee by the news that Miss Cornell was coming that way. You should have seen the cheering multitude which surged around the Tulane stage door in New Orleans, waiting for a glimpse of the star on her way to her hotel. You should have seen those Texas audiences in Amarillo and Dallas and Austin and San Antonio and Houston and Fort Worth, made up of people who had waited months for this opportunity and driven hundreds of miles to see the play. Such response is warming to the heart, but I think Miss Cornell should warn her sisters in the theatre that they must not, therefore, count upon a grateful hinterland to throw out the welcoming red carpet. If the Lunts, for instance, fired by the heroic example set by Miss Cornell and Miss Hayes, should consider forsaking New York and London to follow in their footsteps, they might make the great decision in a moment of graciousness—'Alfred, dear, these people need us so'— or even in a glow of missionary zeal. But their management would, nevertheless, have to fight every step of the way even to get a hearing for them.

In many a town to which no play has come in recent years, I have heard the bereft citizenry saying in aggrieved accents, 'They never send us plays any more,' for all the world as if the drama could be scattered over the land like seeds by a congressman; as if, indeed, some vague undefined department in the National Government had thereby failed in its appointed constitutional task. These discontented ones never think to inquire what would happen if a play actually had the temerity to suggest visiting their fair city. The chances are it would find no theatre available at all. And even the Lunts, on this hypothetical tour of theirs, must be prepared to act away like mad in structures more inappropriate than any Alfred Lunt himself has known since he used to play for pins in the barn at Genesee Depot.

When you play seventy-four cities in a season, you can count on finding theatres in only a few of them, and some of those will be old opera houses so neglected that the star must give up her dream of hot water with which to remove her make-up, huddling as best she may in a community cubby-hole which has not been cleaned since last it was occupied by the late Sol Smith Russell. If no theatre is still left standing, she must dispossess a movie or make shift in a community hall or a high-school auditorium. In Oakland she must share the space with the local basket-ball team and, through the thin partition dividing the sheep from the goats, endure with what philosophy she can muster the pistol shots of the timekeeper on the other side of the dividing wall—strange, anachronistic gunfire sounding faintly through the swordplay which finishes Mercutio. In Memphis she must play in a temple built by a river captain who retired from the Mississippi, got religion and left as his memorial a huge auditorium which seats—in pews—a vastly profitable number of drama lovers, some of them so advantageously placed that by a little craning of their Tennessee necks they can see, over the top of the inadequate curtain, the hastily improvised dressing-room in which Robert Browning or Romeo is emerging shyly from his underclothes.

Such merely physical inconveniences lend a touch of salt to the eternal adventure of pitching one's booth in the market place, but there remains now in the path of any touring company one obstacle which only this generation has encountered. It is a commonplace that the celluloid drama has driven the flesh-and-blood companies from the one-night stands. But are you also aware that the local interests thus engaged are now stubbornly united in an instinctive conspiracy to keep such ancient rivals out of town?

Frankly, the movie houses do not welcome the advent of such a challenge as Katharine Cornell, and in one frustrated city, not a stone's throw from the Great Lakes, they pay the only feasible stage so much a month not to book any plays in the town at all. In a hundred American cities the local movie houses would not let a play be booked on any of their stages. I could name a dozen where they prevented Miss Cornell from playing in their town at all.

The viewpoint of the local management is reasonable enough. The petty lord of a movie house in which she might rear her scenery and play her play could make way for her easily enough and, with a little rehearsal, even teach its elegantly caparisoned ushers the lost art of seating an audience—the forgotten meaning of a reserved seat. But all his colleagues would regard him as a traitor to the common cause, and he himself, after he had collected his momentarily gratifying share of her enormous receipts, would discover that the neighbourhood must have been stinting itself to pay the exceptional price of her entertainment. At all events, he finds that, when he then books a film to follow her, his dependable clientele has spent all its money and his receipts for days to come are so lean that in the end he is no better off for her having passed that way.

Many of that troupe's experiences during the tour they will none of them ever want to forget. They will long remember, I suppose, the leisurely progress from Columbus to Louisville, some of the players making the jump by water, moving serenely down the Ohio, taking their ease in the rocking-chairs on the deck of perhaps the only river boat in the world which is captained by a woman. They will long remember the performance at Amarillo, where a sandstorm competed so successfully for the attention of the audience that in the tender colloquies between Elizabeth Barrett and Robert Browning neither could hear a word the other was saying and under the deafening cannonade upon the roof fell back upon the ancient art of dumb show.

And surely no one in that troupe will forget while he lives the Christmas they spent together in 1933. Christmas Eve—it was a Sunday, you remember—found them trundling through Montana. They were booked to begin a week's engagement in Seattle, and you may be sure that Mr McClintic had joined the troupe in St Paul to witness his great lady's triumph in his home town. All that Sunday there had been prodigious preparations in the purlieus of the dining car. The mere members of the public who were travelling on that train were notified to dine early, as the diner had been pre-empted from 8.30 on. Miss Cornell was giving a Christmas dinner for her company, the whole troupe—actors, electricians, everybody.

There was immense hilarity, with young Marchbanks from *Candida* cracking nuts for Juliet's nurse while Robert Browning and the hated Mr Barrett of Wimpole Street drank to each other's everlasting prosperity in thick railway tumblers of Christmas punch. But even as the last toasts were drunk and the troupe scattered to their berths with much wishing of Merry Christmas and quotations from Tiny Tim, the management was growing uneasy because of telegraphed reports that the December rains were making transit through the state of Washington slow, perilous and incalculable. It had already rained for three and twenty days and nights, and if it kept up much longer, they might have to make the rest of the trip in an ark and give their show, if at all, on the

191

first convenient Ararat. At best, they would be later than they had hoped to be in reaching Seattle.

After they passed Spokane, it began to be doubtful whether they would get there at all. At every pause a telegram would come on board with anxious inquiries from the worried management ahead. The tickets had all been sold for the first performance. Even if the company could not arrive at the appointed time, would the management be justified in sending out word over the radio and catching the evening papers with an announcement that, however late, the troupe would at least arrive in time to give the performance at the scheduled hour? Then, as night fell, they were still proceeding at a snail's pace through rain-drenched darkness far from Seattle. The anxiety shifted to the question whether, even if the curtain could not be sent up as advertised, would they at least be there in time to make it worth while holding the audience fifteen minutes or half an hour? Seven o'clock, eight o'clock, nine o'clock passed, and still they crawled through the darkness, stopping even at one point while hastily mobilised bands of railroad workers flung up a new trestle, over which the train might creep breathless past the wreckage of one which had given way. By this time the company had given up hope. There could be no performance. This meant that, on the following Saturday night, one-eighth would be missing from each salary envelope. It is a rule of the theatre that such deductions can be made whenever a performance is called off through what is blasphemously known as an act of God. It was, therefore, a gloomy bunch of Thespians who rode the last stretch, their noses glued to the streaming windowpanes as the train seemed to crawl over a bridge made of the very faces of the railroad workers who stood aside to let it pass, grim, rain-drenched Mongolian faces lit up in the darkness by the flare of acetylene torches, staring in cold frightening wonder at the perilous passage of these strangers whose necessity had brought them out to work in the night and the rain.

It was an exhausted and disgruntled troupe that finally climbed down on the platform in Seattle at 11.15 p.m. They were just collecting their wits and their baggage when they were pounced upon and galvanised into immediate action by an astonishing piece of news. The audience was still waiting. All the best trucks in Seattle were assembled at the station to grab the scenery and costume trunks, and rush them to the theatre. Tarpaulins were stretched and a hundred umbrellas proffered to protect it as it was being put into the trucks and taken out at the other end.

A line of automobiles were waiting to carry the company to the stage door. At the theatre, or loitering in groups in the lobby of the Olympic Hotel across the street, twelve hundred people were still waiting. Most of them were in evening dress and some of them were sustaining themselves with light midnight snacks. They had waited so long. Would Miss Cornell still play for them? Would she?

But the company must have time to unpack their trunks, put on their make-up and get into the crinolines and gay, shapely pantaloons of 1855. They promised to do it in record time. Meanwhile it seemed a pity to ask that audience to wait any longer with no entertainment of any kind. So, for once in the history of the theatre, the curtain was rung up forthwith and that Seattle gathering, at midnight on Christmas Day, actually saw the stage being set and lighted, saw swing into place the walls of the Victorian prison in which the tyrant of Wimpole Street chained his frail and gifted Andromeda. Each feat of the stage hands received rounds of applause. As the windowed wall of Elizabeth Barrett's room fell into place before the distant canvas glimpses of Wimpole Street and the windows in turn were hung with the rich portieres and valances of yesteryear, the enthusiasm mounted. It grew as the trunks, in full view of the audience, were opened and the costumes doled out by the wardrobe mistress. The actors, in dripping raincoats and horn-rimmed spectacles, lined up like charity boys at a handout, each collecting his ecru pantaloons, his flowered waistcoat, his ruffled shirt and what not. There was a great round of applause for the one member of the troupe who was already in complete costume when he arrived at the theatre— Flush, the guileful and engaging cocker spaniel who has never missed a performance of *The Barretts of Wimpole Street* since the first one, in Detroit some years ago.

But the greatest interest of all, I think, attached to the mysterious and intricate process by which a stage is lighted, a carefully calculated crossplay of beams by which certain parts of the stage are bathed in radiance, and others, in which the action will be less important, are left in shadow. The focal point of *The Barretts of Wimpole Street* is the couch from which Robert Browning rescues the sleeping princess. As Elizabeth Barrett, Miss Cornell must spend the entire first act, probably the longest act in all dramatic literature, supine upon that couch, and it is a matter for very careful calculation to have the lights which play upon it adjusted to the fraction of an inch. For this purpose, to the rapture of Seattle, Jimmy Vincent, the stage manager, stretched himself out and assumed, one after another, all the postures he knew Miss Cornell would later assume. As Mr Vincent is stocky and oriental in appearance, and as the visible gap between his trousers and his waistcoat widened horrifically with every languorous pose into which he tried to fling his arms and head, the effect was stupefying. Then the warning bell rang, the lights in the auditorium went down and the curtain fell, only to rise again with Miss Cornell at her post on the couch. The play was ready to begin.

It was five minutes past one in the morning. The entire troupe—scenery, costumes and all—had arrived in the town less than two hours before and already the curtain was rising, which is probably a record for all time. The excitement, the heady compliment paid by the audience in having waited at all, had acted like wine on the spirits of the troupe and they gave the kind of performance one hopes for on great occasions and never gets. But at the end of the first long act, Miss Cornell was visited by a kind of delayed fatigue. A postponed weariness took possession of her. She felt she must have something, anything, if she was to go on at all with what remained of the play. To Mr McClintic, hovering apprehensively in the offing, she merely said: 'Get me an egg', and rushed to her dressing-room.

Into the streets of Seattle at two o'clock in the morning rushed the faithful McClintic in quest of an egg. Nothing was open except a drug store and a lunch wagon, and the audience, in its long wait, had consumed every morsel of food in that part of town. There wasn't an egg to be had. The kitchens at the Olympic across the street were dark and inexorably locked. As a last desperate measure, McClintic began calling up such surviving citizens of Seattle as he had gone to school with years before. Finally one such appeal aroused someone. A sleepy voice asked who could be calling at such an hour in the morning. It was with some difficulty that he succeeded in identifying himself. 'You remember Guthrie, who used to live in such-and-such a street and used to go to school with you?' Oh, yes, and then what? 'Well,' the voice from the past faltered in its final task, 'can you let me have an egg?' Incidentally, she could and did.

It was a quarter of four in the morning when the final curtain fell. And that blessed audience, feeling, perhaps, that it was too late by this time to go to bed at all, stayed to give more curtain calls than the exhausted troupe had ever heard.

When the tour wound up in Brooklyn, on June 23, Miss Kitty had played to more than half a million of her fellow countrymen. I suppose they will all remember her, but none, I am sure, more fondly than the faithful band in Seattle which, on the day after Christmas, waited until one in the morning for her first curtain to rise. They will ever have a welcoming round of applause to greet her entrance when she is an old, old actress playing the Nurse to the Juliet of some youngster as yet unthought of.

From *Long, Long Ago*, 1943.

A large number of people have written about why they are actors; far too few have ever written about why they are not. One of the latter is however the television talk-show host and sports columnist, Michael Parkinson (b. 1935), who wrote this brief memoir in 1975.

Why I am Not an Actor

RECENTLY I was invited to invest some money in a West End show. Although I'd always strongly fancied the idea of being an 'angel' I turned it down. The show looks as if it will run forever. A short time before that particular example of my feeble business brain at work I was asked to tour the provinces in a play. I refused on the grounds that they were going to bill me as 'well-known TV Personality' instead of 'frustrated Thespian', which is what I really am.

I had a worrying start to my acting career in that the first two plays I appeared in, I played women. Nowadays, no matter what you might think of my face, you'd never be in any danger of mistaking me for a member of the opposite sex. But there was a time when people couldn't wait to stick a frock on me and shove me on stage. The very first time it happened was at infants' school when I played the Queen of Hearts in an epic entitled *The Missing Tarts*.

In those utility days I appeared shrouded in a tent-like dress which my mother had made from a pair of black-out curtains. My blonde wig was shoulder length and made of raffia. Overall I resembled a shrouded haystack. The play was written by one of our teachers, a charming spinster lady of bewildering innocence. For instance she wrote this line of dialogue between myself and my husband:

QUEEN OF HEARTS: Would you like a tart, Percy?
KING OF HEARTS: There's nothing I like better than a nice tart.
QUEEN OF HEARTS: Would you like me to put jam on one and bring it up to bed?

She couldn't understand why the audience broke up at this point, nor, to be frank, could we. I only understood its significance after the headmaster had insisted on a re-write and I had to learn the new lines which substituted 'crumpet' for 'tart'.

195

Things didn't improve at secondary school where I auditioned for any of the male parts in *A Christmas Carol* and ended up in my black-out curtains playing Mrs Cratchitt. I hated her because she was such a soppy cow. Moreover she got me goosed by a Roman spear-carrier from Rotherham in a drama festival which was the night I played her with bruised knuckles and a bloody nose.

It was, however, this part that first brought me to the attention of the critics. The local drama critic, who also doubled as horticultural correspondent, court reporter and sports writer, wrote: 'There was much audience sympathy for Mrs Cratchitt, who last week scored a hat-trick in the Barnsley and District Lge and is a fine cricketer whose father is well-known figure in local pigeon racing circles.' This confusing statement was much appreciated by myself and my family who thought it sorted out the local gossips before they could start putting it around that I was some kind of weirdo who liked wearing frocks.

It wasn't until I was about fourteen or fifteen that I got to be a man on stage. Then I was picked to play a dashing cavalry officer in a romantic comedy opposite a couple of the local beauty queens. As the part called for little other than an evening kissing them on couches and peering down peasant blouses I was well pleased. We entered for the local drama competition and listened eagerly as the adjudicator from Wakefield, or somewhere grand like that, demolished the opposition before arriving at our effort.

He didn't muck about. I think his opening words were: 'This play is rubbish.' He then softened his line as he worked his way through our cast list, saving my performance until last. I was sure he had done so because he had something special to say. He did. He said: 'Finally the part of the young cavalry officer. My only comment on his performance is that it would have been considerably more romantic, dashing and believable had he not been wearing odd socks.'

At that moment I decided to forsake romantic leads in favour of character parts, a decision which led to my break with the legitimate theatre. I played Councillor Albert Parker in J. B. Priestley's *When We Are Married*, a production put on by the local youth club. We had tremendous success with the play, eventually reaching the all-Yorkshire final at Dewsbury, or some such seat of learning. Our chances of being the county champions were ruined by a well-wisher versed in the traditions of the theatre who sent drinks to the dressing-room. Had he sent champagne, as is customary on these great theatrical occasions, then we might have got away with it because none of us would have known how to remove the cork. As it was he sent round three bottles of cheap sherry which, when mixed with a little turpentine, made a magnificent paint stripper.

We were last on and at least three of the cast, myself included, were well drunk for the entire performance. The only major calamity was the actor who played the photographer. He turned green in the middle of his big speech and lurched off to be sick in the wings leaving us to improvise as best we could until he returned looking like one of the walking dead. I retired from the stage soon after and have never trod the boards since.

I did not entirely lose my passion for the theatre. When I started work for a local newspaper I insisted on being sent to cover every drama group production in the area and honed my wit on innumerable productions of *Blithe Spirit* and *Murder in the Red Barn*. I became what I had set out to be, the 'Butcher of Barnsley' but my ultimate ambition to be a drama critic on a national newspaper was thwarted by my own cowardice. Given the chance of a job on a national daily I was warned that the man I had to see could not abide young journalists who wanted to be (a) drama critics, or (b) sports writers. As I wanted to be both I faced a clear choice during the interview.

'What do you want to be, young man?' said the executive. 'Well, I know what I don't want to be, sir,' I said, in craven fashion. 'What's that?' he enquired. 'A drama critic or a sports writer,' I said. 'Quite right. One is a pansy, the other an illiterate,' he replied and was obviously so delighted with this bright young thing sitting opposite that, had I insisted, I have no doubt he would have adopted me as well as giving me the job.

Thus, in a professional sense, I drifted away from the theatre. But my ambitions still lingered. I looked enviously at the succession of marvellous young northern actors like Finney and Kenneth Haigh who strode the stage and had their name in lights while I wasted my talents reporting such earth-shattering events as chip-pan fires in Oldham. Working on the theory that if I couldn't be one of them I could at least touch the hems of their coats I decided to interview my heroes. Mr Haigh wasn't at home the day I called but eventually I did get to Mr Finney. Well, not quite. He was busy doing *Luther* so I interviewed his mother instead.

So that I might know what I was talking about I went to see Albert in the play and, like the rest of the audience, was electrified by the magnificence of his performance. I talked about it to his mother and asked her what she thought at the end when the audience rose and acclaimed her son. 'Well,' she said, 'It was very moving. In fact one or two people were crying, you know. But I kept looking at my son up there on stage and I couldn't help thinking to myself "Oh Albert lad, I don't like your hair-cut".'

This classic piece of parental observation and common sense took me back to the very beginnings of my ambition to be an actor. Being reared in the cinema, where I went four nights a week, I first wanted to be a film star. As I saw it the only obstruction to my career in Hollywood was my name. Now Parkinson is a perfectly serviceable name for a construction company or a manufacturer of boiled sweets or even a disease, but I felt it would not look right alongside the glamorous names of the silver screen like Veronica Lake and Hedy Lamarr.

One day I thought I had the answer to my problem. I read in a magazine that Yma Sumac, a Bolivian princess with an eight-octave range voice, could be Amy Camus, from the Bronx, who had magically transformed her life by simply reversing the spelling of her name. I saw no reason why I should not do the same. I came up with Michael Nosnikrap.

What more can I say?

From *Punch*, 5 November 1975.

Like Terence Rattigan, J. B. Priestley (b. 1894) may not currently be the most fashionable of British dramatists, though his place as one of the leading playwrights and authors of the century remains totally assured. Like the Osborne of The Entertainer *(q.v.) Priestley too saw in the old Edwardian music-halls a metaphor for England, albeit a more optimistic one, and in* Lost Empires *he wrote their best epitaph.*

IT MIGHT be the worst house of the week—and indeed most of the people sitting near me looked stupid—but even so it was wonderful in a way to leave the darkening and chilly streets of Newcastle and then find oneself sitting in the fourth row at the Empire. I think the secret of all these music halls is that while they seemed big—and most of them were —at the same time they seemed warm, cosy, intimate. A lot has been written about the magic of the playhouse, but it has always seemed to me very pale and thin compared with the warmer and deeper magic of the music hall, which attracted more men than women to itself because there was something richly feminine about it, belonging half to some vast tolerant mother and half to some bewitching mistress. I don't say I was putting all this into words as I stared about me that night, saw the orchestral players switch on their lights and try their instruments, noticed fat Mr Broadbent, no longer out of temper, bobbing up, first to smile at two people sitting just in front of me and then to tap with his baton, and heard his orchestra, with its desperate strings as usual fighting a losing battle with the woodwind and brass, scurrying through Grieg's *Norwegian Dances*; but I will swear some such thoughts were going through my head. And for the first time since I had promised to join Uncle Nick, instead of feeling confused, dubious, vaguely apprehensive, I felt quite happy about it. I was still going to be a watercolour painter—nothing could shake me about that—but until I could keep myself by painting, the variety stage, at five pounds a week instead of twenty-two-and-six, would be better than any office.

The first turn was a 'fill-in', a pair of trick cyclists, and of course I wasn't interested in them, only in the people I would be travelling with for the next few months. The first of these, the second act on the programme, were the Colmars, three male acrobats and a girl, Hislop's 'stunner', called Nonie. It was one of those acts, which had always rather bored me, in which the men stood on each other's shoulders and chucked the girl around a lot. (I saw one recently, on a TV circus programme, and it seemed just the same, unchanged in a world of bewildering transformations.) Nonie was rather small and seemed quite young, probably still in her teens, but there was nothing undeveloped about her figure. Her legs were magnificent in their tights, and her full breasts made her glittering bodice rise and fall. And the way she held herself and moved, among the three sweating males, suggested she was tremendously conscious of herself as a female. Her sex came over the footlights like a sharp challenge. In those days of long skirts, stays and demure blouses, we had to guess what girls really looked like; but Nonie Colmar (who plays an important part in this story, so I'm not wasting time on her) triumphantly displayed what a well-shaped girl had to offer. I don't think I was any more lustful than most of us were then, but my mouth almost watered at the sight of her.

Next was Harry G. Burrard, Eccentric Comedian, who came rushing on, with the band playing its loudest, waving his arms and hoarsely breaking at once into one of his hell-for-leather idiotic songs. His makeup and costume—a grotesque ginger wig, a white face and red nose, an enormous collar, a bottle-green tunic and peg-top patched pants—left the audience in no doubt that he was a funny man. But this Monday first house offered him only a few distant giggles. Perhaps like me they didn't think him funny. *Diddy-diddy—oodah—oodah—oodah*, he croaked away, still waving his arms; and nobody cared. I don't think I am being influenced by the knowledge of what happened afterwards if I say that, at first, he made me feel embarrassed, and then, as he went on and on without any encouragement, I began to feel sorry for him. I was near enough to see his eyes, and they seemed to me—though of course I might have been deceiving myself—fixed in a kind of despair. I know I felt relieved when he took himself off, with the band at its loudest again, pretending desperately that a little weary clapping was an ovation.

Uncle Nick was next, the last act before the interval. This was the time he preferred, because it meant that the wings were clear of people waiting to go on. The orchestra opened as usual with part of the *Ballet Egyptien*, and then there was the familiar *Ganga Dun* big set, some kind of glittering Indian temple, which Uncle Nick had designed himself. It looked important and showy, but also its structure and glitter helped his act. I watched it now of course with new and keener eyes, reminding myself that I would soon be taking part in it. Sam and Ben Hayes and Norman Hislop, hardly recognisable in Indian make-up and costume, came backing on, and then Barney, the dwarf, also an Indian now, scuttled across the stage with squeals and backward looks of terror; and finally Cissie Mapes, a gauzily clothed Hindoo maiden, arrived to prostrate herself before some advancing figure off-stage. A gong sounded.

And there—a tall, commanding, sinister figure—was the Indian magician himself, who announced his arrival by letting loose a vivid green thunderflash. There was no doubt that Uncle Nick was a superb showman. Even the stolid fat deadheads sitting all round me, waiting for death rather than for any entertainment, were not entirely unimpressed. But *Ganga Dun*, intent upon magical feats as if they were part of some religious rite, gave no sign that he was aware of the existence of any audience. Unsmiling, grave, he behaved as if they were not there.

At first, from seemingly empty bowls and vases, handed to him by the Hindoo maiden, he produced bunches of flowers, fruit, coloured silks, gold and silver coins; and then he performed the feat, a genuinely Oriental one, of covering a heap of sand with a cloth once, twice, three times, while a magical plant appeared to grow there. The Hindoo maiden was then carried by the magician's slaves and her rigid body placed across two trestles. *Ganga Dun* regarded her sombrely, made some mysterious passes, then beckoned the slaves to remove the trestles. The Hindoo maiden remained there, now apparently unsupported. A few more passes and she slowly rose about two feet higher. The magician passed—or appeared to pass—hoops round her body, to prove that no wires were holding it up. Another gong, another green flash, and the magician was holding her by the hand as she bowed and smiled. But then an angry rival magician, as tall as *Ganga Dun* and nearly as imposing, wearing a turban, a majestic beard, and stiff long robes that hid his feet, arrived rather slowly and shakily, to challenge the magic power of *Ganga*. This he did not in words—nothing was said throughout the act—but by means of various insulting gestures. *Ganga* soon lost his patience, went nearer, summoned the gong and the green flash again—and then there was no rival magician, only the robes in a heap on the floor. It was a very effective trick, and it would have left me puzzled if I hadn't noticed that it was Barney the dwarf who was wearing the beard and turban, so that I guessed he had been raised two feet or so by stilts or something, and that at the end of the trick he was hiding in the heap of robes. But now a pedestal, about four feet high and very fancy, was brought on to the stage, and a white box was placed on top of it. Cissie as Hindoo maiden climbed into the box, and even while its lid, which faced away from the audience, was still slowly closing, the box was lifted off the pedestal, securely roped, then fastened to a hook let down from the flies. The box remained in mid-air for a few moments. The magician scowled at it; there was a roll on the side-drum; as if in despair he plucked a pistol out of his robes and fired three times at the box, which was then lowered and opened, all its sides falling down, and was plainly seen to be empty. There was a chord from the orchestra;

Ganga Dun, aware at last of the audience, bowed to it almost negligently: the act was over. I led the rather scattered applause, but did not succeed in bringing back the magician before the curtain to take a final bow. When the lights went up for the interval, I looked around me. The Monday first-house people looked just as stolid as they had done before. Their sense of wonder had not been touched and aroused, because they had none. If my uncle had brought on three elephants and made them disappear, those people would have hardly raised an eyebrow.

The house manager stood me a Bass in the Circle Bar, which was almost empty. 'Wonderful act—one of the best,' he said again. 'I must have seen that girl-in-the-box trick twenty or thirty times and I still don't know how it's done. You do, I suppose—um?'

'Yes, I do.' I tried not to sound too grand and condescending. He waited, obviously wanting me to tell him how it was done, but I wasn't having any. So now he frowned.

'You can tell him from me, I noticed he cut three minutes out of the act. Naughty—very naughty! I'm supposed to report him to head office for that, but of course I know he wouldn't do it to a full house. Always gets a wonderful reception with the right house. Great Showman—Nick Ollanton—though he can be naughty—very naughty. Staying in front for the next half, I hope? Good! Three very good turns coming on— Ricarlo the juggler—those girls, Susie and Nancy—then Tommy Beamish. You've seen Tommy before, I expect. Wonderful comedian, Tommy—and they worship him up here. He'll have 'em rolling before the week's out. But he may walk through it this first house. He can be a naughty boy too, Tommy. Lovely talent though—lovely. Well, off you go and enjoy yourself. Give 'em a hand if nobody else does.'

Ricarlo was an elegant and graceful though not handsome Italian, probably about forty who worked in full evening dress, and did most of his juggling, which was superb, with a top hat, a cane, and a cigar, to which he added, after a few minutes, a pair of yellow gloves. Throughout the band played, very softly, the same little tune, one I had never heard before, half gay and half melancholy. And indeed there was something half gay and half melancholy about Ricarlo himself and his act. His movements, so graceful and quick, so beautifully timed, had about them a kind of infectious joy; but his dark and big-boned face, with its ebony stare, seemed carved and dyed in melancholy, the sort of blank sadness that I have since noticed many Latin people seem to be sunk into, behind their noisiness and flash of teeth and eyeballs. As I watched him dreamily—there is something almost hypnotic about this sort of juggling —I felt that here was a man I might come to like. And once again I led such scattered applause as he received.

The front cloth of unbelievable shop windows, before which Ricarlo had appeared so elegantly and incongruously, gave place to a garden scene, first in a greenish moonlight, where two girls and three men began singing softly. This of course was the song-and-dance act of *Susie, Nancy and Three Gentlemen*. When the lights went up I saw that the three men were wearing grey morning dress and grey toppers; and I also saw, with an interest that soon rose to excitement, that Susie and Nancy were quite bewitching creatures. Susie, the taller and older and the one I knew was married, was a ripe brunette. Nancy, who looked about eighteen, was a blonde with short curly hair, unusual in those days, a saucy look and manner, and legs that were both ravishing and witty. The whole act was out of the usual music-hall run, more like a visitation from musical comedy, and perhaps a trifle too deliberately 'refained'; the dancing, apart from Nancy's, was careful rather than brilliant; the songs were melodious nothings about Orange Girls and Kitty on the Telephone and so on; and no commanding talent was audible or visible; but—and I'll admit my instant infatuation with the adorable Nancy may have swayed my judgment—the act conveyed something that seemed to vanish from the world not long afterwards, something I never found again in any place of entertainment—a kind of young and innocent gaiety, a bit silly as youth itself can be silly, without any sort of depth in it, any weight of experience, but somehow enchanting and lingering in the memory as an enchantment, so that later, when everything was different, and fragments of the songs returned to my mind, I was at once haunted by a bright lost world that had taken my own youth with it. As for that little Nancy, so pert and saucy and yet somehow so inno-cent, I began to fall in love with her there and then. And as I clapped until my hands ached, and glared at the fat deadheads who turned their idiot faces my way. I thought how wonderful it was that Uncle Nick had asked me to join him, so that I would see this girl again, and again and again, and would soon go backstage where she existed. But I did not really think of her existing in the corridors, passages and spaces there that I had seen and smelt that morning, but in some unchanging sunlit garden, some perpetual Maytime: I was already touched, barmy.

Luckily for me, Tommy Beamish, topping the bill, came on next. I had seen him before, but not in this particular sketch, in which he was 'supported by Miss Julie Blane and Mr Hubert Courtenay, both well known in the West End Theatre'. He was one of those rare comedians who began to make me laugh as soon as they appeared. He was a born comic, a plumpish man with a round cherubic face, usually decorated with an improbably ginger moustache, and with rather bulging eyes that stared in bewilderment or suddenly blazed in droll indignation. He never bothered with the ordinary comedian's patter, told no funny stories, sang no comic songs. He would lose himself in a labyrinth of misunderstandings and cross purposes, and would go on repeating some commonplace phrase or even one word, with deepening bewilderment or growing indignation, like a creature from some other world baffled by this one, until he had only to make the smallest gesture or mutter half a word to produce another roar of laughter from the nearest stalls to the high distant gallery, lost in the smoke. Like all the great variety artistes, he was able through the projection of his stage personality and his marvellous sense of timing to dominate every kind of audience, keeping them hushed and still when it suited him and then releasing their laughter as if he were pressing a trigger. He was the best comedian I ever saw on the stage—I am not forgetting Chaplin, but he belongs to the screen—and I have not seen his equal these past forty years or so; yet now there must be only a few of us, our memories already hazy, who remember him at all.

The sketch they played that night was simple enough in outline. Mr Hubert Courtenay, an old Shakespearian type of actor who suggested he was really the Doge of Venice or the banished Duke of Arden, was an immensely dignified country gentleman. Miss Julie Blane, though she could not keep the mischief out of her splendid eyes, played with some skill his anxious and delicate-minded daughter. They had sent for a vet for poor little Fido, and in his world of dubious communications and infinite cross purposes, Tommy Beamish had found himself summoned to the house, though he was in fact a plumber. The resulting confusion created the atmosphere in which Tommy was at his best. The indignant Courtenay rolled out words like 'prevaricate' and 'dilatory' and 'callousness', which Tommy repeated in amazement, brought back to taste again, chopped in half and flung the pieces about when he felt himself at bay. His slightest reference to plumbing operations, to his astonishment and then despair, were regarded as outrages by the quivering Miss Blane, whom he followed round the stage, sometimes climbing over the furniture, hoping to make it clear to her that he was not some kind of monster. A decent well-meaning man, only anxious to be helpful and impressed by the gentility of his patrons, he floundered into deeper and deeper misunderstandings, sometimes almost ready to cry and at others leaping to a height of blazing indignation. Even the fat deadheads all round me had to laugh, though they hated doing it. And as for me, I laughed so much and so long that often I lost the sight of Tommy in that curious and disturbing red haze which comes with violent laughter just as it does—so we are told, though I have never experienced it—with sudden and terrible anger.

What with the delectable and tantalising Nancy and then the sublime idiocies of Tommy Beamish, I had had as much as I could take and wanted to cool off, so I went out during the final turn, a 'fill-in' trampoline act, caring nothing, like most people then, about the inevitable flickering bioscope that would end the programme. (We never imagined that soon it would help to put an end to Variety itself.) I wandered around for a few minutes, passing the queues now waiting for the second house, my excitement cooling in the Newcastle night air, chilly and sooty like that of most industrial towns then, as if they were really one vast railway station. Then I found the stage door and asked for Uncle Nick's dressing-room.

He was sitting alone, smoking a cigar, still with his make-up on but without his turban. 'Well, Richard, how do you think the act's looking?'

'Better than ever,' I told him. 'Even with that rotten audience.'

'I cut the Magic Ball trick. I can't astonish those blockheads, so why waste one of my cleverest effects? You can watch it tonight from the side—no point in you sitting out front again. I want you to note very carefully from now on everything that young Hislop has to do, and if you can't do it better by the end of the week, then you'll have made a fool of me.' He sounded heavy and grumpy, as if he needed some champagne—there was none in sight—or the applause the second house would give him. 'You stayed on after the interval? No, no, quite right. Get the feel of the whole show. How was Tommy Beamish?'

'Funnier than ever, I thought,' I began enthusiastically, and then checked myself.

Uncle Nick took out his cigar and grunted at it. 'He doesn't like me, and I don't like him. I suppose he's a very successful comedian, but then I don't like comedians. They have to pretend to be even sillier than the people who are watching 'em—and that's saying a lot—and after a time it does something to 'em. Their brains soften, then their characters. Before the week's out, Tommy Beamish often has to be more than half-pissed before he can go on. That Blane woman, who lives with him, has a hell of a time. Here I'm lucky, lad. I haven't to pretend to be sillier than they are but cleverer, and that's all right because I *am* cleverer—though that's not saying much because, as you'll soon find out, most people who come to variety shows are half-witted. I could fool *them* in my sleep. I do my work for about one person out of every two hundred.' There was a rather timid knock, then Cissie Mapes looked in, still a Hindoo maiden.

From *Lost Empires*, 1965.

And so, finally, back to the audience: Ned Sherrin (b. 1931) reports from the stage at Wyndham's where he was to be found throughout 1976 narrating a Stephen Sondheim anthology evening, and the archive then closes, as it opened, with a poem: in this case the appeal by A. P. Herbert (1890–1971) 'To the Lady Behind Me at the Theatre'.

You Out There

YEARS OF sitting in the stalls looking up at the stage did not prepare me for the process in reverse: months of sitting on the stage and looking down at the audience, introducing *Side by Side by Sondheim* at Wyndham's Theatre. It was a fascinating experience.

The entertainment was a collection of the theatre songs of Stephen Sondheim, definitively sung by Millicent Martin, Julia MacKenzie and David Kernan. My role was to act as a sort of guide through this bumpy terrain, which gave me an excuse for more immediate contact.

Sybil Thorndike used to say that there was nothing you could do to predict an audience. They bring their own varied and corporate life into each theatre they jointly and severally enter. 'Some nights,' Dame Sybil confided, 'they're porridge; some nights—electricity.'

As each evening started I made the first furtive check while my three colleagues were singing their heads off. It was often instructive—sad faces, expectant faces, bored or disgruntled faces, faces of unwilling husbands dragged there by purposeful wives, faces already composed for sleep, which settles in as the lights go down and the music starts. Then the first responses to the first spoken words, never an actual laugh; but sometimes a murmur gave a clue to the liveliness of the evening's assembled group.

And every porridge and every electricity night I reflected on Dame Sybil's accuracy.

I had never realised how much one could see from the stage. I could identify people as far back as row J and recognise a sleeping head in N, especially if it was thrown back rather than cunningly posed forward. But if back and middle rows were worth a quick check it was the front rows which provided more consistent entertainment. Some people loved to look up expectantly, seeking a personal contact with the players, others looked resolutely down, too shy to catch an artiste's eye, condemning themselves to seeing nothing of the show above knee level—not a great visual treat as both girls wore long dresses. Many couples held hands, and the choreography of hands which were particularly questing was a continual delight.

One old gentleman of about 80 sat down in the front row flanked by two ladies of about 60. He held hands restlessly and relentlessly with both of them throughout both acts. Millicent Martin had a theory that one was his mistress and the other his blind wife, which seemed to fit the observable facts. A week later a similarly senior lady arrived with two escorts who gave and received the same attentions. Strange! I have a theory that most people think they cannot be seen from the stage.

Sometimes front rows talked animatedly as though a TV screen stood between them and us. At the end of one of David Kernan's more lyrical songs, which he sang with quiet charm, I saw one old lady nudging her neighbour as the last lovely notes died away. She pointed at David's trousers with animation, 'Look,' she said in a clear bright voice, 'turn-ups are coming back.'

One of the most pleasant sensations was to watch a genuinely miserable face relax as the evening went on. I found it hard not to invent scenarios to explain the sadder spectacles: bad day in the city, incipient ulcers, threats of redundancy, anguish at the office. Another melancholy speculation was which seats might not be occupied after the interval. It had to be admitted that the entertainment was not always to everyone's taste and that some occasionally slunk away. A disgruntled television peer boasted to Bernard Levin that he had left at half time and was promptly told he would lose Levin's friendship and esteem if he didn't go back and sit it out. Apparently it worked better the second time around, and he stayed.

Sondheim's dense and literate lyrics were something of a trap for foreigners who were less than fluent. I watched a sad Spanish lady grow sadder and sadder as one evening progressed and her daughter laughed more and more, until late in the second half a smile at last crossed Mama's face as she heard the line, 'I wish that I could speak Spanish', winging out in Millicent Martin's precise pronunciation.

Three Germans spent half a first half discussing their bewilderment in high voices if not High German about five feet away from me and then stumped away up the aisle. I saw the Company Manager pursuing them to pin down the nature of their discontent. 'Ve don't understandt it,' they told him, 'and ve don't understandt vy three must sing unt not talk unt von must talk and not sing?' Had they heard *me* sing the mystery would have been solved.

Persistent returners included a handful of attractive young women who turned up fairly frequently with older gentlemen in the 'tired businessman' category. I assumed they were girls from the escort agencies who channelled their punters our way.

Late arrivals were a problem; but a problem which had to be lived with. My favourite late arrival was Douglas Bunn, the Master of Hickstead, who had been ceaselessly hospitable in Sussex and who came up in July having called a girl friend to ask her if she would like to go and see 'something with Ned Sherrin'. 'Jolly good,' she said, 'he's the Irish showjumper, isn't he?' 'No,' said Douglas patiently, 'it's some sort of theatrical thing.' They arrived at 7.45 to collect their tickets; assumed it was an 8.30 curtain and went off for a couple of scotches to put them in the mood. Returning in good time at 8.20 they found us 20 minutes in. 'Ah,' said Douglas to the helpful usherette on the way downstairs, 'can you fill us in on the plot so far?'

Much as I could see and hear from the stage, I did miss not hearing interval comments, though I daresay sensibilities were sometimes spared by this enforced ignorance. I have always cherished audience remarks.

An American at Stratford after *Julius Caesar*: 'That Brutus! Was he noble!'

Noël Coward to Claudette Colbert after Arthur Miller's autobiographical *After the Fall*: 'I preferred *This is Your Life* as a television programme.'

Two elderly impresarios at the first matinee of Osborne's *Entertainer* with Olivier: 'If that's a play, I'm Mistinguett!'

An American lady at a heavy Chekhov evening: 'It's more a play than a show, isn't it?'

Liz Robertson, the versatile understudy for *Side by Side*, caught a splendid ladies' loo exchange when we were still at the Mermaid Theatre: 1st lady: 'Yes, I quite liked it. Did you like it?' 2nd lady: 'Yes, I quite liked it. Did you like it?' 1st lady: 'Yes. There was something missing though.' 2nd lady: 'Yes, I thought there was something missing too.' 1st lady: 'What do you think it was?' 2nd lady: (After due consideration) 'Could be tap dancing!'

Of course this business of enjoying a privileged vantage point from the stage opens up other risks. 'Coming Round' is an enjoyable nightmare. This theatrical tradition consists of coming round to the Stage Door and visiting the artiste in his dressing-room after the entertainment. I like to see people after the show and I always note those who come back and those who slink away. The feeling is quite irrational. I dislike going round myself when I am in an audience: but that does not stop me interpreting absence as criticism when I am on the other side.

Not all people do it very well. An old amateur theatrical friend of Julia MacKenzie appeared in her dressing-room one night after she had given a standout performance. After a lot of awkward silences he finally managed: 'You doing anything these days?'

I took two American friends-of-a-friend in to congratulate Millicent Martin. They seemed short on charm, but they were very insistent. She sailed in first. 'Oh,' she said, her face dropping, 'but you looked beautiful on stage.' Milly is well able to take that in her stride, but I'm not sure she was prepared for the husband's follow-up: 'You can't fool me,' he waggled a knowing finger under her nose, 'you've done solo work before, and,' encouragingly, 'you'll do solo work again.'

I dined one night at a restaurant a couple of tables away from Milly and an American friend, a girl who had been to see the show and at whom I'd been talking for some two hours from the stage. I joined them for coffee and after another half an hour of conversation a dim light began to shine in the lady's eyes. 'Wait a minute,' she said, 'are you the man who reads out the announcements?' So much for recognition.

A week later the Keith Prowse office sent in a number of their ticket agents to see the show. They had a drink with the cast afterwards. I worked hard for 20 minutes with a nice young woman who had a 'station' somewhere along the Strand. At the end of it she asked what I did.

'I work here for the moment,' I said.

'What as?'

'Sort of on the stage.'

'Oh,' she said. 'Well, you look more sophisticated up there.' It is very salutary.

An evening passed and, watching as the audience warmed, one formed one's own view of the class of Thursday night: but I noticed that the people out there always wanted to have been part of a good audience when they came round, so a ritual conversation was usually observed:

'Were we a good audience?'

'Marvellous.'

'Do audiences always cheer like that at the end?'

'Well, perhaps not quite as much as tonight.'

'No, we thought we were pretty exceptional.'

As a ritual, I found it particularly difficult after a thick bowl of Dame Sybil's porridge. At least it was the nearest I got to acting.

From the *Telegraph Sunday Magazine*, 3 April 1977.

To the Lady Behind Me at the Theatre

Dear Madam, you have seen this play;
I never saw it till today,
You know the details of the plot,
But, let me tell you, I do not.
The author seeks to keep from me
The murderer's identity.
And you are not a friend of his
If you keep shouting who it is.
The actors in their funny way
Have several funny things to say,
But they do not amuse me more
If you have said them just before;
The merit of the drama lies,
I understand, in some surprise;
But the surprise must now be small
Since you have just foretold it all.
The lady you have brought with you
Is, I infer, a half-wit too,
But I can understand the piece
Without assistance from your niece.
In short, foul woman, it would suit
Me just as well if you were mute,
In fact, to make my meaning plain,
I trust you will not speak again.
And—may I add one human touch?—
Don't breathe upon my neck so much.

From *Punch*, 1948.